Technology for Unleashing Creativity

Essential Music Technology: The Prestissimo Series
Richard McCready, Series Editor

Digital Organization Tips for Music Teachers
Robby Burns

Recording Tips for Music Educators
A Practical Guide for Recording School Groups
Ronald E. Kearns

iPractice
Technology in the 21st Century Music Practice Room
Jennifer Mishra and Barbara Fast

Technology Tips for Ensemble Teachers
Peter J. Perry

Practical Music Education Technology
Richard Dammers and Marjorie LoPresti

Interactive Visual Ideas for Musical Classroom Activities: Tips for Music Teachers
Catherine Dwinal

Technology for Unleashing Creativity: Practical Tips and Tools for Music Educators
Steve Giddings

Technology for Unleashing Creativity

Practical Tips and Tools for Music Educators

Steve Giddings

OXFORD
UNIVERSITY PRESS

OXFORD
UNIVERSITY PRESS

Oxford University Press is a department of the University of Oxford. It furthers the University's objective of excellence in research, scholarship, and education by publishing worldwide. Oxford is a registered trade mark of Oxford University Press in the UK and certain other countries.

Published in the United States of America by Oxford University Press
198 Madison Avenue, New York, NY 10016, United States of America.

Library of Congress Cataloging-in-Publication Data
Names: Giddings, Steve, 1985– author.
Title: Technology for unleashing creativity : practical tips and tools
for music educators / Steve Giddings.
Description: [1.] | New York : Oxford University Press, 2022. |
Includes bibliographical references and index.
Identifiers: LCCN 2021056051 (print) | LCCN 2021056052 (ebook) |
ISBN 9780197570746 (paperback) | ISBN 9780197570739 (hardback) |
ISBN 9780197570753 (epub) | ISBN 9780197570777
Subjects: LCSH: Music—Instruction and study—Technological innovations. |
Computer music—Instruction and study. |
Electronic music—Instruction and study.
Classification: LCC MT1.G42 T43 2022 (print) |
LCC MT1.G42 (ebook) | DDC 780.7/7—dc23
LC record available at https://lccn.loc.gov/2021056051
LC ebook record available at https://lccn.loc.gov/2021056052

DOI: 10.1093/oso/9780197570739.001.0001

9 8 7 6 5 4 3 2 1

Paperback printed by Marquis, Canada
Hardback printed by Bridgeport National Bindery, Inc., United States of America

For all the music educators and learners who need it.

Contents

Foreword

It is perhaps a cliché that the world of music education is changing. After all, we can see and document change in music education simply by looking objectively at the methods by which music has been taught and learned over the course of history. Music is essentially an aural art taught by aural tradition, and we can see through examination and observation how there has never really been a time when music education has been stagnant or has rested in its desire to pass its joys on to the next learners. Examining a textbook from even since the turn of the century can highlight the number of changes that have occurred since its publication.

In truth, it is our society and our students that are changing and entreating us music educators to change along with them. Good music teachers are constantly adapting their methodologies to reflect new pedagogies, even though the methods they learned back in their undergraduate or graduate studies may be well out of date. They might possibly have been taught to teach by using the same methodologies that are employed in those not very old texts, and are now expected to teach things they never learned in college.

The COVID-19 pandemic of 2020–2021 forced a lot of us music educators to examine what methods were successful in our teaching, methods that were simply not possible in isolated conditions. Rehearsing together became practically non-existent, private instruction became incredibly difficult and frustrating, and any form of collaborative work required a whole new way of thinking. Thankfully, many new resources were available to teachers, and companies such as Music First, Ableton, Smart Music, Avid, Acoustica, Soundtrap, and Hal Leonard were very generous in making new tools available to teachers to help them bridge the gap back to in-person instruction.

These digital tools and methods have done more than just be a stopgap to tide music education over until normality returns. Many teachers and students have discovered new skills and competencies that they would not have considered before. Being able to create, sequence, record, edit, and publish their own music has become an invaluable set of skills for music students. Even though these possibilities have been there for many years, the pandemic has allowed these skills to be recognized and lauded. The National Core Arts Standards in the United States and the regional standards adopted in Canadian Arts curricula both specifically include creating and making music as core competencies. Many teachers have been able to include more of this creating and making into their music curricula while performance was nigh impossible, and many have discovered how much joy and relevance this inclusion has brought to their students' musical studies.

Steve Giddings, the author of this book, has spent his entire teaching career in exploring and refining his methods in this creating and making role, and he is a proven master teacher in this field. He has brought his considerable knowledge and experience, and somehow managed to condense it into this one volume. Though there are enough ideas here to fill many books, the aim of the *Prestissimo* series is to provide teachers with that one volume of essential material for their circumstances, that one-stop shopping cart of methods to infuse music technology into their classroom. In this way, readers of this book will find before them a wealth of road-tested, successful ideas to help keep creativity alive in the classroom as they transition out of the pandemic and into a new era of music making. Wise teachers will be able to select from the material presented herein and present engaging lessons and activities that students will enjoy, and that will strengthen their musical skills and experience. Reading this book will provide much optimism and relief for those who are struggling with adapting to the new technologies, and new inspiration for those who are already successful.

Richard A. McCready
Series Editor

Acknowledgements

I love teaching music, but writing has been a hidden passion for me that I didn't know existed until beginning in 2007, when I published my first article in the *Canadian Music Educator Journal* (*CMEJ*). Later, through more publications with the *CMEJ*, and then blog posts, that passion began to grow. My website, www.stevesmusicroom.com, was designed for teachers but also developed in me a love of sharing lessons and helping other teachers. I published my first book in 2017 (*Rock Coach*) and my second one in 2020 (*Creative Musicking*) under my own publishing company name. In between those books, I began writing a column for the *CMEJ* (although the column was put on hold for the writing of this book). This book is the result of the mixing together of all those projects, many of which are recycled and adapted for this book.

I am humbled that I was asked to write this book for this series. Thank you to Richard McCready, Norman Hirschy, and Michelle Chen for the guidance and encouragement throughout this process. Even though this is my third book, it is the first for a major publisher and I doubted myself at many points. Thank you to the *CMEJ* for giving permission to include a number of articles I had written for them over the years. Of course, my wife, Jenn, has been more supportive and amazing than ever. Even though she was working through her master's degree while I was writing this book, she has been understanding. Thank you also to my extended family, my friends, and colleagues near and far who have supported me in this endeavour. Your support did not go unnoticed.

Introduction
Modern Music Education

When Music Education Changed Forever

2020 will go down as the year everything changed. All of a sudden—and in some cases, literally overnight—schools all over the world went online in the wake of a global pandemic. Struggling music teachers were told they must transition their music making, normally in a group, into an online format over Zoom, Google Meet, Microsoft Teams, and Skype. It was not an easy feat, because as we all quickly found out, the technology did not yet exist to have synchronous rehearsals in groups. Many teachers stepped up to the challenge and many began to realize that music, the way it had been taught for generations, did not work in this format. It became blatantly obvious that music education needed to change to accommodate or face fading into obscurity. There was a hole to be filled that had only a few shovelfuls of dirt at the bottom: individual creativity and the creative process but also the widespread use of technology. The realization that music *can* be created individually in someone's basement with a computer and some user-friendly software was huge. More music teachers began using technology than ever before, coming out of their comfort zones and enhancing their online lessons with creative technology. It was the proverbial kick in the pants we all needed to bring our music learning and music teaching up to the modern digital age. Even after it was all over, and things began to seem that they were getting back to normal, many of the new discoveries found during the school shutdowns stuck, as teachers took the best of both to help learners thrive as musicians in an increasingly digital world.

The Proposal

When I was asked to write this book, it was February 2020—a very different time. The world was on the brink of a worldwide pandemic, but nobody knew. After I met with my editors (through Zoom before it was cool) I came up with a brainstorming document based on the conversation we had before everything shut down. By then everything was changing *very* quickly. Things were becoming serious and music teachers were figuring out the changed reality. I thought at one point, by the time this book is released, everyone will already know

Technology for Unleashing Creativity. Steve Giddings, Oxford University Press. © Oxford University Press 2022.
DOI: 10.1093/oso/9780197570739.003.0001

about technology and how to be creative with it, because at that point we had no choice. As time went on and I was able to get my head around the pandemic, I realized (with some encouragement) that this book is exactly what music teachers need right now and in a post-pandemic world. Creativity and technology have long been forgotten and this was a perfect opportunity to help those teachers embrace those shortcomings of music education.

The Musical Paradigm Shift

The way music is taught must reflect the musical landscape that exists outside of our schools. In school music making usually involves Orff, Kodály, the American band model, or an orchestra with instruments not usually (or ever) seen outside of the classroom or academia. Orff percussion, recorder, and other typical elementary school instruments are designed for—or convenient for—the purpose of education, but not necessarily for their practical application in the real world. Choral programs are throwbacks to the church choirs that were popular throughout much of history. These traditional models and approaches certainly have benefits and many have stood the test of time. Consider, though, how music is made outside of school and into the lifetime. Most centres include a community band or choir that involves those adults who played an instrument in school—and these community ensembles really exist because of their existence *in* schools. Outside of those, professional wind bands—for the most part—exist only in the military, and choirs in churches. Don't get me wrong; these activities are certainly meaningful extensions into the lifelong learning landscape, but then consider the number of persons who engage in that kind of music making beyond the school walls. I have a feeling it is nowhere near the number of persons who were in band in school. And, considering that roughly 60% of my own learners do *not* choose to take music (which in my province is band) after Grade 6, I want them to have had experience with the skills that will help them engage with music in a meaningful way *outside* of school. It is common for a bedroom guitarist to record themselves playing while using a digital audio workstation (DAW). It is common to use YouTube to learn how to play something on the piano. It is common to create original music by using available technologies and musical instruments and it is common to do all of these things among friend groups or individually. Most, if not all, of the music that exists outside of school is produced by using computers or some type of analog or digital technology.

The Other 80%

The concept of the other 80% is not new. Since traditional music programs began dwindling, music educators have been trying to find more ways to keep learners in those programs. Lucy Green in her 2002 book (*How Popular Musicians Learn: A Way Ahead for Music Education.* Aldershot, UK: Ashgate Publishing) explores the concept of informal learning approaches of popular musicians and why kids opt to drop music or decide not to take music in school in the first place. Simply put, they are not interested in the music and music making that is taught in school, but are highly motivated and musical outside of school. Technology and using technology specifically to unleash creativity is one of those many ways to engage the other 80% in our programs.[1] For those teaching in areas where music is required (general music, or similar programs), technology and creativity are ways to engage those unengaged learners in music and your opportunity as a music educator to instill relevant skills for active lifelong music making, but also giving those learners a reason to continue in music education in some capacity. For those of you teaching at secondary schools where music is not required, creativity and technology are key ways to reach those learners who are outside of traditional ensembles and who may or may not be engaged in active music making outside of your school walls.

Traditionally, we like to think that the skills we express unto our learners in elementary music, band, and orchestra programs are the skills that will extend through to encourage lifelong learning and engagement with music, that those skills of sight-reading European staff notation and playing a wind or string instrument to an extremely high level will be the skills that are needed to play music beyond the walls of our classrooms and into the future, right? After all, they will be able to read other people's music and be able to play any music they want, right? Well, yes to some degree: they *will* be able to play any music written in European staff notation that they want, but many musics—outside of Western classical and jazz—are not notated with staff notation, or not notated at all! I would argue that the most beneficial skills we can impart onto our learners are those skills of creativity and technological music literacy. I'll explain:

Creativity Skills

Reading European staff notation is definitely helpful in *some* musical situations and those who can read well can learn other pieces of music that are notated in that form. However, if a learner has developed the ability/confidence to be creative through improvisation and composition, they will truly be able to play any music they want, and in partnership with copious amounts of by-ear learning (which will be discussed) that ability to literally play anything they want will be enhanced and broadened. Consider that if a learner can create *their own* music, *without* notation, they are exponentially more likely to keep playing because they won't need the sheet music to play it. If they are able to jam with other musicians, then they can engage in conversation with other musicians, without notation. In addition to this benefit, if they have developed the ability to learn music by ear efficiently, they will be able to play anything they want, whenever they want without the crutch of the sheet music in front of them. Not to say that music is a language, because I don't believe it to be one in its truest sense, but learning music should be exactly the same as *learning* a language. Before we start school, we've had at least five years of figuring out the language through improvising and conversing with professionals *way* before we learned how to read. Musical skills should be

---

1. David Williams and Rick Dammers, "The Other 80% Music Home," *Music Creativity through Technology*, March 28, 2021, https://musiccreativity.org.

acquired in the exact same way. These are the musical literacy skills for the modern musician. Consider this chart and refer back to it to help you conceptualize this (see Table 0.1):

TABLE 0.1 Language and Musical Skills Chart*

Language Skill	Equivalent Musical Skill
Reading and understanding multiple forms of text	Reading and understanding multiple forms of notation (European staff, Nashville Numbers, tablature, etc.)
Having and engaging in a conversation	Jamming with other musicians
Reciting a phrase or sentence back after just hearing it once	Being able to hear a musical phrase and repeat it, or play by ear
Telling a story, either orally or through written word	Being able to improvise, or compose a piece of music
Using many different media to express views (printing, cursive, keyboarding, word processors, pencils, pens)	Being able to play multiple instruments and use many workstations well (instruments, notation software, DAWs, sound gear, etc.)

* Adapted from Giddings, *Creative Musicking* (2020).

Technology Skills

Technology and music are inextricably linked. Considering that most of the music produced today is composed by using computers or in partnership with technology, it is only logical that our learners develop these skills to be able to produce their own music by using technology. Understanding the basics of DAWs is an essential technology skill to help foster creativity in our learners. DAWs are designed to help learners make great music in a matter of minutes. Music notation software is used to notate music in the traditional sense and can be used in partnership with DAWs to make music (explored more in depth later). A very common phenomenon of the digital age is the ability to find a relevant instructional video on YouTube and be able to learn from that video. YouTube learning (as I've called it) is a skill that requires a heightened level of critical thinking and diligence. If a learner finds a great "How to play . . ." video on YouTube and wants to go through it, they need to be able to have the discipline to go through it on their own, stop or go back when they need to, and be able to self-assess on the fly. From there, they can make their own arrangements on the basis of what they know. Jam tracks are another useful resource found all over YouTube to help learners jam with other musicians in a less intimidating way than in a live, real-time setting. All of these skills and technologies directly impact a learner's ability to engage with music throughout the lifetime. These technologies make creativity more accessible, therefore increasing the likelihood of lifelong musical learning through creativity.*

My Journey with Technology and Creativity

My journey with technology is not unlike that of many millennials born in the mid-1980s. I made mix tapes (like, real ones on actual cassette tapes) by staying up "late" to listen to the

* Section adapted from work originally published in the *Canadian Music Educator Journal* 61, no. 4 (2020): 41–44.

radio for that favourite song. I witnessed the rise and fall of Napster, and learned what an MP3 file was and the differences in bit rates associated with them. I grew up with the invention of the Internet (dial-up, I might add) and learned it as I went. I learned much of my knowledge about technology through trial and error throughout my life. In Grade 6 when I was 11, I did a science fair project on how CDs and CD players work, giving me one of my first exposures to high-fidelity sound and digital music. My dad picked up a used electric guitar for me when I was 13 or so because he knew I liked music. And even though I didn't understand it at the time, that was my first real experience with electronic amplification. These experiences certainly shaped my understanding of music technology while I was growing up, but then into high school and university I really got into trombone and drums, which traditionally use little, if any, digital technology or amplification. From then on, my experience with music technology was limited. I used Finale to arrange parts and create lessons for various projects in my university and early teaching career. I was certainly no guru, but I was able to get around the software. I had used Audacity on a semi-regular basis throughout my late high school and university career for various projects here and there. I even took an electronic-music special-topics course during my university program, in which Audacity was used. So, my experience with a DAW was restricted (pretty much) to Audacity, until I recorded my first studio album with my alternative rock band, The Sidewalks, when I saw a "real" DAW in action utilized by a master producer. In that same band, I learned a lot about amplification, microphones, sound systems, and various other ways of making music through technology. I learned even more as I began teaching music. Also, once I had learned to "let go" after my degree, I was able to begin learning how to be creative without overthinking it or being scared to be "wrong." Everything I know about music technology and creativity has been acquired outside of school in popular music groups or on the job as a music teacher. This book will help you with the learning part so you can be the best creative music technology coach you can be for learners.

Who Will Benefit from This Book?

This book caters to and is created for K–12 music educators by helping them to understand that combining creativity skills with music technology is of paramount importance in the musical landscape that exists outside of our walls in the modern world. Not only that, but music technology is also inherently creative as a tool, and has the ability to enliven the creativity in even the most reluctant learners. On top of this benefit, these skills help to reflect the music making that is prevalent in our modern society—modern skills for modern musicians.

Of course, this book doesn't stop there. Throughout the pages of this book, I will try to help you understand the relationships between music, technology, and creativity and how technology can help tap into their musicianship while fostering collaboration, creativity, and lifelong learning in learners. I will present with you teacher-tested lesson plans, real-life ideas, learner-centred approaches, and strategies for inserting creative technology into your classrooms. They may challenge you to reimagine what music education can look like in schools, or give you accessible, practical ways to enhance what you already have to reach more of the school population. This book might be specifically catered to you if you are among the following:

1. The music teacher who has been asked to integrate technology into their classroom, but has no idea where to begin
2. The music teacher who is looking for guidance on how to encourage greater learner autonomy in their classrooms
3. The music teacher who describes themselves as not "tech savvy," is somewhat intimidated by technology, and needs a friendly technology coach to help them
4. The music teacher who wants some tips to help facilitate more creativity in their classrooms
5. The music teacher who wants to find new ways to engage their learners in music
6. The music education student looking for resources and ideas for their new classrooms
7. The music teacher ready to challenge their traditional thinking about how music is taught and learned
8. The music educator who wants to be able to continue using creative music technology in meaningful and authentic ways

Whichever one of these points describes you, you are likely to glean some ideas and ways of thinking from this book. Even if you don't feel that these points describe you, I am sure you will find something useful within these pages that you and your learners will love.

"Possible Applications" and K–12 Learners

Throughout this book, there are lesson ideas, but also many of the creative technologies mentioned are accompanied by a "Possible Applications" section. These sections are designed to give general ideas on how to use these specific technologies or software in your classrooms in authentic, practical, and creative ways. Some are geared toward a particular ensemble; others are geared toward particular grade levels, but the vast majority are designed to be general enough to adapt for any grade level or ensemble that you happen to facilitate. This being said, the ideas in these sections of the book are more or less ready to use for Grades 4 through 12 with little, if any, adaptation. There are, however, additional factors that might be taken into consideration when you are facilitating creative music technology with primary grades (K–3) by using these sections:

Use Touch-Screen Devices

Fine motor skills for five-to-seven-year-olds are often not as advanced as they are in older learners, meaning that cumbersome keyboards and mouse pads on Chromebooks might be a barrier to many in this age group. Some schools use touch-screen devices for their youngest learners and Chromebooks for their oldest.

GarageBand on iPad has some very intuitive virtual instruments for small hands, a topic that is explored in Chapter 4, and ScratchJr is a wonderfully age-appropriate app for mobile touch-screen devices used for coding that is discussed in Chapter 7. Chrome Music

Lab, discussed in Chapter 6, can be accessed on any device with an Internet connection and is a wonderful tool utilized well in touch-screen environments. Chrome Music Lab's simplified interface also caters well to primary learners. Other apps that work well on touch-screen devices are Blob Opera, BandLab Mobile, BeepBox, and Cornelius Composer, which are all discussed throughout this book.

Work Together as a Large Group

As a way to begin your youngest learners on music technology, composing with the technology as one large group can be very effective. Use a projector and compose music together. Groups at this age level can often be difficult to facilitate, as many do not yet possess the social skills or the ability to work with others in a productive way.

Some good examples in this book are "Composing as an Entire Class with GarageBand for iOS (K–12)" and "Listening Map and Arrangement Activity (Grades K–3)," both in Chapter 4. "Second Lesson Idea: Remix by Using Stems" (also in Chapter 4) by using BandLab for Education also has some adaptations for primary learners. "K–3 Snowflake Project" in Chapter 6 is also another great example of utilizing group activities for primary learners with creative technology. A found-sounds activity using Audacity to make a soundscape or story together is one example mentioned in Chapter 4 as well. There are many other activities that take this particular adaptation for your youngest learners into account. These are good places to begin.

Budget More Time Than You Would for Older Grades

It is common for K–3 learners to forget their log-in information, meaning they will take longer to log in. Other than this challenge, it just takes them longer to do most things independently.

Keep Them Moving

Learners between the ages of five and seven crave movement. Limit the talking and have them move as much as you can. If you are composing a piece on the projector together, have them get up and move to what they have so far. Have them show you how it makes them feel, or move to the beat of the music if there is a discernable pulse. They don't need to be moving all the time; just make sure they are not sitting for long periods of time. Once the piece is composed, put together movement stations where learners move to manipulatives like ribbons, or using puppets or their feet.

"Listening Map and Arrangement Activity" in Chapter 4 prescribes to this principle by using movement before and after the arrangement process. Another one to incorporate the movement aspect would be the "K–3 Snowflake Project" in Chapter 6, wherein basic concepts like pulse, rhythm, and contour can be reinforced along the way through movement.

Use Pencil and Paper First

Have learners draw their compositions or arrangements first and then the facilitator arranges their composition into a DAW so they can be heard as in "Listening Map and Arrangement Activity" and "K–3 Snowflake Project." Also, using ScratchJr or a number of other apps, designing a video game character with pencil and paper, and then composing its theme music is another way to incorporate this adaptation. These video game ideas are scattered throughout but can be used with Chrome Music Lab, BeepBox, Paint Composer, and others.

Give the "Illusion of Choice"

Obviously, as you will read, it is important to give autonomy to learners so they feel they are part of the compositional team. I say "illusion" because you are not giving learners free rein; you are narrowing the choices they can make but still giving them the autonomy. It is important that for young learners, giving the choice between two or three loops (as an example) and having them vote will give the impression that their opinion matters and that they are being given a voice in the music-making process.

BandLab for Education and Soundtrap for Education, discussed in Chapter 4, are both ways to create and choose precomposed loops for learners to use. Quantiloop, explored in Chapter 10, is also another great looping app that is easy to use for young learners. Using Chrome Music Lab, you can give learners a precomposed piece from a link and can add something like a rhythm track. These are easy ways to begin narrowing down choices for learners. There are many opportunities for this approach throughout the book.

Set Up Technology Stations

Another way to adapt creative technology activities to Primary learners is to have different technologies set up at each station and have them rotate through every five minutes or so. It doesn't have to be complicated; one station could have Song Maker from Chrome Music Lab set up, and another one of the other apps within the same suite (explored later). The number of stations and the time spent at each will depend largely on how long your classes are. Some other stations that might be useful for young learners are Incredibox, Blob Opera, Groove Pizza, 808303.studio, MakeyMakey Piano, and TypeDrummer. These are all discussed throughout this book.

1

Creativity in Music Education

The terms "creativity" and "musician" were once inseparable. In the classical world, based on the conservatory approach, the creativity part has seemed to have all but disappeared. Yes, we are all creative beasts in some form, but in classical music and music education in general, creativity typically equates with being able to recreate a piece of music slightly differently from the way someone else does. For the most part, the instructions on how to play the piece of music are written directly onto the page, and the only part up for debate is how the instructions are to be "interpreted" by the musician playing that piece. Even then, there are generally accepted ways to interpret a piece of music that are considered conventional and stylistically appropriate. In every other genre of music outside of classical (and jazz to some degree), creativity and creating something new is part of being a musician and is never separated from that, nor does it rely solely on reproducing other people's music to exist.

Music Making

The term "music making" has come to encapsulate this mindset. I know that I was brought up to believe that when I was playing from sheet music in a wind band that I was "making" music. To some degree this is true, because the music really only exists in its natural form after it has been performed by a musician who can read that notation. However, considering that music is not literally being made in this scenario, but instead reproduced from iconic symbols that represent pitch and rhythm that have already been created and written onto a page, "recreating" might be a better fit. Recreating something that has already been written out is not an inherently creative act. Reciting is not creating. Even the US National Standards state that the second step in the creative process for all group types (ensembles, too) is to "Plan and *Make*," which includes "selecting and developing composed or improvised ideas into draft musical works," and preserving drafts of *imagined* work that serve a "variety of purposes and contexts."[1] As a person who also writes music curriculum for his home province,

---

1. NAfME, "Core Music Standards" 2014, https://nafme.org/my-classroom/standards/core-music-standards/

Technology for Unleashing Creativity. Steve Giddings, Oxford University Press. © Oxford University Press 2022.
DOI: 10.1093/oso/9780197570739.003.0002

I know that their use of the word "imagined" was a deliberate choice. It's one that evokes the idea of using one's imagination to form ideas, which brings me to my next point.

Bloom's Taxonomy

In the United States and Canada, most curricula are designed by using Bloom's Taxonomy as the primary conceptualizing approach. Bloom's revised taxonomy suggests that the highest level of thinking and learning is creating. For those unfamiliar with Bloom's Taxonomy, it's been traditionally conceptualized as a hierarchy of cognitive skills that guide many curricula around the world. In almost every pictorial, it is represented as a pyramid hierarchy, with "Create" at the top. There are six levels (Figure 1.1).

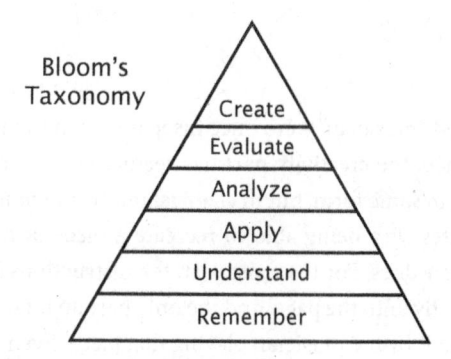

FIGURE 1.1 The traditional pyramid style of Bloom's Taxonomy

All good teaching goes through Bloom's hierarchy, whether we know it or not. In many performance-based programs we often stop at Apply and never quite get to Create. Creating and creativity are at the core of all musics; unfortunately, this is not the case with traditional music teaching and learning. As Dobbins (1980) puts it, "the capacities for creative self-expression and spontaneous conversational interaction indicate a person's proficiency in the use of a verbal language. The most exactly equivalent music skill is that of improvisation."[2]

My Experience with Creativity

The only time I've felt creative in "school music" was on the drums in the school jazz band; other than that, it was in rock bands *outside* of school. Sure, I did a few (and I *mean* few) improvised solos in the university jazz band, but the first time I considered myself a composer and a creative trombonist was with my original ska/alternative rock band, The Sidewalks. We've all heard, "Oh, you're a musician; you must be creative!" Music is the only art form for which this is not necessarily synonymous. I've considered myself to be a musician since Grade 5 but not once in that whole school music experience do I remember getting to create

2. Bill Dobbins, "Improvisation: An Essential Element of Musical Proficiency," *Music Educators' Journal* 66, no. 5 (1980): 36–41.

my own music, aside from that very limited time on the drums in the jazz band (even then, the creativity was minimal). In reality, the only reason I was even on drums in the first place was because I was mostly self-taught and did a ton of creating at home by myself, and wanted to try something new.

Turning Bloom on His Head

Imagine if you will, flipping Bloom's taxonomy on its head (see Figure 1.2). I'm not talking about a flipped classroom; I'm talking about *starting* with Creating and "ending" with Remembering. Traditionally, Bloom's Taxonomy is conceptualized like this: Once learners have gone through all the steps of learning, *then* they can create something new. And it is commonly understood that learners cannot create before they understand what they are doing. What I am suggesting is to start with Creating and move naturally, back and forth through the "hierarchy" in a much more intuitive way. In this model, the hierarchy doesn't really exist anymore—just learning. Learners *discover* music through creating it themselves. Instead, Creating is the foundation, not the exception.

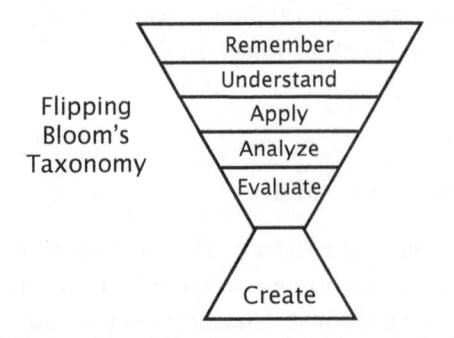

Flipping Bloom's Taxonomy

Remember
Understand
Apply
Analyze
Evaluate

Create

FIGURE 1.2 An example of Flipping Bloom's Taxonomy where create is the foundation

Creativity in US and Canadian Curricula

The National Core Music Standards describes "create" as to "conceive and develop new artistic ideas, such as an improvisation, composition, or arrangement, into a work."[3] *The Oxford English Dictionary* defines it as to "bring something into existence." If we use those definitions, recreating a piece of music doesn't cut it for ticking off the box for creating—although some form of re-creation, or copying, helps in developing the ear to musical conventions and idiomatics in any genre (discussed later).

In the United States, the National Core Arts Standards govern what each state's curriculum will look like. Each state, county, or district adapts those standards on the basis of

---

3. NAfME, "Core Music Standards Glossary," 2014, https://nafme.org/wp-content/uploads/2014/06/Core-Music-Standards-Glossary.pdf

regional differences that naturally exist within those entities. "Creating" is the first pillar of the National Core Arts Standards, which also include the first three (of 11) Anchor Standards:

1. Generate and conceptualize artistic ideas and work.
2. Organize and develop artistic ideas and work.
3. Refine and complete artistic work.

The National Association for Music Education has the music standards broken down into five strands that include:

1. PK–8 General Music
2. Composition/Theory
3. Music Technology
4. Guitar/Keyboard/Harmonizing Instruments
5. Ensemble

Out of those five strands (with the exception of popular music groups), Ensembles, in their traditional classical or church music forms, have the most trouble facilitating both creativity and technology in authentic, meaningful ways. Even though Create is a pillar of the core curriculum, it is still somewhat ignored in many music education circles.

In Canadian Curricula

In Canada, there are no national standards. There is no federal education minister, just 13 provincial/territorial ones. Each province/territory is solely responsible for education, meaning that they each have free rein to administer and write their own curricula. They can adapt another province's (or country's) curriculum to fit theirs if they so wish. This being said, a regional music curriculum was written for music programs in the four Atlantic provinces in 2001 and called the Foundation for the Atlantic Canada Arts Education Curriculum. By now it is certainly dated but many of the curricula in Atlantic Canada are based on this document, some loosely, and some more rigidly.

The Atlantic Canadian Curriculum has three "pillars," one of which is Creating, Making, and Presenting. Within that, there are two General Curriculum Outcomes (GCOs), or Anchor Standards of sorts:

1. Students will be expected to explore, challenge, develop, and express ideas, using the skills, language, techniques, and processes of the arts.
2. Students will be expected to create and/or present, collaboratively and independently, expressive products in the arts for a range of audiences and purposes.[4]

4.　PEI (Prince Edward Island) Government, "Foundation for the Atlantic Canada Arts Education Curriculum," 2001, https://www.princeedwardisland.ca/sites/default/files/publications/eelc_arts_foundation_document.pdf

They seem to suggest, in the basis of these two GCOs, that performing precomposed music in large ensembles is not the only expectation of this program. These GCOs certainly are inclusive of large ensemble music, but they also imply that it should not be the only form of expression.

There are even a few mentions of technology and "electronic sources" throughout the document, meaning this stuff should have been happening in music classrooms all over Atlantic Canada long before the publication of *this* book—but it wasn't.

The Issue

So, creativity is written into the documents, but why is music education so reluctant to give learners their own voice and the opportunity to express their creativity? Part of the issue is the wording of the documents themselves and the other is the training that preservice music teachers receive in University. In the Atlantic Canadian documents, at least, the common iteration under Creating, Making, and Presenting is mostly aimed at interpreting a precomposed piece of music, as opposed to creating original music. The closest it comes to mentioning this is the directive to "use a variety of notational systems to represent musical thoughts and ideas," but that takes into account only the ability to use a notational system to write ideas, and doesn't really address creativity and originality at all. Many times, kids will have much more complex musical ideas than they are able to express on paper (explored more, later in this book). I applaud the document for including the wording "a variety of notational systems," which opens the door for so many other ways of musicking.

It is all too common for a public-school music teacher to be trained in a conservatory where being creative and being creative through technology are silently frowned upon—unless, of course, you go on to "study" composition (you can't study composition, really; you just compose). Not only are composition majors encouraged to be creative, but they are also encouraged to use notation software and DAWs. In fact, composition is so separated at the conservatory that it is almost impossible to be both a performer *and* a composer. During the time of the "greats of classical music" it was expected that any trained musician could play, compose, improvise, and play by ear. Now, reading European staff notation seems to be the only valued skill within that field. If you are lucky enough to "study" composition, you become almost God-like, because the typical conservatory-trained musician (non-composer) cannot exist without the pre-written music of the composer—someone else's ink seems to become the only thing that matters. The voices of the people are lost.

Children's Inherent Creativity and the Perfection Illusion

Because of my classical training, like many others I've developed a misplaced emphasis on perfection rather than on the creative process. Children, for instance, don't have any of the inhibitions of a trained musician. In a TED Talk by creativity advocate and scholar, the late Sir Ken Robinson, he mentions that children from a very young age are not afraid to be wrong. If they don't know, they "just give it a go"—they improvise.[5] Unfortunately, he says, creativity is educated out of us early on. We become too well "trained." He points out that "if you're not prepared to be wrong, you'll never come up with anything original." I have had more years of training to be a musician than the kids I primarily teach have been alive and yet they seem to have composition figured out! There have been multiple rock bands at my school in separate years that have written and performed their own songs. A number of bands have had their songs recorded. One of those groups was ACR, and their song "Don't Go" can be heard at the following address: http://stevesmusicroom.webstarts.com/uploads/ Don_t_Go_-_A_C_R_.mp3. I am impressed every time a group composes a song together. At the same time, because they didn't have all of the training that I have had, these learners just did what they thought sounded good. Their fear of imperfection didn't get in the way, because it was non-existent. And when musicians of any age are using DAWs and other creative technologies to compose, many times no instruction is given other than that the piece must have a beginning, a middle, and an end. Even with these minimal parameters, some of the stuff learners come up with is incredible.*

Since the beginning of my studies for my classical music degree, I've suffered from pretty severe performance anxiety. It's a feeling I don't often get when performing within a group, unless I have to play an exposed written part. When I'm performing popular music or I'm in an improvised setting in a jazz band, for example, I never get performance anxiety. This shows itself only in classical music performance settings or if there is a notated solo part. My fear of imperfection doesn't get in the way when I'm improvising, because it has become something I'm used to and the thing is, nobody else knows what it's "supposed" to sound like. Sometimes, neither do I! Many times, I just close my eyes and play.

Changing the Mindset and "Letting Go" of Theory

An understanding of theory is essential for any musician. However, there *is* a balance, and depending on what genre or instrument you play will dramatically affect the theory you need to know. This is especially true of the classically trained musician, who tends to emphasize music theory (of 17th- and 18th-century Western European musicians) and may see it as an unbreakable law, many times to the detriment of their creative spark. What I mean is, if you know theory, don't "unlearn" it; just let go of it and be free *from* it because it can be restrictive. What we are unintentionally led to believe during our studies for our classical degrees is that Bach's rules of voice leading and harmony were the *only* set of rules that existed. This belief is partly due to an overemphasis on his style, a narrow focus that *can* be toxic in that it creates something of a hierarchy of musical compositional methods, because of the simple exclusion of other genres. If a "rule" of voice leading were to be broken, it was thought that it would

---

* Portions of this section were previously published in the *Canadian Music Educator Journal* 55, no. 2 (2013): 44–46.

5.   Ken Robinson, "Do Schools Kill Creativity?" video, October 2, 2020, https://www.ted.com/talks/sir_ken_robinson_do_schools_kill_creativity/up-next?language=en

not sound good enough. How many times during your studies for your degree did you see or hear a parallel fifth and think, "*BLASPHEMY! How could they do such a thing?*" Bach's style was just that, a style—one of many other styles of music before, during, and after it.

We often forget that music theory, for any genre of music, comes *after* some famous people already figured it out themselves—it's descriptive; not prescriptive, meaning that those musicians did what sounded good and a group of people got together long afterward to analyze and explain why their music sounded so good. Composition and improvisation can be significantly inhibited by learning music theory too early, because of the indoctrinated misconception that music *must* follow these strict rules. In fact, every genre and style of music has their own set of music theory. For example, the blues does not really follow any Western European model, and it can't truly be analyzed through that lens. To put this in perspective, in a typical 12-bar blues, all the chords are major tonalities, but the melodies are based on the minor pentatonic scale with a blue note (♭5, as we call it). Conventional common-practice-period theory would lead you to believe that mixing a major chord tonality with minor-based melodies would not sound very good—but it does.

Think about it another way: I guarantee you that Bach didn't sit down at his organ with the intention of coming up with an incredibly complex theoretical doctrine before he started composing; he just played whatever he liked, and wrote it down if it sounded good. If he didn't like it, it didn't make it onto the page. Even Bach learned to compose music first by copying other composers (or by copying a recording, if you will).[6] Eventually, he found a method that worked for him because it sounded good and made him money. Classical composers today are held on a much higher musical pedestal than other types of conservatory-trained musicians. The only characteristic that sets them apart from popular music composers and songwriters is that the classical composer has to write it down in a standard form for the "interpreters" (the classical musicians) to perform. Otherwise, it might not get heard. But with modern technology, DAWs, and notation software becoming ever more sophisticated, are musicians even needed to perform the scratchings of a classical composer? Perhaps this is a musing for another time. And considering the reach of the Internet as a resource and the ability to share anything over it, having music created in a DAW that can be posted online for anyone to hear in its purest form has the ability to reach *far* more audience members than a concert hall does.

Notes Are Overrated

Note reading is important, but not to the extent that traditional music education has led us all to believe. As with theory, there needs to be a balance. Many rock and popular musicians don't start out knowing *any* notation, and that's okay. Popular genres focus more on learning by ear, going by feel, and listening intently—skills that traditional music education has the tendency to put on the sidelines. Another chunk of popular musicians will understand some

---

6. Christoph Wolff, and Walter Emery, "Bach, Johann Sebastian," Grove Music Online, accessed November 27, 2021, https://doi.org/10.1093/gmo/9781561592630.article.6002278195

forms of shorthand notation like tablature or Nashville Numbers (discussed later). I would argue that a person who plays rock music primarily, learning European staff notation may not be overly useful for them, as the primary vehicle for transmitting the music is via audio recording. Also, the instrument a person plays will largely determine what notational systems (if any) that person should learn. A producer of beats (a composer of backing hip-hop or electronic music tracks) in a DAW, for example, would likely never need to learn to read European staff notation, because the medium they are working with has its own notational system and they work directly with sound, not the depiction of sound. My point is that conservatory-trained musicians must free themselves, so to speak, from the constraints that an overreliance on notation and theory can have on their creativity. Remember this: aural and visual complexity is often mistaken for quality. Keep it simple!

Learning by Ear, Creativity, and Technology

What does learning by ear have to do with creativity? To be creative, a person has to use their ear in a different way to anticipate where the next note or chord will go. Learning by ear helps to develop the ability to hear the idiomatic tendencies of a particular instrument or genre. Over time, this skill helps the creator of the music to be able to hear where the next chord or note should (or could) go during the creative process. I experienced this first-hand when I learned both guitar and drums by ear. For example, on the guitar, there is a very commonly played chord extension that starts on the D chord, then the D^{sus4} chord and then back to the D chord, simply because of how the chord is voiced and the shape of the chord on the instrument. This idiomatic pattern is heard in a plethora of songs from "American Pie" to Bon Jovi's "Dead or Alive" and to Pearl Jam's "Last Kiss." It is extremely easy to pinpoint and can be recognized instantaneously. The exact same parallels can be drawn between this chord use and technology skills. Patterns that are common will become instantly recognizable as well as sounds and effects commonly used. It is important, however, that this pattern recognition is not to be confused with ear training (used in the conservatory model), which will be discussed in another chapter.

Improvisation versus Composition: What's the Difference?

What Is Improvisation?

It seems, when traditionally trained musicians think of improvisation, jazz improv is instantly where their minds go, that when we improvise, we believe we have to sound amazing the first time and understand all the theory behind it. But it's not true. Those amazing improvisers had to start somewhere, and all learners really need to know to improvise is just three notes! Just listen to any song on the radio, and I mean *really* listen. How many notes do the melodies actually use? Chances are it's only between three and five! What we often don't understand, though, is that improvisation is the "gateway drug" to composition—you can't have one without the other. Improvisation can certainly be a means unto itself but to create a composition of your own you *have* to improvise first, or if you like, present the material for the composition.

What Is Composition?

Composition is also thought of as something that's *way* more complicated and complex than it actually is. Compositions are simply improvisations that have been set in stone, so to speak. They have not necessarily been written down in staff notation but could be drawn, coloured, or recorded with an audio recording device. Any recording of an improvisation can become the composition. If a musician improvises in the recording studio, the result can then become the composition. For example, Slash's guitar solos were no doubt improvised in-studio (or crafted in the pre-production stage) but have become part of the composition, and it would be difficult now to hear those iconic solos any differently from the way they are on the radio. In my own experience recording with my band, the solos heard on the record were not necessarily even played in one take. Many of the solos on the album were improvised at separate times and pieced together by the recording engineer to create a well-crafted composition that *sounded* improvised in one take. Once the albums had been released, the solos on the albums were very similar to what we would then play in a live setting. Anything can be recorded nowadays with apps on our phones—literal recording studios in our pockets.

2

Technology in Music Education

Music and technology have been intertwined since the dawn of the art form and have always been connected to new ways of producing sounds and making new musics. Even though technology has been intertwined with music since its inception, and since the dawn of sound recording has expanded to include multitrack recording, musical instrument digital interface (MIDI), and other digital recording, music education has been slow to catch up. But where does this reluctance to accept technology come from? Aside from music education's general resistance to change, there are some other factors, as follows.

Curriculum in the United States and Canada

Technology in Canadian Curricula

It seems that the curriculum is only part of the problem. The Foundation for the Atlantic Canada Arts Education Curriculum does mention technology and there is even an outcome to address it, which states, "Students will be expected to understand the role of technologies in creating and responding to expressive works." It is careful in its wording in that it doesn't say to "use" and understand, or to "explore" and understand these technologies. The best it can muster for technology is the instruments that produce music or sounds by stating, "Recognize individual orchestral, band, and keyboard instruments and their families by sight and sound." Of course, these are mechanical, not to mention incredibly Eurocentric, and, frankly, not digital technology. About as close as the document gets to digital technology is "understand that changing technologies have produced new opportunities for musical expression." So, again, know it exists but don't worry about understanding it even though music technology was well integrated into music outside of school by 2001, when the standards were written.

All of the basics of digital music production existed in 2001. Multitrack recording was invented in the 1950s, and MIDI in the 1980s. Looping was also well established. These are still widely used technologies. The gear has gotten smaller, easier to use, more affordable, and more accessible, and all of the basic concepts of how these technologies work are still true.

Technology for Unleashing Creativity. Steve Giddings, Oxford University Press. © Oxford University Press 2022.
DOI: 10.1093/oso/9780197570739.003.0003

Certainly, in 2001, digital recording and sound reproduction existed, but part of the issue is not the curriculum, but the teacher training received (which continues to be a problem). Outside of classical music, and even jazz to some degree, digital technology is widely used to produce original music, perform music, and record music. In the conservatory model, exposure to sound production and audio engineering is very little. This means that it is perpetuated from the teacher training and that limited knowledge is passed into the curricula that are written by teachers, and then to the learners of those curricula. Many times, it is even completely ignored by the teacher in the classroom because of their lack of exposure to modern digital music technology or their complete disrespect for music made with a computer.

Another important factor to note is that many of the technologies available in the 1990s and early 2000s were not as cheap or accessible as they are today. Cloud-based free technologies (which you will learn about in this book) were either non-existent or primitive in their forms but there were a number of open-sourced technologies like Audacity, and some simpler MIDI software that could have been utilized at the time.

Technology in the US National Standards

Unlike the Atlantic Canadian Foundations Curriculum, the US National standards do not include technology as either one of the four pillars or in the 11 Anchor Standards. In the combination of the five streams mentioned previously, the word "technology" appears only 13 times. Oddly enough, there are three that don't mention it even once: Music Technology (!?), Guitar/Keyboard Harmonizing Instruments, and Ensemble. To be fair, the Music Technology stream gets more specific with technology and uses the words "analog" (six times), and "digital" (49 times). No other stream mentions those words. Strangely, too, not once do the words "technology," "analog," or "digital" appear in the Guitar/Keyboard Harmonizing Instruments, or Ensemble strands. Seeing as guitar- and keyboard-based music largely utilizes analog and digital technologies in the form of amplifiers, onboard computers, MIDI controllers (which are devices used to communicate musical information to a computer which are often in the form of a keyboard), and other computer-generated sound effects, it seems somewhat hard to understand why these technologies are neglected. Outside of classical-based ensembles, analog and digital technology is used regularly to make sounds and produce original music. It is safe to assume, on the basis of the National Standards, that unless you are a teacher of music technology, analog and digital technologies will be largely overlooked in a typical music classroom.

Teacher Training

Have you ever noticed that informally trained musicians tend to have a much more extensive knowledge and understanding of musical technology than those trained in a conservatory-style university program? They tend to also know a great deal about music and how it is made, but on a (sometimes) deeper level than a conservatory-trained musician. I remember in my university teacher training, between 2003 and 2008, the most we talked about with regard to technology in music teaching was pressing "play" on a CD player—no joke! Much of the time, "technology in music education" is interpreted as the musical instruments and the mechanical properties of those instruments. It is applied and interpreted in an historical context, as in the development of modern musical instruments. In the Prince Edward Island (PEI) curriculum, developed around the same time as the Atlantic Canadian Foundations document. There are explicit examples of using analog and digital music technology in the Grade 1 to 6 music classroom, but from what I understand through teaching in PEI, these ideas either have not been widely adopted or are completely ignored. I am sure many North American situations are very similar. Robert Komaniecki puts it succinctly in a tweet (Figure 2.1).

Robert Komaniecki
@Komaniecki_R
                                                                                                    ...

Just thinking about how my music PhD required me to demonstrate proficiency in French and German, but not in any notation software or DAW

2:25 PM · Sep 23, 2020 · Twitter Web App

51 Retweets   **9** Quote Tweets   **524** Likes

FIGURE 2.1 Robert Komaniecki tweet describing his thoughts on how his PhD didn't require proficiency in any DAW

The Big Three

For a curriculum I helped to develop that was based on the Atlantic Foundations document, I proposed three subsections for musical technology: mechanical, analog, and digital.

So you might be wondering. "What do you mean by these headings?" I'll explain.

Mechanical—This category includes any physical musical instrument that is non-electric or nondigital.

How a piston valve on a trumpet works is mechanical. How a key on a tenor recorder works is mechanical. It is still technology that helped to advance the playability of particular instruments and make them easier to play, even though they aren't digital or electronic. What the advancement looks like depends largely on the time period the improvement was added.

Analog—These devices use electricity but still have a physical presence.

A reel-to-reel tape recorder is an analog recording technology. A nondigital mixing board with physical faders and knobs is an analog technology, and the microphone is also analog. They don't need computers to work, just electrical signals and amplification. Another common analog technology is the electric guitar.

> Digital—These technologies mostly exist on a computer in binary code, which is a series of 0s and 1s that are used to communicate to a computer.

They exist in the "cloud," within your computer, and on your phone. In essence, if the functionality uses a computer chip it is considered a digital technology. Some digital technologies take the form of guitar amplifiers, pianos/keyboards, and mixing boards and are run by a computer installed within the software to run them. Digital technologies are not to be confused with virtual, as virtual instruments (discussed in a later chapter) exist only as software and need a computer or a MIDI controller to work.

It is important that when we are discussing technology in music education, we understand that these three are still in use and have multiple purposes in modern music making. When someone or something is playing and performing music, all of these types of technologies coexist, working together or separately at any given moment. For example, as a music educator you might be coaching a trumpet player (mechanical), a drummer (mechanical), an electric guitar player (analog), a keyboard player (digital), and a trombone player (mechanical) who are all recording in a studio (digital) and be able to understand all these technologies and how they work separately or together to make music.

The "Old" Way

There seems to be this notion in some circles that if music isn't recorded in European staff notation or played on a "real" instrument, the composer of that music, and the music itself, are "lesser." The typical visual of a composer (or songwriter) is a person sitting with their piano or guitar while they are slavishly writing out notes or lyrics with fantastic romanticism like this (Figure 2.2):

FIGURE 2.2 Brooding Beethoven at the piano

But what if a music composer looked like this? (Figure 2.3):

FIGURE 2.3 Composer at a DAW

Over the years, songwriting, has come to describe any number of methods and processes for writing songs in popular styles. It's traditionally thought of as one or two people sitting at a piano (in the Tin Pan Alley days), or a guitar and writing chord progressions to go with melodies or melodies with rough lyrics to go with chord progressions. It's the way popular music has been written for decades, and it's called the melody-and-lyrics approach to songwriting. It's the kind we all imagine when we think of popular music composers writing music. Nashville is still heavily steeped in this approach to songwriting. I mean, if it ain't broke, don't fix it.

The word "producer" has developed a new meaning as well. In music and most of the performing and recording arts, a producer is the person who oversees the production or the recording process and may have some creative input into the final product. In electronic music composition and many popular music styles (especially rap, hip-hop, and pop) the word "producer" has become synonymous with the word "composer." Another common word in the music world that has taken on a new meaning is the word "beat." In electronic and popular musics, "beat" has a more complex meaning than it does in classical musics. In traditional music teaching, it refers to the pulse in music. In electronic and popular musics, it refers to pulse, but also refers to a precomposed backing track, a drum-machine pattern, or a drum-kit groove. A person who composes backing tracks for an emcee to rap over is called a beatmaker.

The Track-and-Hook Approach

Since the early 2000s, the track-and-hook approach has become the preferred method for writing hit songs. In this approach, producers prepare what is essentially a backing track that is fully produced and fleshed out before adding a melody to it. The melody is contracted out, so to speak, to melody writers, or topliners who write melodic hooks (the part of the song that catches the ear of the listener) and then sends it back to the producer. The topliner doesn't even have to be in the studio to add their melody lines. That is the beauty of technology nowadays. Soundtrap and BandLab (see Chapter 6) both facilitate this method of writing songs with relative ease. Because of the accessibility of different forms of this technology, producers may send their beats out to 20 different topliners for their take. Topliners are usually in the position of writing melodies because they were selected to be hook writers for factory-like music production. It's not unheard of, either, to have a topliner improvise a line over a producer's track with a little bit of Auto-Tune on to help them improvise without worrying about getting every single note perfect. Auto-Tune, in this scenario, helps the topliner to improvise unhindered.[1] It can also be used as a choice musical timbre within a song—as compositional material.

Canadian rapper Drake uses Auto-Tune as a timbre for his voice in recordings. Cher, a bit later in her career, used Auto-Tune (after everyone knew she could already sing!) as a choice musical timbre for her voice. There are situations in which Auto-Tune is a useful tool for composing and that the negative reaction it tends to receive from even trained musicians is unfounded.

Sometimes a particular song is written with a certain artist in mind. This practice is standard in both the Nashville country music industry, in which the lyrics-and-melody approach dominates, and in the mainstream pop industry, in which the track-and-hook approach dominates. The moral of this story is that both work and they both get the same result—an original musical composition.

Harmony to Texture

For the purposes of discussions throughout this book, classical and classical-based music will refer to music within the Western European classical canon and the musics based from it that primarily exist in schools and universities. To make a classical piece of music more interesting, composers and performers of classical music often add dynamics (the louds and softs) or harmony to a melody to enhance its appeal. In recorded and electronic-based music produced on computers, the primary vehicle for generating interest is texture (or rhythm). This is mainly due to audio compression, in which the louds and softs are equalled out so that everything on a track is of consistent volume and tone. But the music itself, mostly based on repeating patterns and amplification, lends itself very well to subtle textural changes to draw in the listener. Dynamics and harmony are not necessarily the go-to element of the music

---

1. John Seabrook, *The Song Machine: Inside the Hit Factory*, (New York: W. W. Norton and Company, 2015).

producer or beatmaker, as they often rely on textural enhancements instead to get the musical point across. In Netflix's original "Song Exploder," hip-hop artist and musician Ty Dolla $ign says, "To me, music is all about textures."[2]

The Use of Amplification

Many modern instruments rely on some form of amplification to make a sound. Those instruments include, but are not limited to, the electric guitar, bass, electronic drums, and digital keyboards. Heavily distorted electric guitar, for instance, depending on the type of distortion used, certainly cannot portray even the slightest change in dynamics without controlling the volume. Many rock bands and popular music ensembles rely on analog and digital technology to exist. A band can't even really rehearse without amplification from some sort of technical equipment. These groups also rely heavily on texture but, depending on the instruments involved in a live show, can give dynamic contrasts when needed. Chapter 4 will go into much more depth on the equipment to facilitate creativity in scenarios like these.

Technology for Technology's Sake

Technology has long been neglected in music education. And even since the Tanglewood Symposium of 1967, not much has changed. Keeping in mind that most people in the developed world today have supercomputers in their pockets and that computers in 1967 were the size of entire rooms, Declaration 5 states that "developments in educational technology, education television, programmed instruction, and computer-assisted instruction should be applied to music study and research."[3] At the time, and up until the 1990s, the old adage "Technology for Technology's sake" could have very much applied to education in schools. Technology was purchased without many educational benefits attached. Today, the benefits are clear, and while the whole of education is jumping on board, music education seems to be lagging behind. Some might argue that to be talking about Technology for Technology's Sake in this day and age is moot, because we've already won! But consider the vast amount of technology in society and in the music industry that never darkens the doorway of the music room.

2. Hrishikesh Hirway, prod. Song Exploder. Tremelo Productions, 2020. https://www.netflix.com/watch/81025977.

3. Tanglewood, "1967 Tanglewood Symposium," Accessed March 28, 2021. tanglewoodsymposium.blogspot.com/p/the-tanglewood-declaration.html.

3

The Informal Learning Approach

Informal Learning

Informal learning is not a new idea in education. It's how people have learned outside of school and before public education since the beginning of time. In music education, however, we sometimes forget that music can be learned informally. And it is—all the time, especially in popular genres. In fact, most music ever made was created informally. If taught authentically, popular music, creativity, and technology lend themselves well to informal learning approaches. But what is informal learning, and what does it look like, anyway? Informal learning essentially involves learning methods outside of a formal school setting. In music, this usually involves the following:

1. Learning music that they choose, and identify with
2. Learning by listening and copying recordings initially on a trial-and-error basis
3. Playing and learning alongside friends
4. Acquiring knowledge in holistic, haphazard ways, and learners navigate the learning themselves
5. Integrating listening, performing, composing, and improvising throughout the learning process[1]

Authenticity

Authentic learning means that the goals and learning processes are realistic and culturally relevant, and meet learners' needs.[2] Authentic learning is also a term that is used in diverse global music contexts, and in popular music ones as well. It applies very well to technology instruction, too. Letting learners of creative technology play and explore is much more "culturally relevant" to the way this musical technology is learned in the world outside of school

---

1. Lucy Green, *Hear, Listen, Play! How to Free Your Students' Aural, Improvisation, and Performance Skills* (New York: Oxford University Press, 2014).

2. Evelein Frits, "Pop and World Music in Dutch Music Education: Two Cases of Authentic Learning in Music Teacher Education and Secondary Music Education," *International Journal of Music Education* 24, no. 2 (2006): 178–187, doi:10.1177/0255761406065479, 183.

Technology for Unleashing Creativity. Steve Giddings, Oxford University Press. © Oxford University Press 2022.
DOI: 10.1093/oso/9780197570739.003.0004

than the way it is in traditional learning. This comparison will be discussed later in the chapter but it is worth noting now that much of the music tech, and creative music tech specifically, is learned primarily through trial and error without any formal training. Thus, the term "culturally relevant" can be used here. It is a prominent subculture within the modern music world. This means that a shift in the way we teach and deliver curriculum needs reinventing.

Becoming the Facilitator

Of course, there is a bit of an ebb and flow for the teacher in this regard. To fully let learners engage in informal learning, some control does have to be forfeited. This means that the teacher becomes a facilitator of learning, and the kids become learners instead of students. It puts the onus on the children to learn, and the teacher to facilitate that learning. What great teachers of young children are good at is facilitating informal learning through what they call play-based learning. Essentially, it's taking the play-based approaches of early childhood educators, kindergarten teachers, and applying them in an age-appropriate way that is, ultimately, discovery learning. The ebb and flow that I mentioned earlier refers to being able to go between letting the learners do all of the learning and being able to coach them in the right direction. I like to refer to myself as their music coach, as opposed to their teacher.

The following are ways teachers can think to begin relinquishing control of the classroom to facilitate learning from the informal learning approach.

Have an Open Mind and Learn with Students

When learning with students you are keeping one step ahead of them or, in many cases, *in* step with them. You may even be behind where the learners are, and that's okay. In doing so, you will learn in the way students are naturally inclined to learn a new concept or skill. They, too, learn best when they teach somebody else. It is reflective of Vygotsky's theory of the zones of proximal development (ZPD)[3] (Figure 3.1).

The ZPD is "the distance between the actual developmental level as determined by independent problem solving and the level of potential development as determined through problem solving under adult guidance, or in collaboration with more capable peers."[4] From this definition, the teacher would be considered the more capable peer or the *coach*. You could also do as the theory suggests and have the students teach one another. This practice also aligns with the informal learning research of Lucy Green, who suggests that the teacher should be the *facilitator* and let the students do most of the teaching.[5] Having the students be in charge *will* take longer to reach the end goal, but it will take some of

3.   L. S. Vygotsky, *Mind in Society: Development of Higher Psychological Processes* (Cambridge, Massachusetts: Harvard University Press, 1978).

4.   Ibid.

5.   Lucy Green, *Music, Informal Learning and the School: A New Classroom Pedagogy* (Aldershot, UK: Ashgate Publishing, 2008).

the pressure off you, and just imagine the real-life experiences that will take place here! Keep in mind that this is a learner-centred process-based approach, so taking as long as the learners need is important.

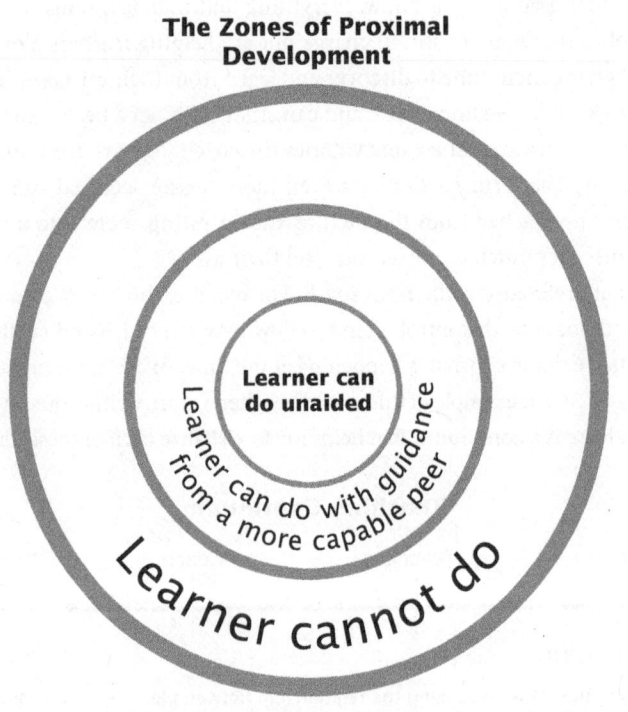

The Zones of Proximal Development

Learner can do unaided

Learner can do with guidance from a more capable peer

Learner cannot do

FIGURE 3.1 A pictorial describing the Zones of Proximal Development as developed by Lev Vygotsky

Trust the Kids—They Know More Than You Think They Do

We tend not to give learners enough credit. The fact is that you don't even need to know how to work the technology, because oftentimes the kids will have it figured out or will be able to figure it out rather quickly. Your students, many times, know more than you think they do.

Lucy Green's research took her into classrooms by working with real students and teachers in real schools. Teachers involved with this project "unanimously agreed that . . . using informal learning practices in the classroom has generally changed [their] approach to teaching for the better."[6] Teachers admitted that they were repeatedly surprised by their learners and that, in general, their expectations had been too low. They did not give learners enough credit for what they were actually capable of doing. Throughout this project, the teachers and the researcher realized that the main theme for the success of learners involved in this project was that of autonomy. Learners were given choice and freedom and therefore were presented with the opportunity to discover learning on their own.

6. Ibid.

Think of Yourself as a Coach or Facilitator

Thinking of yourself as a coach or facilitator can greatly decrease the pressure on you and help make learning *with* your students a very positive experience. The label of *teacher* adds a level of stress that assumes you know everything and puts less onus on the learner. The term *coach* implies that you are still in charge but are helping learners along to reach their goals while still giving them time to discover and learn from their mistakes. Think of a sports coach—a coach can still give homework and can still drill if need be, but in the end the onus is on the players to perform at the game without the coach, to learn from their mistakes and fix them on the fly. The term *facilitator* is even more learner-centred still by almost completely removing the teacher from the picture and inserting them into a supervisory role while students discover much of the learning on their own.

My personal preference is the term *coach*. For me, it is the happy medium between too much control and not enough control. I tend to flow between coach and facilitator, depending on what students are doing or what is happening at the time. In certain situations, more of a facilitator role is needed. An example of this would be when we are writing our own songs and creating new ideas. Here is a continuum that helps me to visualize each of these terms (Figure 3.2):

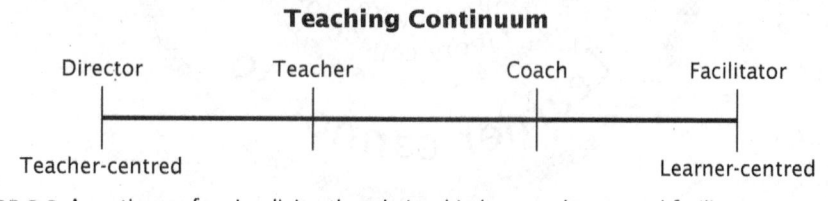

FIGURE 3.2 A continuum for visualizing the relationship between learner and facilitator

The term *learner*, like the term *facilitator* is a much less formal way to think of the word but also shifts the *teacher-student* relationship to *facilitator-learner*. *Student*, like the term *director* or *teacher*, implies a very rigid type of learning and does not consider the explorative aspect of learning in general. I don't direct or teach; I facilitate.

The overall theme when you are beginning to engage with informal learning as a teacher is to let go of your control so that the student can become the learner. The teacher becomes the facilitator who promotes learning by setting up the environment. For vernacular and popular musics (many of which are composed by using technology), this approach is incredibly useful and authentic in the way those genres are traditionally learned—a great tool for engaging learners in music in ways they never thought possible in a school setting.

The Benefits of Learning Informally

You may be thinking, "Okay, Steve, sounds cool, but why can't I just keep doing what I'm doing?" The answer is that you can, but consider the skills that are missing in a strictly traditional, formal setting. If we consider learning music as akin to learning a language, then the skills needed to fully understand music as a language must be acquired. We need to open up what we mean when we think about "music literacy." Music literacy is not just reading and writing notes and rhythms—it encompasses so much more, as referred to in the introduction of this book.

Musicians trained in formal settings tend to emphasize the understanding of European staff notation and writing it out without giving students opportunities to have their own conversations, tell their own stories, play by ear, or improvise and compose. Informal learning approaches open up the learning process and naturally give meaningful, real-life musical experiences to learners other than just reading and writing. I don't want to get too political, but informal learning is not a top-down dictatorship the way traditional music learning tends to be. It's a true liberal democracy (aside from the learners not getting to elect their facilitator) wherein every learner has agency over their learning and can make decisions for their own musical journey with the guidance of a leader. Agency in education can be a very powerful force.*

Some Resources for Informal Learning

If you want to learn more about informal learning in a music setting, here are a few resources to peruse:

> *How Popular Musicians Learn* (Ashgate Publishing, 2002), by Lucy Green
> *Music, Informal Learning, and the School* (Ashgate Publishing, 2008), by Lucy Green
> *Hear, Listen, Play* (Oxford University Press, 2014), by Lucy Green
> *21st Century Music Education* (Canadian Music Educators' Association, 2016) by Ruth Wright, Carol Benyon, and Betty Anne Younker, eds.
> *Rock Coach* (Steve's Music Room Publishing, 2017) by Steve Giddings (wait, I know that guy!)
> *Coaching a Popular Music Ensemble* (McLemore Ave Music, 2019) by Steve Holley
> *Creative Musicking* (Steve's Music Room Publishing, 2020) by Steve Giddings

Informal Learning and Technology

With regard to music technology fluency, the five tenets of informal learning certainly apply. Many times, in North America at least, skills in creative music technology and other musical technology are learned informally. Even sound engineers and recording producers often learn all of their skills outside of a formal school setting. YouTube videos and tutorials are plentiful (akin to the 1967 Tanglewood Symposium's mention of teaching videos). Many of my friends and fellow musicians who have primarily learned their craft informally can discern the difference between specific types of effects in electronic music and can even discern the difference between 3kHz and 2kHz in an isolated track. Those who work in live sound tend to possess a vast knowledge of the industry standards and without formal training work with North America's top acts. And in this

---

* Portions of this section were originally published in the *Canadian Music Educator Journal* 60, no. 4 (2019): 33–36.

way, using informal learning approaches to facilitate learning of music technology is culturally relevant and authentic.

Let's Play It by Ear

Playing by ear, at one time, was not only a skill that popular musicians utilized—it was part of being a whole musician. When I was pursuing my undergrad at music school between 2003 and 2008, learning music by ear was discouraged, frowned upon, and considered a "lesser" form of music learning when compared to reading precomposed music written in European staff notation. Much of this bias was implicit due, again, to an overreliance and hyperfocus on one thing. Even though it was considered lesser, only a few of us could actually do it, and my thought was that if it was so much lesser, why couldn't we all do it? Playing by ear is a foundational musical skill that classically trained musicians have lost because of depending too much on European staff notation. We just have to find a way to "let go" and spend more time letting our learners copy and create their own music. The informal learning approach helps us to achieve those musical goals we have been neglecting in music education all this time.[†]

Copying Recorded Music versus Ear Training

Copying music that you hear is how the ear is developed. Think of it as language acquisition; you copy the sounds first, for years before reading comprehension begins. In music school, "ear training" is often a separate course that is done in complete isolation from ensemble and solo work and the exercises are not even executed on their primary instrument! Good ears can be developed in this way, but the most effective, authentic, and worthwhile method for ear training is to copy recordings and do it in a way that complements ensemble and solo work. Think about it like this: when a popular musician wants to learn a new song, they don't search for the sheet music; instead, they listen to the recording and learn it by ear. In most cases, they search it online by using readily available technology. In so doing, the musician is able to develop their ear in a much more natural way because over time they will be able to recognize patterns in other songs more quickly than if it was done in isolation. As well, if there is a new skill that needs to be learned to perform the song, the new skill will be learned, too. What is important to note here is that learning by ear in this way makes it vastly easier to improvise because the patterns within the music are much more easily recognized. It can later carry over into notation reading and make that skill much easier to acquire as well (if that is your goal, of course).

Lucy Green, a long-time scholar of informal learning approaches in the United Kingdom, has lots to say about learning music by ear. A tenet of informal learning involves

---

† Portions of this section were adapted from an article originally published in the *Canadian Music Educator Journal* vol. 60, no. 2 (2019): 34–36.

learning music by ear from a recording, as referenced earlier. During her first study, published in 2002, she observed that

> the informal learning practices of popular musicians, especially listening, copying [learning by ear] and improvising can lead to the development of what can be called very "good ears." Although their aural abilities are not necessarily any better than those of classical musicians, they are likely to be better sooner and, moreover, to be possessed by the vast majority of the players involved, rather than the few.[7]

This observation suggests that the immersiveness of learning by ear from a recording might be a superior method to developing the ear than the traditional non-immersive approach common in conservatory training.

In her 2014 book, *Hear, Listen, Play!* (HeLP), Green presents concrete examples of how the informal learning model using ear-based learning can look when administered in a variety of school music settings with tips for the teacher on how to approach it and what to expect in those situations. For part of the research in the book, Green was able to conduct an experiment with a control group of learners (those who did not use any HeLP strategies) and their HeLP groups who had experience with HeLP strategies. Learners were paired with others who had similar experiences and ages but were from different study groups. Then, "each student listened to a short recording of a melody played twice on a piano. The student was then given the starting note and key chord, but nothing else, and was asked to play the melody back on their instrument, by ear."[8] Students were all assessed on the following criteria with the help of the ABRSM (the assessment body for music in the UK):

pitch accuracy
contour accuracy
rhythmic accuracy
closure (whether they attempted to complete the melody or not)
tempo accuracy
overall performance

They found that *"all the children in the group who had used the HeLP strategies achieved higher marks on every criterion than did the students who had not used the HeLP strategies"* (italics added). Although Lucy Green herself said that more research is needed in this area, these findings are significant.

Rap music is the exception here. Many rappers learn their craft through informal means but recreating is not normal in that music-making culture as the next section explains.

---

7. Lucy Green, *How Popular Musicians Learn: A Way Ahead for Music Education* (Aldershot, UK: Ashgate Publishing, 2002).

8. Green, 2014

The Hip-Hop Advantage

Copying and performing the music of other musicians is expected in most Western musical cultures from classical to rock and jazz. In jazz circles specifically (also very much rooted in Black American artforms), if a musician doesn't know how to play a song that is called during an open jam session, they are ridiculed. In rap music specifically it's inauthentic and even *disrespectful* to copy another emcee's lyrics and sound. This is why there are almost no rap covers. Other rappers call it biting, and the unwritten rule is that you are not to steal (or bite) any other rapper's verses or sound. It is similar to jazz wherein a musician is expected to play their own solo in a performance, but not the one from the recording. On the other hand, in rock music playing the original solo is seen as paying homage to the original artist.[9] Also in rock music, reproducing the solos and the songs exactly as they are on the recordings is incredibly common and, in some cases, expected. I mean, there are cover bands devoted to reproducing exactly a chosen band or artist. Also, covering a song but changing the stylistic approach and using the same recognizable melodies and chord progressions to create a completely new listening experience is also common and encouraged. Of course in classical music, particularly in nineteenth century music, it is expected the musician play exactly as it was intended in the "recording" (the sheet music) and straying from that is considered incredibly disrespectful (the exact opposite of rap).

In rap music, which is almost entirely composed on computers using samples (of other people's music) and precomposed beats, the lyrics and verses of a rapper cannot be reproduced. Those must be original. What this suggests to me is that rap music is an inherently and intentionally creative artform. The music must come from within, and must be identifiable only to that emcee. As the Flipping Bloom's Taxonomy discussion from earlier suggests, this philosophy also means that it *is* possible to create without first having recreated. This has far-reaching implications for creativity and the informal learning opportunities within a school to help bridge the gap between music-making practices inside of school and those outside of school and into the lifetime.

In Questlove's 2018 book, *Creative Quest*, he describes creativity as being incredibly important to hip-hop, but then poses it another way by stating instead that perhaps we should think about "how important hip-hop is to creativity."[10] If there were a "continuum of creativity" of sorts, hip-hop music would be on the extremely creative end, and classical (in the conservatory model), would be on the other. The reason all of this context about hip-hop music is important is that there is a lot that music education as a whole can learn about hip-hop culture and specifically how extremely creative and tech-savvy the artform is compared to other forms of music creation. Music education has a lot to learn from hip-hop culture with regard to the creativity and the use of technology to create music.

---

9. Adam Neely, "Rap Cover Songs Don't Exist (and Here's Why)," video, September 22, 2020, https://www.yout ube.com/watch?v=D_mh1Rq35ZM.

10. Questlove, *Creative Quest* (New York: Ecco, 2018), 147.

How Informal Learning Might Look in Your General Music Classroom

Recently, I facilitated an informal learning scenario in my classroom with Grade 6 learners using Chromebooks and fretted instruments. This approach can certainly be adapted for Grades 5 through 12. Here is what it looked like.

Phase 1: To Begin

Prior to this project, we had learned a few chord shapes on guitars together as a class. The students learned by copying my hand shapes and getting comfortable with reading chord diagrams, making sure their fingers were in the right places to form the chord or in a comfortable position that worked for them. The songs we learned together were "Eleanor Rigby" by the Beatles (C, Em), "Songbird" by Oasis (G, Em), "Best Day of My Life" by American Authors (D, G, [Bm]), and "Last Kiss" by Pearl Jam (G, Em, C, D). As you may notice, we were building up to "Last Kiss," which is a four-chord song with all the chords they knew up to that point. For beginners, I had them choose between the simplified shapes or the full shapes.

Phase 2: Any Requests?

When I knew they had a handle on the shapes, I asked the class for requests. At that point, I introduced UltimateGuitar.com. It's a fantastic website designed for learning popular songs and, many times, classical selections, too. Recently, it's been updated with strumming patterns for some tunes, but it usually has tabs, chord diagrams, lyrics, and the ability to switch between guitar, ukulele, and piano. There is an auto-scroll feature at the bottom of the page, as well as a transpose function, too. Often, if learners type "[song name] chords" into Google, UltimateGuitar.com is the first hit that comes up. Because it's a crowd-sourced site, the songs can occasionally be incorrect, so either choose the latest version of the song or when you notice a mistake use it as a teachable moment about making sure to really listen or set the learners up by playing the two different chords against the recording and see if they can hear the one that fits better. Figure 3.3 (next page) shows a number of the features on this website.

We went through the same learning process as always with any new chords. If a song had tablature come up, we talked about how to read it and what it means. Every class had the base of G, Em, C, and D, but depending on the song each class chose, they could go in different directions after this, as is perfectly acceptable in the informal learning world. Being a learner-based model, it focuses on the process and what the individual learner needs/wants instead of what the facilitator thinks everyone wants/needs.

Phase 3: Authentic Informal Learning

Once I had thought the learners had a good understanding of how to read chord charts for new chords and how UltimateGuitar.com worked, it became time for Phase 3. Phase 3

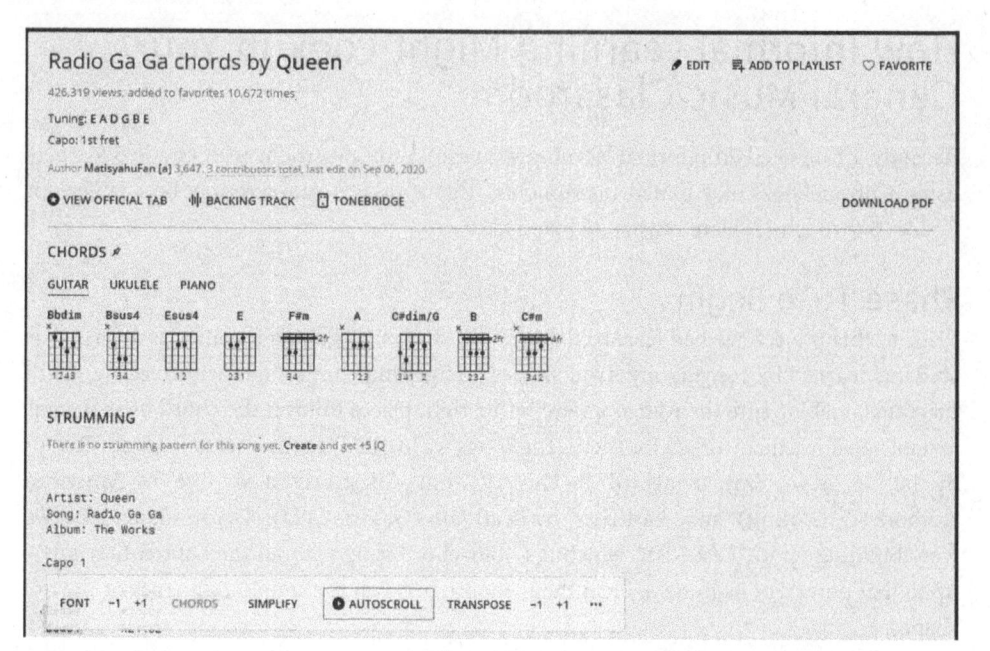

FIGURE 3.3 Screen shot of the UltimateGuitar.com interface showing the chords for the song "Radio Ga Ga"

included getting Chromebooks out for each learner and letting them decide if they wanted to work in pairs or individually, choosing any song they wanted and figuring out how to play it by using UltimateGuitar.com. Now, the most authentic version of this would be to have thrown them into the deep end, so to speak, in Phase 1. The model I employed, however, gave each learner a base to go from, while still allowing everyone to learn what they wanted. Some got heavily into tab and some into chords. Some wanted to sing and play the song, and others just wanted the chords. It depended on where the learners were and what interested them. At that point, I acted as coach and facilitator, learning new songs with them and exploring the best ways to solve problems of fingering or tabs that looked confusing. I had YouTube set up in the middle of the room with headphones so the learners could hear their song; the essence of learning in this way is more listening—immersing themselves in the culture, if you will. If your school has ways to play music at learner laptops, this would be a better approach so they can hear it more easily and more often. An important step in this process is being able to know how the song actually goes. Since the chord charts give only so much information, listening is paramount.

Later in this phase, some learners wanted to try the ukulele, and UltimateGuitar.com has an option for ukulele chords, as well as piano chord diagrams. I completely endorsed this venture because it was exploratory learning and discovery learning at its best. They instantly discovered the similarities between the guitar and the uke. For example, they would notice that the D shape on the guitar is the G shape on the ukulele (everything is up a fourth). Many really enjoyed the agency this difference provided, and they were still learning the exact same concepts and skills. And they were beginning to create their own mini-arrangements without prompting, by choosing the instrument to play it on. An extension of this exercise would be to actually have them create their own arrangements by using UltimateGuitar.com as a guide for their creative ideas. From there, learners might have ideas to expand on the experience by using loops from Chrome Music Lab or using a drum machine.

How It Might Look in Your Traditional Instrumental Music Classroom

Classical music ensembles like wind bands can learn informally, too. There can be some amazing learning moments by using UltimateGuitar.com in a large ensemble format. If you want to learn a pop song (or classical work) on any instrument, you and your learners do the following:

Choose a song they want to play.

Learn the melody by ear. Giving them the first note could be helpful, but this depends on the aural learning experience of your learners.

Look up the chords on UltimateGuitar.com and have everyone learn to play the root notes (thus beginning a wonderful conversation about triads).

If it's in a strange key for your learners (which it likely will be), UltimateGuitar.com has a transpose function. It could be a great way to explore new keys! Being able to play along with the recording is beneficial and a lot of fun for your young musicians. Learners can easily transpose a track in BandLab, Soundtrap, or Audacity (although Audacity distorts a little) if needed (these DAWs will be explored later in the book).

Begin to learn what notes are in particular chords and write everything down in shorthand notation.

This is where arrangement comes into play. The learners could even record their parts into a notation software or an audio recording into a DAW, or preserve it in MIDI notation.

Add the melody back in and have the learners figure out what instruments play what parts.

Give them the control. If it sounds good, it's probably good.

This exercise could be effective either in a whole group or, if you have individual practice rooms, in small groups. I've done this with a small group of intermediate-level Brass players. We learned "Happy" by Farrell Williams by ear and arranged it with a backing karaoke track from YouTube. By the way, "Happy" is in F minor, so it works well for band learners. Also, there are backing tracks around for pretty much every song, and they can be transposed in most cloud-based DAWs, but there is also the Chrome Transpose Extension, which can transpose any online video in real time. Find it in the Chrome Store.

This exercise can be accomplished with classical music as well. Have them learn a classical melody by ear and listen for any inner parts by following the same process as before. Another simple way to include informal learning practices is to have your learners choose all of the repertoire for the year. Since band and orchestra musics are likely not genres that learners would normally hear, you might try setting up some listening stations to have them hear some selections they could choose from. Or give them even more liberty and direct them straight to JW Pepper in small groups to hear a number of arrangements to select. The site could be where they are assigned homework to find a piece of music that would work for their ensemble with some guidelines.

Following are some other ways to implement the tenets of informal learning through technology to help nourish the whole musician in your instrumental music program.

MuseScore

If you've ever used MuseScore you would know that its online community is vast. There is a plethora of music written in European staff notation perfect for wind bands, orchestras, and small ensembles. All learners have to do is find them and you can see and listen to the scores right on the site. Of course, because the pieces are all crowd sourced, you will have to likely explain to learners that some of the music on there is simply not designed to be played on wind instruments and might have been better composed with MIDI in a DAW. With this online community, users can find thousands of compositions and arrangements by professionals and amateurs alike. To be able to use the scores and manipulate them, a yearly subscription is required. Even still, this could be a fantastic way to find new music and give learners agency over the music they play.[‡]

Getting Creative

An extension of this exercise would be to download a piece in MIDI (explored later) and open it in your software of choice (DAW or notation software) and change the instrument sounds or some of the notes to make a new song. You could even add another part to the music. In a DAW like BandLab or Soundtrap, have learners add a drum machine or a loop that might fit for the style of music they are working with. In the wind-band genre, classical is king, but making a cool hybrid composition combining modern digital elements and the classical piece of music can be incredibly freeing for you and your learners. Using Moonlight Sonata (or any piece of music or arrangement), try the following:

Make a new classical arrangement in a notation software.
Create a completely new piece of music with the bones of the "Moonlight Sonata."
Keep the bassline and compose a new melody to go along with it.
Add a loop that works using a DAW.
Add a drum-machine sequence.

These ideas can be easily adapted for any choir, band, or orchestral group.

‡ Portions of this section were originally published in the *Canadian Music Educator Journal* 60, no. 4 (2019): 33–36.

Conclusion

Adding informal learning approaches doesn't have to be an entire revamp of your program. It could be adding in simple ways to give more choice and voice to learners in your room and making the learning activities bridge the in-school and out-of-school divide. You may be already adding informal learning approaches to your teaching in ways you didn't realize. Informal learning is a theme that will be recurring throughout this book, so all of the activities and ideas should be viewed through that lens.

4

Digital Audio Workstations

Digital technology is creativity's greatest ally. Without digital technology, musical creativity becomes much more difficult to access. The step of learning a traditional instrument, which takes years to master, can be skipped and learners can get right to creating their own master-pieces, and with little tech know-how.

DAWs make creating original music incredibly easy; they are used to record and pro-duce the music we hear every day. The sounds may be produced entirely by computer or can be produced in partnership with acoustic instruments via audio recording. The Beatles were among the first masters of the recording studio, recording their own sounds but also producing new sounds that did not previously exist. Most of their later albums were pro-duced and composed entirely in the studio, and were never actually able to be performed outside that environment because the sounds and techniques they made could not be re-produced live. Thus, the composition existed in the studio only. Since that time, DAWs have become ever more sophisticated, making their musical possibilities endless. The move from analog (reel-to-reel tapes) to digital made this technology exponentially more ac-cessible and creative. And in the post–COVID-19 landscape, collaborative music-making software that teaches modern musicianship skills is incredibly valuable.[*]

The Industry Standards

You may have heard of some of the more popular industry standards like ProTools, Cubase, Ableton Live, FL Studio, or Logic Pro. They are all capable of the same processes and there-fore can all record sounds, produce sounds, add effects to recorded sounds, and do multi-track recording. They all have MIDI abilities with built-in virtual instruments and the ability to plug in a keyboard or pad controller through USB. There are also ways to produce beats, and compose by using loops and drum machines. Some producers prefer the functionality or layout of one DAW over another and some are better in particular contexts than others. All

---

[*] Paragraph adapted from Steve Giddings, "The Creative Magic of Digital Audio Workstations: Technology to Unlock Creativity in Your Learners," *Canadian Music Educator Journal* 61, no. 4 (2020): 41–44.

Technology for Unleashing Creativity. Steve Giddings, Oxford University Press. © Oxford University Press 2022.
DOI: 10.1093/oso/9780197570739.003.0005

of these proprietary, desktop-based softwares have free trial versions or "lite" versions of their software that typically require the purchase of some piece of hardware like an audio interface or a MIDI controller. This simple fact makes these softwares somewhat difficult to acquire, and to be able to have them installed on a lot of different stand-alone machines makes them a bit expensive for starting up, but would definitely be useful to work towards.

Ableton Live has a great website for learning how to use DAWs and the language that is commonly associated with using these types of software. Their website is geared to learners in Grades 4 through 9 and teaches the basics of how to use it and the music literacy required for it. Here is the site: https://learningmusic.ableton.com.

Having stand-alone computers available with some of this software on it would be useful, as the software we will be discussing throughout this chapter has particular limitations that more advanced versions of the industry standards are capable of.

Ethan Hein, co-author with Will Kuhn of *Electronic Music School* (Oxford University Press, 2021) and inventor of GroovePizza (explored later), has an amazingly useful Twitter account. In tweet form he gave a quick overview of the strengths and purposes of each of the industry standards plus some others that could be useful. Here is the abridged form.

Good for Professional-Level Production

Ableton Live (Windows, Mac) and Logic Pro (Mac only) are both expensive but Logic is less so. Reaper is a free DAW for Windows computers and can produce professional-quality recordings if you are dedicated to figuring out the software, but it doesn't come with any virtual instruments or loops.

Good for Hip-Hop Producers

FL Studio (Windows, Mac) evolved from Fruity Loops, which was an Internet app of the late 1990s.

Good for Recording Live Musicians

Pro Tools (Windows, Mac) or Cubase (Windows, Mac) are good choices. I would add Audacity for an all-around open-source DAW for recording live musicians. If you know what you are doing, you can get a lot from it with all the plug-ins and updates available for it.

For Cloud-Based Devices

BandLab, and Soundtrap both run entirely in the browser so work great for Chromebooks. They are pretty good all-round DAWs for the money. I will have more to say on these shortly.

Alternatives for Schools

Of course, the industry standards are expensive, and many of the "lite" or "free" versions do require a purchase of some piece of hardware or some type of membership. Thankfully, there are online, free, or free-to-use alternatives that are much more appealing to schools getting started. Here they are.

GarageBand

GarageBand comes standard for all Macbooks, and Mac desktop computers. It can be downloaded on any iOS device as well and the mobile version is extremely intuitive and is generally very good at most things. The only downside is that it is not available on Android, Windows, or any other non-Apple product—it is exclusive to Mac. Figure 4.1 is a screenshot of it in action.

FIGURE 4.1 Drum machine in GarageBand for iOS

BandLab

BandLab has much of the functionality of any free DAW, but what sets it apart from GarageBand software is that it is completely online and collaborative. Learners can collaborate with anyone from around the world. They can invite collaborators much the same way as with Google Docs, and collaborators can work on the same project together remotely. Another wonderful feature of BandLab is the BandLab for Education option, which has a walled garden, meaning that it creates a closed network within a school, in which learners can collaborate. It also has a library of constantly upgraded loops and sounds and maintains a good chunk of the functionality of any more costly DAW. The Education section is constantly being upgraded, too, but currently does not have the same functionality as the non-educational accounts. Some of the collaborative features are pared down and a couple of other features are different from the non-education ones. BandLab has a good online community and forum just within its website and most questions can be answered there. Facebook and other social media sites are good resources for BandLab troubleshooting. Figure 4.2 shows the main tracks screen in BandLab online.

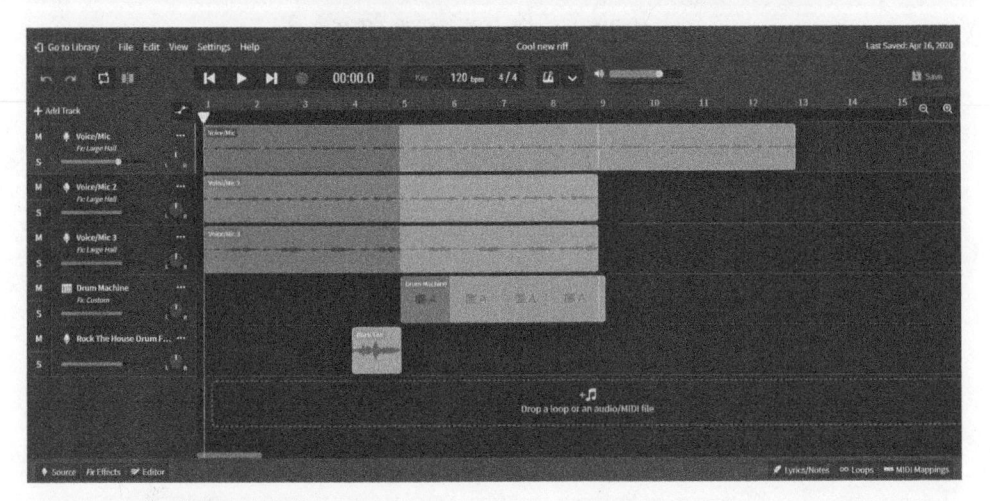

FIGURE 4.2 BandLab main editor screen

In 2018, BandLab purchased Cakewalk, which was a lesser-known professional-level DAW available for purchase before that time. BandLab has made Cakewalk completely free as a downloadable piece of software for any desktop. It has the ability to customize the user's experience level with short text-based tutorials built in—a great option for a larger professional DAW for one or two dedicated desktop devices in your music room. If you are a bit techier, this one needs a few workarounds to get going properly, but it is comparable to the industry standards. There is a help and troubleshooting page on the BandLab website.

Soundtrap

Soundtrap is a functional DAW comparable to BandLab with a walled garden much like BandLab with its equivalent Soundtrap for Education. Many prefer it to BandLab for the brilliantly collaborative features on the Education section. It can work very much the way a Google Doc does, with multiple people working on the same project, remotely, even in the Education section. Soundtrap is free for individual accounts; it's just that some features will be disabled unless you pay for a personal subscription. In Soundtrap for Education it's a little different: a school *has* to pay to use it on a subscription basis. If your school can afford it, I recommend using it. It costs $299.00 (USD) for 50 seats for one year. If you need more seats, you will have to pay more. During the COVID-19 pandemic, Soundtrap had been offering a free 90-day trial for Education accounts. The full version includes access to Auto-Tune software, a podcasting package, and lots more loop packs as well. If the funds are not there to subscribe, BandLab is a fantastic, free alternative. Each has its own limitations and each has its own mobile app version, which were mentioned previously but will be discussed throughout the book. However, it should be noted that BandLab for Education and Soundtrap for Education accounts are not supported currently on mobile. Figures 4.3 and 4.4 show some of the features in Soundtrap.

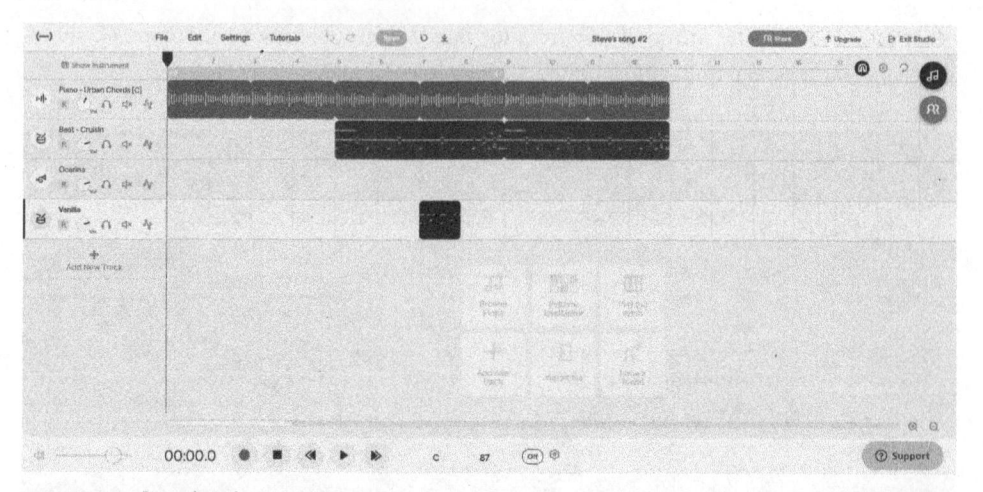

FIGURE 4.3 Soundtrap's main track screen

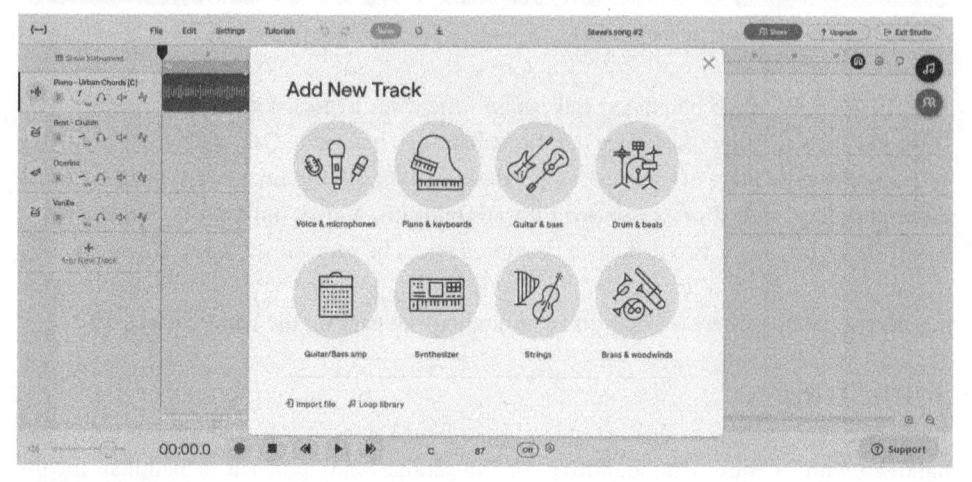

FIGURE 4.4 Soundtrap's options screen

Soundtrap is acclaimed for its voice-to-text podcasting tools and for including Antares Auto-Tune tool for any of its paid versions.

Audacity

Audacity is a free open-source DAW that has been popular for many years among amateur producers. Because it is open source, the code for it can be freely manipulated by others on a volunteer basis, thus keeping it free. (Many open-source softwares are not as intuitive as the proprietary softwares are, simply because there is no tech person on the payroll.) Audacity does have much of the same functionality of any other DAW with regard to sound recording and there are online help forums for it, too, if there is something specific you need to do. If recording and manipulating audio is your main goal, Audacity is a great place to begin. Figure 4.5 shows Audacity's main screen with a few options.

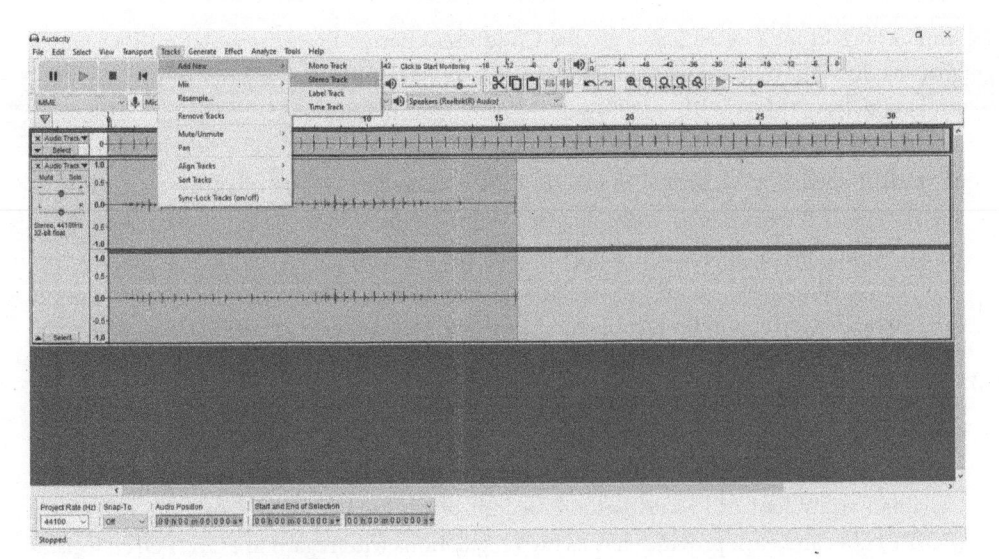

FIGURE 4.5 Audacity's main screen

Soundation

Soundation could be another option for a cloud-based DAW, but because its site does not have a walled garden, it is not compliant with the Children's Online Privacy Protection Act (COPPA), meaning users are open to collaboration outside of the school and learners would have access to social media from within their accounts. Learners would have to be at least 13 years of age and need permission from their guardians to use the technology in school. The free version has lots of options for composing with loops and recording sounds but the paid versions (charged monthly) unlock many more features that become available. This being said, Soundation4Education—a COPPA-compliant education version of Soundation—is exclusively distributed and managed by MusicFirst Classroom. Schools with access to the software packages available in MusicFirst Classroom will have access to Soundation4Education.

What Is COPPA?

The COPPA is a United States federal law that governs the collection of personal information for students under 13 years of age by online service providers, and website operators. BandLab for Education and Soundtrap for Education, for which personal information is collected to create an account to save mixes and music in the cloud and to use the collaborative features, both have the COPPA-compliant walled garden for Education purposes. This means that learners under 13 within a school can sign up on the education side of the site safely into a closed network created by the teacher within that school, much as learners can in a Google Classroom. Without the walled garden, learners would be exposed to anyone of any age using the cloud-based app from around the world and be able to converse and collaborate with them, creating a potentially unsafe environment. Within an educational institution, using a COPPA-compliant cloud-based DAW is a safe way to interact with the technology. Other similar laws in the United States are the Children's Internet Protections Act (CIPA), which governs districts' requirements to filter obscene or harmful material from all Internet-connected devices. This law also requires districts to educate learners about Digital Citizenship. The Family Education Rights and Privacy Act (FERPA) governs and protects the privacy of student education records. If a site is COPPA-compliant, it will often have a part of its site stating such compliance. This safeguard is important to look for in using online apps in which signing up for an account is required for use.

In Canada, there are no specific laws governing children's online privacy, but there is the Personal Information Protection and Electronic Documents Act (PIPEDA) as well as the Digital Privacy Act, both of which are much less straightforward but do regulate what companies do with personal information. When you are researching child online protections, the Canadian Government site has tips and a "Lesson Plan" for teaching kids how to be safe online. As well, there are many provinces that have their own very similar PIPEDA laws. The Canadian equivalent of FERPA is the Freedom of Information and Protection of Privacy (FOIPP) laws and each province has its own regulations with regard to FOIP/FOIPP legislation. Even though COPPA is a US federal law, it is very convenient for Canadian users until such time as Canada has its own such law.

There are some other legal terms you may come across when you are using some of this software, as discussed in the following sections.

What Is Fair Dealing/Fair Use?

Fair Use (United States) and Fair Dealing (Canada) are the laws governing the use of copyrighted material. When a facilitator or learner is composing a parody of a copyrighted work, the new work would likely be protected from legal action under the Fair Use/Dealing laws in your region. Using portions of copyrighted work for educational purposes also falls under this legislation. Each Fair Use/Fair Dealing law is slightly different from country to country and I do not claim to be an expert in copyright law; therefore, doing some research on your own with regard to Fair Dealing in your region will be helpful. Pamphlets are often distributed to Canadian K–12 schools with guidelines on what educational institutions can do with copyrighted material. There is also a useful Canadian Fair Dealing tool online at http://www.fairdealingdecisiontool.ca/DecisionTool.

What Is Royalty-Free Music?

The loops and music in BandLab and Soundtrap, and often in other DAWs, too, are royalty free. This means that they are free to use without attribution both personally and commercially for any project. Users cannot resell those loops and sounds as loops, but as long as they are used to make something new they are free to use without penalty. For producing podcasts and other similar productions, there are royalty-free music sites of precomposed tracks to use with those projects as well. BandLab has more information about the use of these sounds on its site.

What Is Copyright-Free Music?

Copyright-free means that the copyright for that particular work has run out or the creator has declared the work to be in the public domain. These works are rare to come by but they do exist. Keep in mind, too, that even if the audio recording of a work is copyright free, that doesn't mean that the written sheet music is as well.

What Is MIDI?

The best way I can describe MIDI is that it is a file type that holds pitch, rhythm, and tempo information so that a computer can read and understand it. MIDI is an incredibly versatile file type that most notation softwares and DAWs can understand. Many electronic keyboards have a bank of MIDI sounds, and so do DAWs. They can be accessed right on the computer by turning your regular computer keyboard (QWERTY) into a piano (known as a virtual instrument) or by connecting a MIDI device (like a piano keyboard) through USB on your computer to control the MIDI sounds. Older models have five-pin MIDI inputs and outputs (see Figure 4.6) that need an adapter to fit into your USB port. Often, there are instruments called MIDI controllers and their sole purpose is to be used for virtual instruments. Without hooking into a computer with MIDI sounds they do not work (see Figure 4.7).

The sounds you hear on the playback of a notation software like Finale are produced by using MIDI protocols. An incredibly useful feature of MIDI is that it allows DAWs and notation softwares to speak to each other, too. If learners create a melody in any notation software, they can export it as MIDI and then import it as MIDI to a DAW and vice versa.

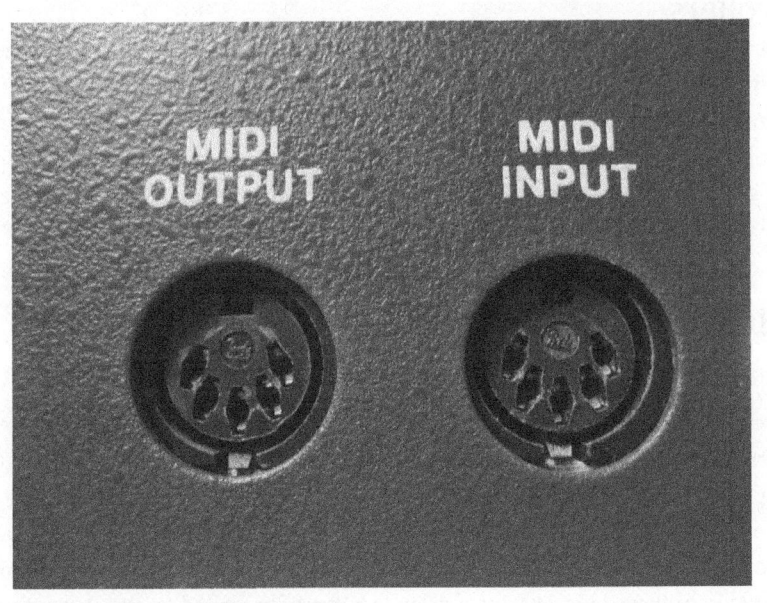

FIGURE 4.6 Classic MIDI input and output jacks

FIGURE 4.7 Pad and keyboard MIDI controller from AKAI

What Is a MIDI Map or MIDI Mapping?

There is often a MIDI map button included in your DAW. When the button is clicked, a lot of the virtual knobs and tracks light up or change colour. This capability is how learners can assign particular actions to the physical knobs, faders, and switches on their MIDI controllers. In BandLab, at least, if learners want to control the volume of a track with their MIDI controller, click "MIDI Mappings," and then the button they want assigned, and wiggle the knob or press the button on the MIDI controller they want it assigned to—and that's it.

Controllers

There are all kinds of non-keyboard MIDI controllers that exist to help non-keyboard players express their creativity in more natural and intuitive ways that work for them. There are also pad controllers, drum controllers, guitar controllers, and even wind controllers, which will all be explored later. MIDI controllers are designed to be a game controller of sorts for virtual music instruments that exist on DAWs. Virtual instruments and their possibilities will be explored more in depth in later chapters.

Hardware

MIDI controllers are useful tools for manipulating virtual instruments and other MIDI information. There are some pieces of hardware/gear you may need to get going on DAWs with your learners other than MIDI controllers. Keep in mind that learners can do pretty much anything they need to do without this gear, but one specific problem they will not easily be able to solve without some extra gear is latency. Latency is the time it takes for your device hardware to convert an analog signal (your voice or an instrument) to a digital one, which is measured in milliseconds, causing a delay in a carefully crafted track, even with a click (a metronome). Learners will really begin to notice latency if they are tracking multiple parts separately. GarageBand, being a native Apple product and software based, has next-to-zero latency. A driver is the software that runs any piece of hardware on your machine, like a speaker or microphone. Most of the proprietary, desktop-based DAWs will autocorrect the hardware latency on your device.

On cloud-based DAWs like BandLab or Soundtrap, the signal not only has to be converted to digital, but also has to travel through the Internet to the host computers, which are likely in another country. The result is that even with hardware latency correction, there will be added latency from this travel time. Soundtrap's site claims that on an Apple device, there will be close-to-zero latency. For all other devices and platforms, there will be some latency, and occasionally quite a lot. It may also depend on your Internet connection. Soundtrap has a small amount of latency on non-Apple machines, a delay that can be improved with an audio interface. BandLab usually has quite a lot of latency as a default. BandLab has a unique function under "Settings" called "Latency Test," with which it will automatically correct the latency between your recording and your machine. The only issue it has is that sometimes it doesn't work, meaning an interface is needed to help correct it mostly because the sound can be isolated more easily using headphones for the latency test (Figure 4.8).

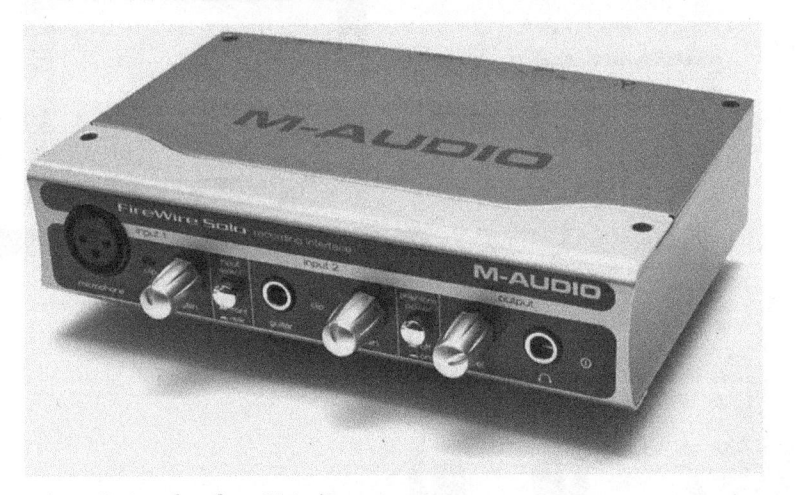

FIGURE 4.8 An audio interface from M-Audio

An interface takes the analog signal from your recorded sound (through a microphone) and converts it into digital with next-to-zero latency. Just to be sure, you can download audio stream input/output (ASIO) audio drivers for your machine from asio4all.org if you are using a cloud-based DAW on a PC or Mac device. These tend to be the go-to audio drivers for recording. If you remember from previously, drivers are the software that runs any hardware on your machine. In this case, the ASIO driver would run the hardware in charge of audio going in and out of your machine. However, it is not often possible to download anything like this to Chromebooks. If you are using Windows or other desktop devices, these drivers would be essential. If you are using an audio interface, you will need a good set of headphones, too, with a ¼" stereo end (Figure 4.9).

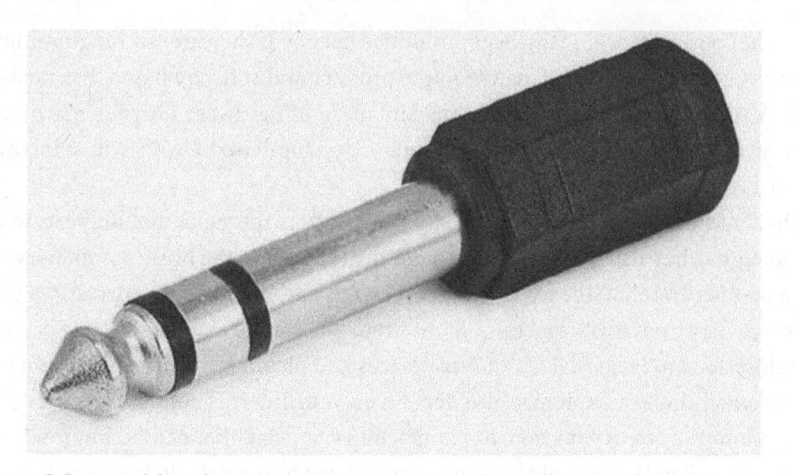

FIGURE 4.9 3.5mm to 1/4″ adapter common in many recording or live sound situations

Plugging in your audio interface

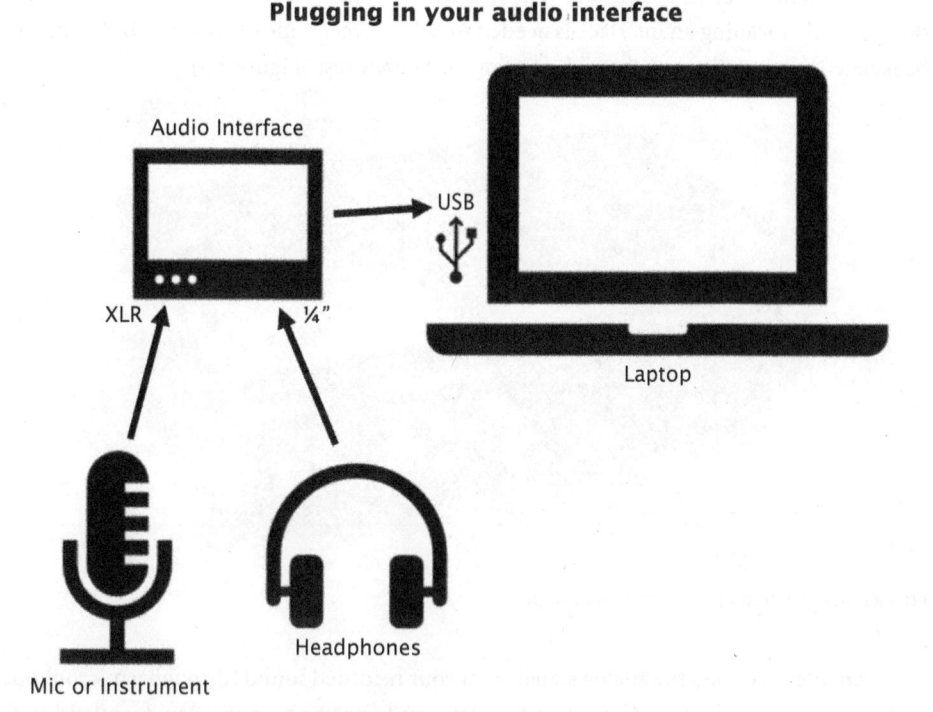

FIGURE 4.10 How to plug in the audio interface to your device

Learners can plug a microphone or an instrument such as an electric guitar directly into the interface, which is connected to the computer. Bus-powered (or USB-port powered) audio interfaces are easy to use and just plug and play right into the USB port of learners' machines without needing to be plugged into a wall outlet for power. Older models need separate drivers to run and can be somewhat challenging to configure if you're a beginner. So, to review, if you have

a bus-powered audio interface
headphones with a ¼″ stereo cable end
a microphone with XLR (mic cable) to plug it in,

then learners should be good to go to record sounds with next-to-zero latency. Figure 4.10 is a diagram of how these plug in to one other.

BandLab Link

BandLab does sell its own interfaces. The company sells both analog (3.5mm tip-ring-ring-sleeve, or TRRS) and digital (universal serial bus, or USB) interfaces that serve different purposes. The analog interfaces are designed to be portable and can plug into a phone for use with BandLab's mobile app by using a 3.5mm connection. The digital interfaces are the ones that give next-to-zero latency on your laptops or desktops with a USB connection. Any interface I have used with either BandLab or Soundtrap seems to work well. Focusrite Scarlet interfaces are popular, and they often come with a "lite" version of the industry standard DAWs like Ableton Live or Pro Tools. If your school needs many interfaces (as most schools would) the Behringer UM-ONE bus-powered interface is be a good choice for the price, but does not come with any software.

BandLab has recently released the BandLab Mini interface designed for mobile devices and similar to the iRig interfaces, which will be explored later.

Portable Recording Studios

There are also portable recordings studios that I have used to record rock groups at my school. One particular device that I have used is the BOSS Micro-BR. This device has been replaced by the BR-80, but is the size of a phone and is a versatile, high-quality recording studio that can be used to make professional multitrack recordings.

Common File Types

Regardless of which DAW being used, each has its own project file types that are unique to the software being used. For example, Audacity has the AUP (Audacity project file) extension for any active projects that were either created in Audacity or being edited within it. Only until "Export" is selected can users choose a file type in which to save it to convert the project file into a universal format across platforms. During the export process, all multitracked parts will be bumped into one track as a "Good Copy" of sorts. This action is commonly referred to as mixing down. In the exported or mixed-down file, all tracks can no longer be edited separately. Users can also export tracks separately to be used in other programs. In BandLab and other similar cloud-based DAWs they do not use specific file types, because no project files are being saved to the hard drive of the computer using it. Learners still must export files if they wish to use them outside of those DAWs.

For some file types learners will likely come across, see Table 4.1.

TABLE 4.1 Common file Types in DAWs

Uncompressed, or "Lossless"

WAV   A common uncompressed file type with high sound quality. There is no loss of quality when you are exporting to a WAV file (hence the term lossless). The file size is much larger than an MP3 file, which averages about 1 megabyte (MB) per minute, while WAV files can range from between 10 and 16 MB per minute of sound.

AIFF Another non-compressed file type developed by Apple. You will likely come across it only on Apple devices.

Compressed, or "Lossy"

MP3   A very common compressed sound file. A compressed file takes up less hard disk space and became popular for file downloads in the late 1990s and early 2000s because of its small file size (usually around 4 MB at roughly a megabyte per minute). Those in the industry describe MP3 files as "lossy" because to achieve the small file size, parts of the sound spectrum are cut, which results in a loss of sound quality. The average person wouldn't normally hear a difference unless they heard a non-compressed file side by side with a compressed one.

M4A Another increasingly common lossy file type.

OGG Another compressed audio file type.

FLAC Another less common compressed audio file type. Great for storing large numbers of music files.

MIDI files

MID/MIDI   These are both MIDI file types and can be manipulated and created in most popular DAWs. MIDI is musical information for a computer, so it is not to be treated as a sound file like WAV or MP3.

Windows Files

WMP/WMA   These are Windows Media Player files and are pretty much exclusive to Windows Media Player. When music is downloaded to a Windows Media Player, it is often converted to a WMA or WMP file. The problem is when you try to import a WMA or WMP file to a DAW to use it in a project, most times DAWs can't read them unless they are converted to a more common file type.

Common Video Files

MPEG   This is a Windows video file type. DAWs typically don't read video files and least often a Windows-specific file type. Why am I telling you this if DAWs don't read it? Because it is a pretty common video file type that you will come across.

AVI Another common video file type.

MP4 A common compressed video file type often used for storing video files.

File Converters

If learners need to convert a file so that it can be used in a DAW, there are always online file converters. If you look up file converters online, you will notice that there are plenty. Any one of them will work for these purposes. However, keep in mind that MIDI and sound files are not interchangeable and neither are video and sound files, although there are some programs like Melodyne that can convert an audio file into MIDI. Some desktop-based DAWs have built-in ways to convert audio to MIDI as well.

What Are Stem Files?

Stem files are individual separate tracks of each complete component of a recorded mix. They are usually in WAV format and can be imported separately to be used in a remix, for example. A vocal stem for a song would be only the fully produced vocal parts for that song, whereas a guitar stem would be only the guitar part of a recorded mix. Some desktop-based DAWs have stem creation tools. In most DAWs, stems can be made by exporting individual tracks of a multitrack recording. This step is similar to exporting parts in a notation software. How can learners find stems of popular songs to use in remixes and for other purposes? That will be tackled later in this chapter.

How DAWs Can Be Used in Your Classroom

All of the lessons and ideas here can work for any DAW you happen to have because they all have similar features, but some DAWs have features specific to that DAW. For the most part, though, these lessons are cross-compatible.

Composing as an Entire Class with GarageBand for iOS (Grades K–12)

One way—especially if your school has only one iPad—to get learners composing and hooked on composing is to project the iPad onto a screen and collect input from learners about where to take it. Here are my suggestions for the process.

You need the following:

an iPad
an LCD projector

a VGA to Lightning adapter (or video graphics array [VGA] to 30-pin adapter for iPads earlier than fourth generation, ca. 2012)

See Figure 4.11 for how to set up an iPad to a projector.

Connecting an iPad to a Projector

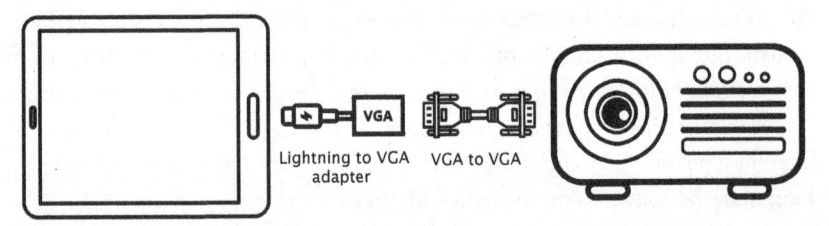

Lightning to VGA   VGA to VGA
adapter

Depending on the age of your projector, VGA to VGA or HDMI to
HDMI cables will be provided. If your projector is HDMI, a
Lightning to HDMI adapter will be needed.

Please note if you are using HDMI that audio is treated differently than VGA because HDMI
overrides the audio and video meaning audio will often go to the projector by default.

FIGURE 4.11 How to connect an iPad to a projector and other useful information to be successful

FIGURE 4.12 The Smart Guitar auto play interface in GarageBand for iOS

How It Works

Once the iPad has been hooked up to the projector by using the adapter, take suggestions from learners on what instruments to start with. Most virtual instruments on GarageBand have a choice between using the following settings: "smart," scale, or notes. GarageBand gives a choice of the following instruments: guitar, keyboard, drums, bass, erhu, and pipa. I recommend starting with one of the "smart" instruments as those particular instruments autogenerate preset loops in the particular chord the user selects (Figure 4.12). Take three suggestions from the class and vote on the most popular choice.

This next part of the lesson depends on what the learners have chosen, but let's pretend—for the sake of simplicity—that they chose "Smart Guitar." It will default to the key of C on an acoustic guitar, with autoplay off. At this point, have them choose a different key if you like. There are four autoplay options to choose from on every instrument, but there are also several types of those instruments to choose from. Just for a guitar, there is a choice between a few different types and they each have four unique autoplay patterns. Autoplay is where the preset loop material comes from, so begin with these.

This exercise can go in any direction from here, but the patterns and flow stay pretty much the same throughout. As each one is added, begin adding the loops to the tracks view so that learners can see the way the loops interact. Once learners have a clear A section, coach them into adding a B section by changing something without making it sound like a completely different song.

Culminating Activities or Variations

For individual compositions, if your school is one-on-one iPads or even five or six to work with, you could use the previous plan as a mini-lesson and then have learners experiment and create with the app on their own or in small groups. Tell them their piece needs a beginning, a middle, and an end.

With older groups, you could have a day or two when those learners who own Apple devices bring them to school to use for composing.

For band instrument arrangements, learners can use GarageBand to create a loop or a longer composition to play along to. Learners could play their instruments and write out parts that fits, or they might improvise their parts and then record them through the microphone function on their devices that is built into the GarageBand app. You could set parameters for their composition: for instance, how many notes they are allowed to use, what scales they can use, or what rhythms to help them to reinforce a particular concept. In the scale function of these virtual instruments, there is a choice of scales. Figure 4.13 shows many of the scales to choose from within the app.

A variation of this approach could be that learners are given the melody to work with and asked to come up with harmony or complementary parts that fit the given melody and record each part into the DAW. This exercise can be done with or without notation. They can use the DAW to work out ideas or write them on paper first and use the DAW recording for their final product.

Using GarageBand's Live Loops (explored in Chapter 10), have learners compose a piece of music in a distinct form and have a dance party while they perform it for the class like a DJ show.

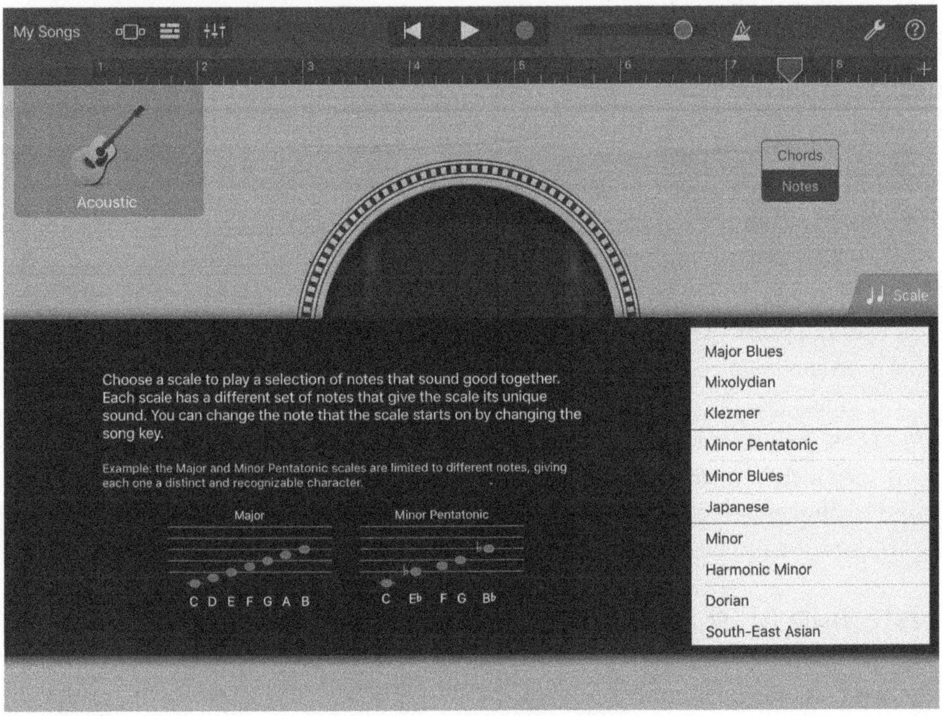

FIGURE 4.13 The choice of scales to play with in GarageBand for iOS

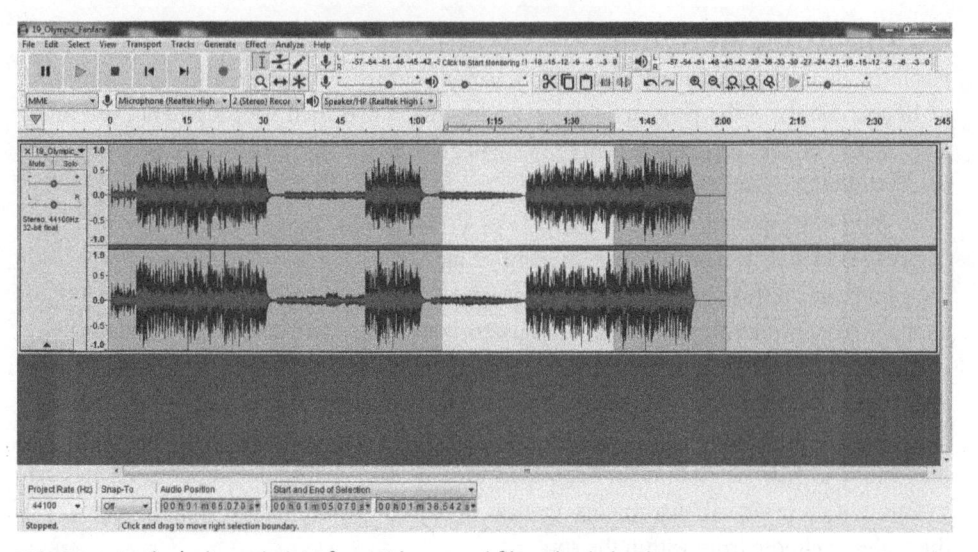

FIGURE 4.14 Audacity main interface with a sound file uploaded to it

Audacity

Audacity (Figure 4.14) has a good chunk of the functionality of some of the industry standards. You can download it for free by using a quick Google search. As mentioned, it is open source so it can do a lot, and is completely free. There are plug-ins and workarounds that can pretty much make it do anything you need.

Though Audacity does not have built-in loops or virtual instruments, here are some ways you and your learners could use this software.

Multitrack recording—Using a nice set of microphones and a headphone amplifier, learners can produce a respectable recording of any group.

Electroacoustic compositions—Audacity has enough functionality to be able to create sounds that sound like other sounds or new sounds that do not currently exist. Learners can become their very own Karlheinz Stockhausen.

Cut and paste—The software makes it fairly easy to cut out other parts and insert them in another place within the same composition. Learners could *literally* rearrange the music (see the section "Listening Map and Arrangement Activity").

Look for found sounds and record them into the software—using a good quality condenser microphone, take it "on the road" and record the sounds of your school hallways or the sounds found in the schoolyard and create a soundscape from it or create an audio-book story.

Listening Map and Arrangement Activity (Grades K–3)

This lesson has been adapted from a longer, more step-by-step lesson for primary learners that I previously published in *Creative Musicking*. The concept of this lesson can be adapted for any grade level and be used with any piece of music as an introduction to DAWs.

Step 1: Choose a piece of music, which can be in any style or genre. You could even ask your learners what they want to use (in keeping with the philosophy of the informal learning approach).

Step 2: Depending on the grade level, you may want to have a prepared listening map, or give learners the opportunity to create their own listening maps. For younger learners, I prepare a colouring sheet that matches the listening map or piece of music we chose. For this activity, using pencil to paper (GASP!) is recommended so that the arrangement can be digitized in a DAW later (and displayed around the classroom).

Step 3: Once learners have a listening map prepared, for younger learners they are going to be rearranging the piece of music by using "analog" old-fashioned copy and paste: scissors, glue, and paper. They cut out each section of the listening map and rearrange them on a new piece of paper in a way that makes the map easy to follow.

Step 4: Once learners have their new arrangements prepared, load the original piece of music to Audacity and rearrange the sound file to match the new arrangement. They can now hear their new arrangement! If learners pasted sections upside down or backwards try using the "Reverse" feature in the "Effects" section of Audacity.

Examples of new paper arrangements are as follows.

For this particular project, I used "Olympic Fanfare" by Leo Arneau, so our original prepared listening map was an Olympic running track with the instruments and sections on it (Figures 4.15 and 4.16).

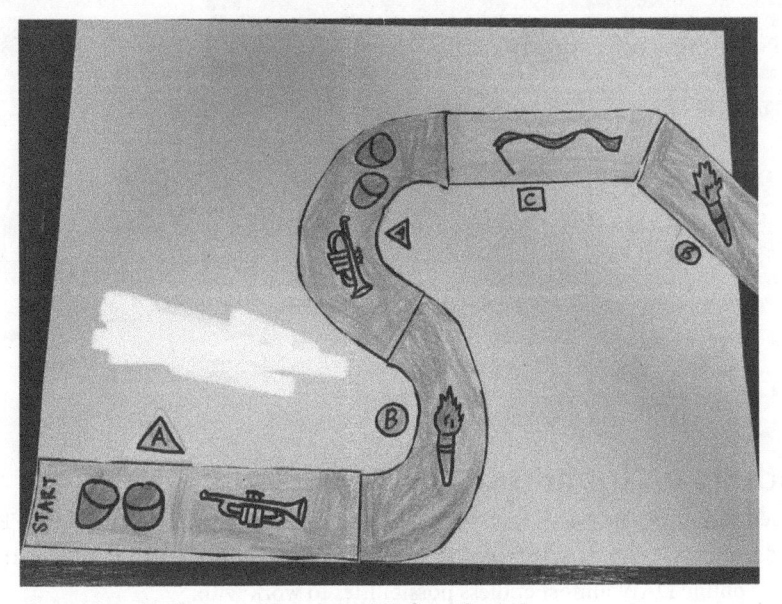

FIGURE 4.15 An example of a cut–and-paste project from Grade 2

FIGURE 4.16 Another example of a cut-and-paste project

A variation of this project would be to make a virtual listening map on Google JamBoard or Google Docs by using only emojis, and rearranging it from there, and then digitizing it in Audacity or another DAW.

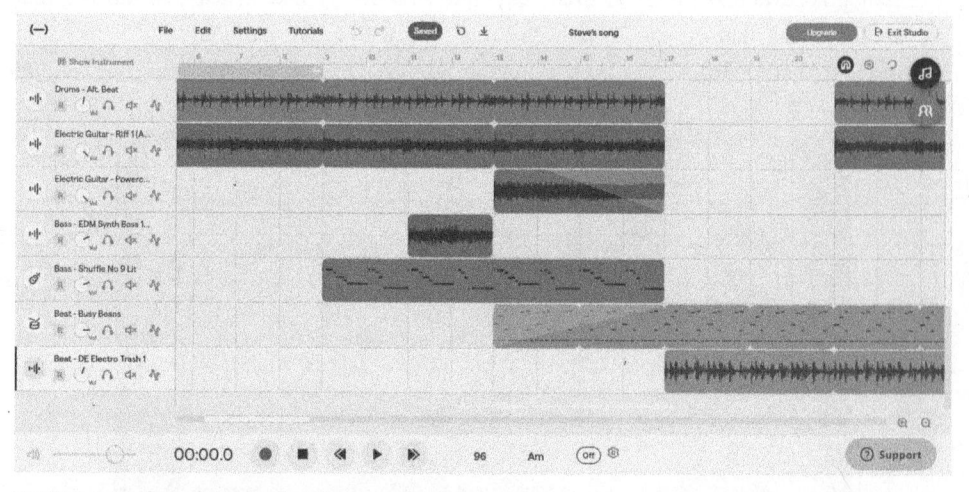

FIGURE 4.17 Soundtrap track editor introduction screen

Soundtrap at Soundtrap.com

Mentioned earlier, Soundtrap (Figure 4.17) is a cloud-based DAW with a paid COPPA-compliant Education section. It is very versatile, with loops, recording, and virtual instruments, giving this online DAW almost endless possibilities to work with.

Here are some ways you could use this online app in your classroom.

Have band learners play all four parts of a quartet and record each track by using the software, or have them create their own harmonies for a particular melody by using multitrack recording.

Have learners compose four-beat rhythmic patterns, to insert into a song.

Have learners rearrange and recompose the sample tracks provided by the developer.

Have one group of learners compose the track and then another learner or group of learners in the class provide the vocal part or the melodic material (as per the track-and-hook approach).

Compose a track as a group or individually by using only the included royalty-free loops.

Use it in combination with more "traditional" methods of composition. For example: compose a track and then play a live solo over it or perform a composed vocal or instrumental part with the track.

Use it as a backing track for rhythm activities.

Use it to compose a backing track to go with any composition.

Use it to compose a drum track if your group needs a drummer with the drum machine or loop packs.

Soundtrap also has an intuitive podcasting function that includes a voice-to-text feature that can be edited by text and by sound.

Have learners choose a person to interview on a specific topic and create a podcast episode.

Have them choose a topic to research that is music related and, instead of a presentation, have them create a podcast episode or series explaining it.

All of the music for the episode can be produced in Soundtrap itself to create a professional-sounding podcast.

BandLab Lesson Ideas

In BandLab for Education (COPPA-compliant) learners will need to set up an account to access, and then much as with a Google Classroom, they will need to join a class that the facilitator sets up for them. This set-up is similar in Soundtrap for Education as well.

Loops Composition

When I introduce BandLab for Education, I like to use Loops because it gets kids creating good-sounding music in minutes (Figure 4.18). They are instantly hooked.

Step 1: Introduce learners to loops as a class and have them notice words like bpm (beats per minute), bars, key, and other useful music terms.

Begin with a drum loop and see which one learners would like to use. Have it go for eight bars and layer another loop beginning at the fourth bar. Add each layer in four-measure increments so that learners can see what they are listening for and understand the importance

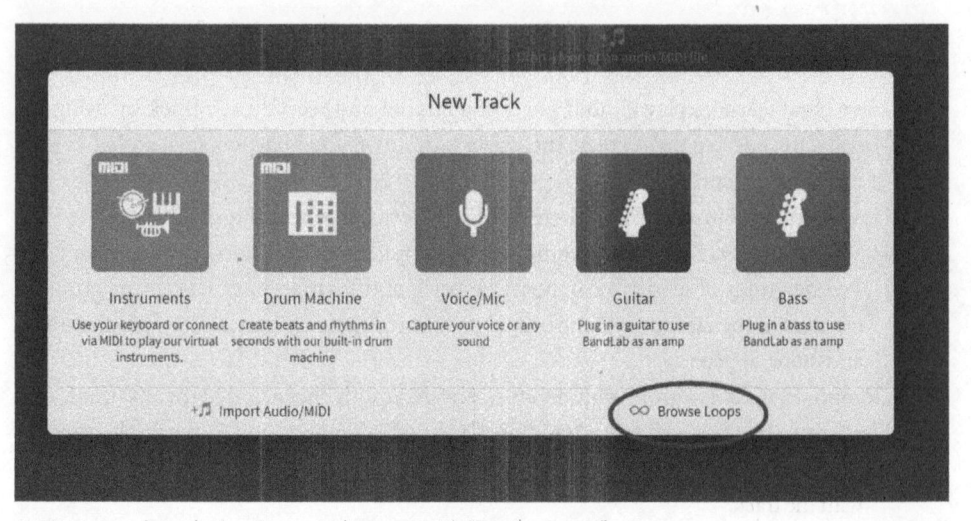

FIGURE 4.18 Introducing Loops to learners with "Browse Loops"

of the four-bar phrase in Western music. The loop can be previewed in this pane and then the learners can click and drag the loop into a track to use it. It is important that learners understand that using multiple bass loops from the same pack will sound as though they were competing for attention. Show them how different elements (guitar, bass, synth, rhythm) can work together to create a whole piece. Some more simple loops might sound boring on their own, but put into context will sound fantastic. Figure 4.19 shows the loops view in BandLab.

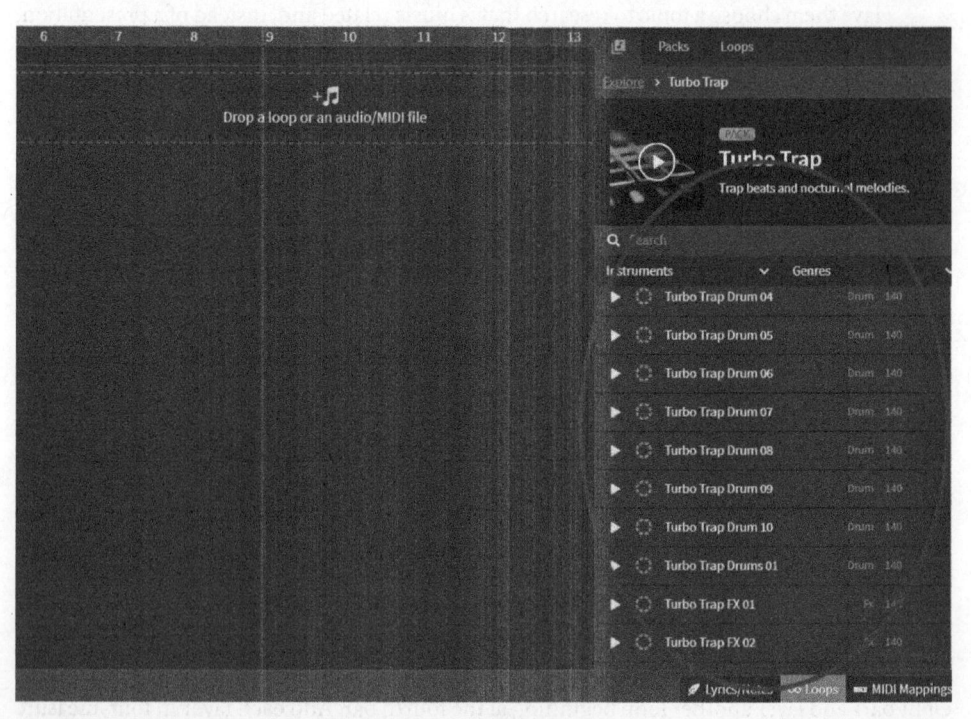

FIGURE 4.19 BandLab's Loops view with the list of loops to choose from on the right hand side

Step 2: Have learners try it out on their devices.

Give them ample time to experiment, explore, and create with the loops before you give an assignment. I usually take one of my class periods of 30 minutes to have them sign up with their school Google accounts and get into the classroom.

Step 3: Give them an assignment by selecting the class from your dashboard and give the following assignment: create a piece of music by using loops that has a beginning, a middle, and an end.

That is literally all you will need to tell them (of course, if composing and expressing their own ideas is new, then you will need to explain what this means). I always present it as if it were a story: stories always have beginnings, and then something happens in the middle, and finally there is a resolution. I've also assigned projects that have asked learners to compose a piece that is at minimum in ABA form. Use the language that your group of learners are familiar with. Figure 4.20 shows the assignment view in BandLab for Education.

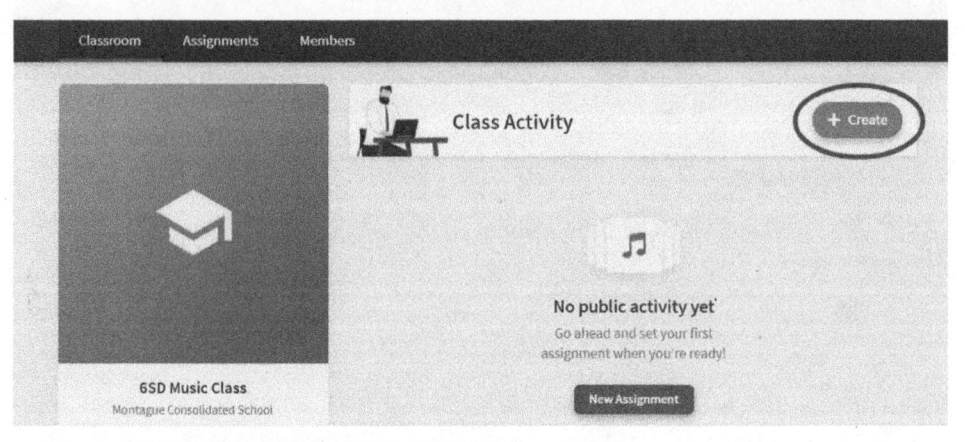

FIGURE 4.20 Assignment view in BandLab for Education

Step 4: As they compose their music, assume the facilitator role and coach them through the process. Remember: there is no such things as right or wrong if the music sounds good. Give suggestions, not directions.
Step 5: Be amazed.

Second Lesson Idea: Remix by Using Stems

For this project, you will need vocal stem files from popular songs. I asked around some Facebook groups for some original stems and there are also a number of other sites that will provide stems for various songs. When I type stem files into the Google Search, this is one of the questions that come up (Figure 4.21).

Another way, if stem files are not an option, is to purchase a cappella vocal parts on Amazon Music for $0.99 each. For the search, make sure you select "Digital Music" in the drop-down menu and put "Acapella hits bpm" in the search field (Figure 4.22). These files aren't the original studio recording stems but are recreations that sound pretty close and are designed for the purpose of a remix. The downsides to going this approach are that the versions don't sound exactly like the originals and they will likely be much faster versions (BandLab has the ability to alter tempo).

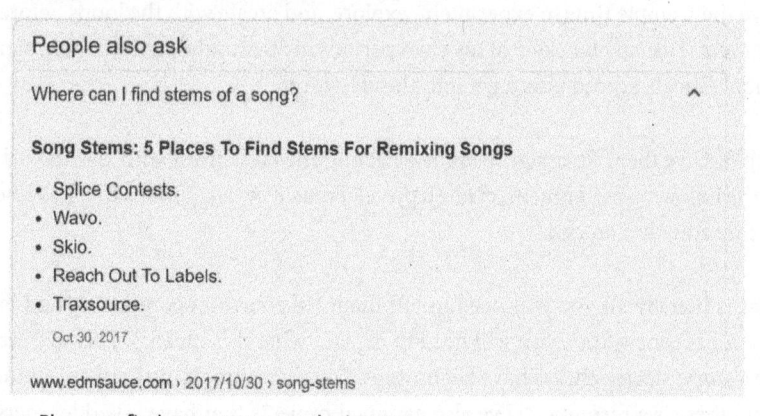

FIGURE 4.21 Places to find song stems on the Internet

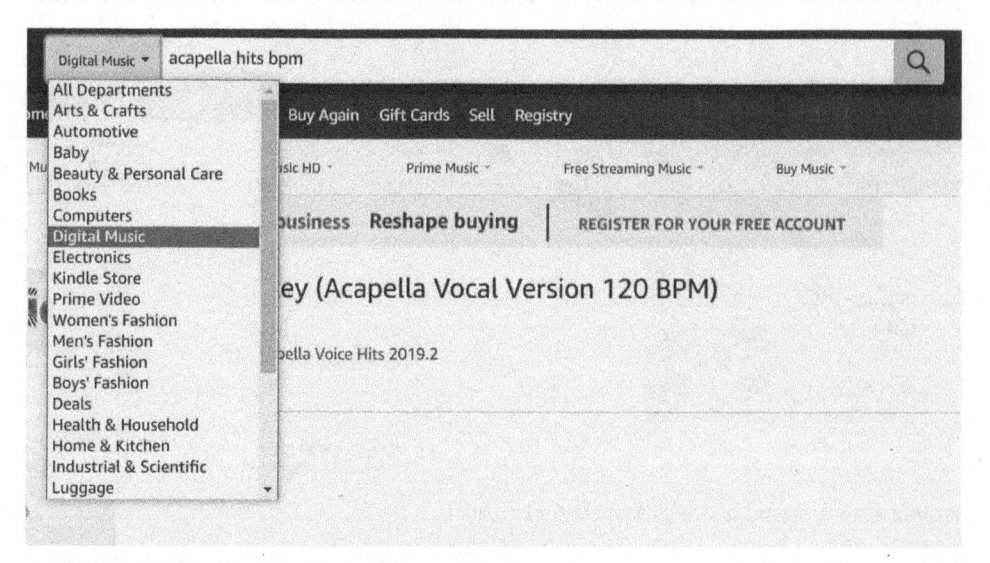

FIGURE 4.22 "Digital Music" search in Amazon Music

Step 1: Import the vocal audio file into BandLab. Set the bpm to the bpm of the track and do not adjust when prompted. Set the key to the key of the track.

Step 2: Label each section of the track: verse, pre-chorus, chorus. . . .

Step 3: Save and assign to your class in BandLab.

Step 4: Ask learners to insert a rhythm track to fit that goes well with the song.

Step 5: Explain that the choruses typically have thicker texture and that there should be a difference texturally between each part.

Step 6: See what the learners come up with.

I tried this exact lesson on my own and remixed Ed Sheeran's "Shape of You" with a vocal stem file to a basement-grunge-band version by using loops (Figure 4.23). It sounds awesome, by the way.

FIGURE 4.23 "Shape of You" remix as a basement grunge band

This idea was adapted from Mix Major–Electronic Music School on YouTube. They have fantastic video tutorials for BandLab. Here is the link to that particular video that I mentioned that goes through setting up a remix with your learners: http://tiny.cc/bkw3tz.

Adapting for Primary Learners

This lesson can certainly be adapted for primary learners (K–3). Instead of having them remix an entire song, have them remix only a chorus, having them work with a smaller portion of the song. Or as a group, give them a few choices and work on one together, and then loop it and practice keeping the beat through movement or a similar activity. They will still love remixing a song they know, and you are much less likely to run into alignment issues that sometimes occur with much longer tracks.

Ending a Song

Learners tend to have trouble figuring out the best way to end their song. They will often end abruptly without a final resolution. Here are some ideas you could present to them:

Show them a studio fade where a particular loop or group of loops keeps playing but fades into nothing until the end.

This technique was super common in a lot of 1980s music. Select the automation button (Figure 4.24) beside the "Add Track" button. This step lets learners adjust the fade and the pan of the track.

FIGURE 4.24 The automation icon from the top left corner of the main BandLab screen

Let the final loop go back to the first beat and end it after that.
Find an unexpected, but tasteful part within the loop to end on. It doesn't have to be on the tonic; it just should sound intentional.

TABLE 4.2 Overview of DAW features

Feature	Ableton Live	Cubase	FL Studio	Logic Pro	Pro Tools	Audacity	GarageBand	BandLab	Cakewalk	Soundtrap/Education
Price	$$$$ Many tiers with various pricing options	$$$	$$ With a choice of tiers	$$	$$$	FREE	FREE	FREE	FREE	FREE/$$
Operating System	Windows, Mac	Windows, Mac	Windows, Mac	Mac	Windows, Mac	Windows, Mac	Mac, iOS	Windows, Mac, Chromebook	Windows	Windows, Mac, Chromebook
Cloud-Based								✓		✓
Desktop-Based	✓	✓	✓	✓	✓	✓		✓	✓	✓
Mobile Version?		✓	✓	✓	✓		✓	✓ Education not supported on mobile		✓ Education not supported on mobile
COPPA/FERPA-Compliant								✓ Education side		✓ Education side
Can Work with MIDI	✓	✓	✓	✓	✓		✓	✓	✓	✓
Contains Loops	✓	✓	✓	✓	✓	✓	✓	✓	✓	✓

Do a workdown wherein one loop is taken out one four-bar phrase at a time until there is one left and end it after that.

The Studio Fade (Conclusion)

DAWs are one of the many tools learners can use when creating their own original music. They may also be the most creative and comprehensive musical tools that learners will come across. To create music with European notation, one needs to possess a number of skills that take time to acquire. DAWs give learners the ability to focus on the creative process and modern-music literacy skills the instant they sit down with it. They can create good-sounding original music in minutes, with little practice. Sure, it is different from what we envision when we think of composing, but this is part of the contemporary landscape. So we, as music educators, need to begin to embrace it. European notation is useful for reproducing music that was composed before the DAW, but sometimes it can get in the way of good, unhindered musical creativity. Of course, in the end, there is a balance, but why put up a barrier to creativity if it doesn't need to be there?

These DAWs are incredibly versatile and the possibilities for their creative uses are endless. And in partnership with other online and offline apps, those possibilities can come to life in a serious way. Since most of the common file types are universal, cross-compatibility between many different pieces of software is easy. In the next chapter, you will be introduced to softwares that focus on using European staff notation called notation software. Table 4.2 shows all the DAWs that were mentioned in the chapter and compares all of their functionalities and abilities.

5

Notation Software

The creative technology tool that most music educators would be familiar with is notation software. Whether we were required to use it during our training or not, it is something we all have at least a baseline knowledge of. It's a type of sequencer that displays sounds in European staff notation, like a word processor for written staff music. The default for notation softwares is European staff notation, but staff notation is not the only way to write or preserve a piece of music. Earlier in the book, we discussed the idea that staff notation is sometimes an impediment to creativity in music, because we often think that something has to be written down for it to be a composition, but the writing of this complex form of notation is the part that could get in the way. So, as important as it is, be wary of an overreliance on it. Compositions, of course, can be written down, but they can also be audio recorded or videoed to be considered a composition. Also, when a curriculum document says something like "use standard and non-standard notation to express ideas" (i.e., MU:Cr2.1.E.5b in the National Standards) it doesn't typically mean to use exclusively staff notation. Standard just means that anyone who knows that particular form of notation will be able to read it and understand it no matter where they are from. There are many different forms of standard music notation just in North America alone. I'm not saying to not use notation software; quite the opposite. Use it to preserve (record) ideas but know that these ideas certainly do not *need* to be expressed in staff notation and that it is often only used to compose and arrange music that is intended for other human musicians to play.

Standardized Musical Notation Systems

European staff notation is pretty great. I mean, if a group of musicians know how to read staff notation, they can read down a piece of music and play it as it was intended to be played the first time without hearing it first; a pretty impressive skill to non-musicians and musicians alike. However, it certainly isn't perfect.

One of the major flaws in European staff notation is key signatures. Even the most skilled staff-notation readers make mistakes in playing in C-flat or any other hard-to-read

Technology for Unleashing Creativity. Steve Giddings, Oxford University Press. © Oxford University Press 2022.
DOI: 10.1093/oso/9780197570739.003.0006

key signature with lots of flats or sharps. Accidentals, double flats, and double sharps just add another layer to the confusion. I know that classical composers will say differently, but do we *really* need F-sharp major *and* G-flat major? C-flat *and* B? C-sharp *and* D-flat? You get my drift. It seems that there have been people who recognized this multitude of key signatures as a problem, too, and came up with a system called simplified music notation to try to curb this issue by using shaped note heads to indicate accidentals (pointed ones for sharps and trapezoids for flats).

Another glaring flaw with staff notation is time signatures. The rule for the top number applies in most situations, and the same with the bottom, but "what gets the beat" works only until it's not a "4" anymore. When the bottom number is "8," based on the rules we were taught, the eighth notes would presumably get the beat. Instead, it ends up being the dotted quarter-note that gets the beat.

The naming system in English-speaking North America is a little strange, too. A quarter note is only a quarter of a whole measure in $\frac{4}{4}$ time and considered to be quarter of a whole note. It's still called a quarter note in $\frac{3}{4}$ time, wherein it should be called a third note (three beats to a measure) and still called a quarter note in $\frac{2}{4}$ time, wherein it should be called a half note. The practice of indicating uninterrupted sound lasting for a whole measure in any time signature using a whole note (much as the whole rest is used) has fallen out of favour and applies only to $\frac{4}{4}$ now. Also, the word "note" is used to describe a rhythm *and* a pitch, which are not the same thing. In my opinion, a better system is the French naming system because the rhythms are called what they look like instead of how they relate to $\frac{4}{4}$ time. Take a look:

whole note = ronde (round)
half note = blanche (white)
quarter note = noir (black)
eighth note = croche (hook)
sixteenth note = double-croche (double-hook)

The rhythm notation itself is actually one of the most useful aspects of staff notation. Rhythm notation has the ability to notate *any* duration of sound. That's why a lot of other notational systems have adopted European rhythm notation into their standardization.

Here are the other standardized notation systems in common use just in North America.

Tablature (Tab)

Systems of tablature in Western notation date back at least to the early 14th century. In modern times, tab is used often—and many times exclusively—as a notation system for fretted instruments. Guitar has a six-line "staff," while bass and ukulele have four. Numbers indicate what frets to press down; stacked numbers indicate harmony or a chord. There are many other unique markings in tab to mean any number of musical elements. In some instances, the system utilizes Western rhythm notation to indicate rhythm, but the ultimate purpose of modern tab is to transmit or notate a piece of music that is already well known by the player. It has a different purpose from that of staff notation.

Think of tab as the notation for the age of the digital recording. It is designed to be used in partnership *with* the recording. Learners using tablature almost always know how the song goes before they look it up. Horn players in funk bands or any non-jazz popular ensemble have been known to use a form of tab for horn players called soul tab. I've used it myself. It's a combination of note names and European rhythm notation that communicate a part to the performer.

There are three main types of tablature:

1. Internet tab—often transcribed by amateurs and can be found easily on sites like UltimateGuitar.com.
   There is often no indication of rhythm, but occasionally attempts are made to imply some type of rhythmic value. Standard letter fonts are used to transcribe in a word processor instead of specific tab fonts or notation software (Figure 5.1). And, although the notation is confusing for a non-tab reader, as long as the reader knows the song, it isn't an issue.
2. Tab with rhythm notation—tab with stick notation above the fret numbers (Figure 5.2).
3. Tab with staff notation—tab paired in a parallel system with European staff notation (Figure 5.3).

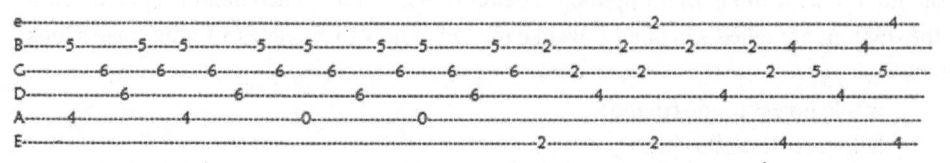

FIGURE 5.1 Example of piece by Steve Giddings written in Internet tab

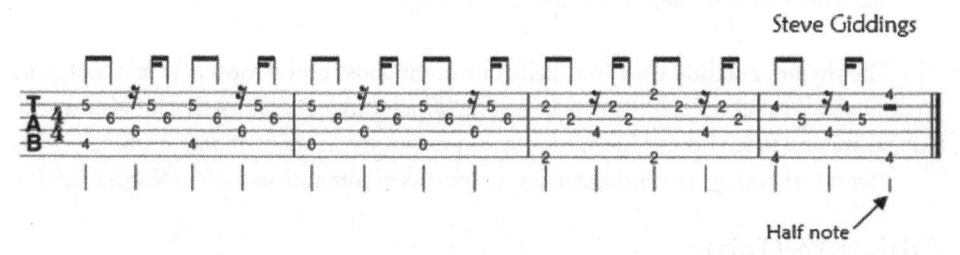

FIGURE 5.2 Example of piece by Steve Giddings written with tab a stick notation

FIGURE 5.3 Example of the same piece by Steve Giddings written in tab with staff notation

Nashville Numbers System

Nashville Numbers are used primarily in the Nashville country music scene and it's a versatile and effective system for communicating a piece of music to a musician. It uses numbers to represent scale degrees and also has its own system of markings to indicate many other musical elements. It is designed to give the chordal structure of a song and can sometimes communicate melody by using (again) Western stick rhythm notation combined with scale degrees or can give strumming pattern information, too. It is most similar to the figured bass of the Baroque and Classical periods. It serves the same purpose as figured bass but instead it uses Arabic numbers to indicate scale-degree chords instead of a bass clef staff with numbers to represent intervals. The scale-degree numbers facilitate easy transposition, and the charts do allow for and expect some element of improvisation much as figured bass did. Figure 5.4 shows how Nashville Numbers is written and then how it would be interpreted in the key of C. The line underneath the 4 and 5 indicate that there are two chords in one measure.

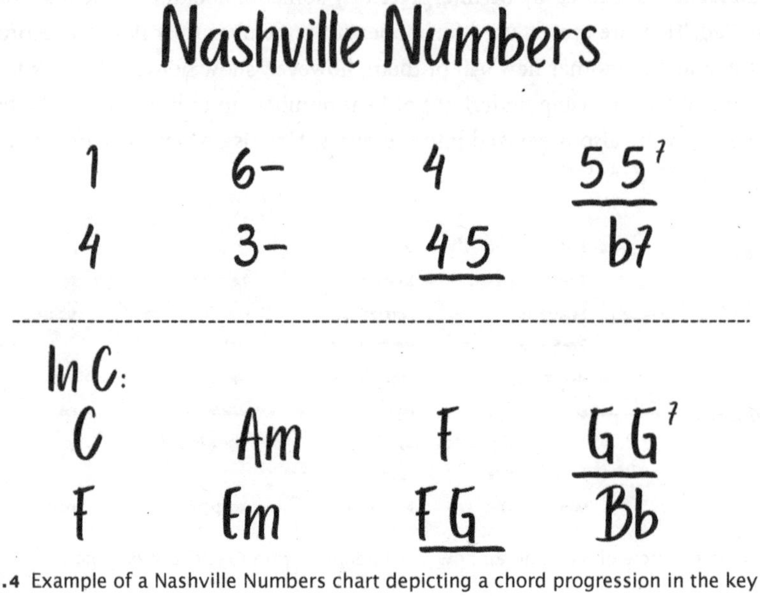

Nashville Numbers

$$1 \quad 6- \quad 4 \quad 5\ 5^7$$
$$4 \quad 3- \quad \underline{4\ 5} \quad \overline{b7}$$

In C:
$$C \quad Am \quad F \quad \underline{G\ G^7}$$
$$F \quad Em \quad \underline{F\ G} \quad \overline{Bb}$$

FIGURE 5.4 Example of a Nashville Numbers chart depicting a chord progression in the key of C.

Chas Williams, author of the book *The Nashville Number System* (first published in 1988), has a great series of videos that explain the system well.

Chord Charts and Lead Sheets

Chord charts and lead sheets (collectively known as "charts") are typically written on a five-line staff, use slashes to indicated beat or rhythm, and have the chord names written above the staff. They may also have melodic material written in. The player is to follow the chart as closely as they can. Some embellishment is expected, though. These charts are extremely common in jazz settings. Musicians who can read staff notation can often interpret these with relative ease.

Lyric Sheets

Lyric sheets have the words of a song with chords written above. Often, the chords are written above the syllable where the chord changes. They are commonly found on the Internet on sites like UltimateGuitar.com and are used much like tablature; the player typically already knows how the song goes. There are a few variations but most are fairly standardized. It should not be assumed that a person who can read staff notation can interpret a chord chart accurately without first having heard the song. They are usually made in a word processor of some type, as these are text-based charts.

Rap Flow Charts

Emcees (rappers) write out their flow in what's called a flow chart. A flow in rap is the relationship between the rhythm and the words and how it interacts with the beat. Since words and rhythm are the most important tenets of rap, it just makes sense. It's not standardized in the same way that staff notation and Nashville Numbers are, so flow charts vary on the basis of the individual, but can easily be interpreted by someone looking at them as long as the beat is notated. They are mostly used for rappers to remember their flow for recording purposes or for study of another flow. All of them, however, show how the lyrics interact with the beat of the music by using underlines or beat numbers to indicate where the beat lands in the lyrics. They are also organized into measures. Here is one example of how a rap flow chart could look (Figure 5.5).

Beat numbers →	1	2	3	4
	The day I	lose it will	be a mira -	de
Measure →	Boxed in	Limited	no	cubicle
	Rock it black and	white like a	panda	This de-
	signer got me	gigs in At -	lanta.	
Rest on the beat →	Who	run it? ____the	answer is	me
	Strapped	up like I	gotta inju -	ry.
	Hate	comes from those	who wish	they were---
	you! The so -	lution is to	keep on	being you.

FIGURE 5.5 An example of a digital rap flow chart adapted from *Creative Musicking*

Figure 5.5 shows how the beat numbers are lined up above the part of the word that gets the beat. The blank spaces are rests. It was written for the purpose of showing how diverse it could be, meaning that there is no obvious flow pattern at all. If you would like to know more about how rap and rap flow charts work, I recommend Edwards (2009).[1]

Digital Audio Workstations

As we already discussed, with a DAW learners actually have the ability to see the sounds being produced. There is no notation per se, but the sounds on the screen become a notation

---

1. Paul Edwards, *How to Rap: The Art and Science of the Hip-Hop MC* (Chicago: Chicago Review Press, 2009).

of sorts. There is no need for using traditional notation, aside from perhaps mapping out the form of the song in the planning or outlining stage. As well, music composed in a DAW will sound the same every time because there is no human error or interpretation to change it.

And when you are using MIDI, there are squares and rectangles resembling neumes from the Middle Ages or, more recently, a piano roll (from a player piano). MIDI notation is often called MIDI piano roll notation (or grid notation) for its resemblance and similar function to a player piano's piano roll (see Figure 5.6). It is standard notation across all MIDI composing software from Chrome Music Lab to BeepBox, with only slight variations.

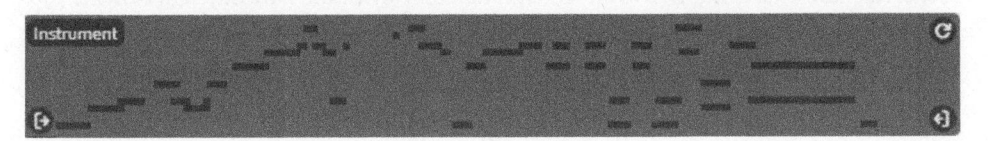

FIGURE 5.6 An example of MIDI piano-roll notation in BandLab

Chromatic Colour System

This system has become standardized among educational circles (with slight variations) and is used in many different ways from Boomwhackers to Chrome Music Lab (discussed later). It is an incredibly visual way to indicate pitch. In this system, C is always red. I have seen the occasional variation on this system but for the most part, it has been standardized.

Time Unit Box System (TUBS)

This is the system that drum machines work from. I often use it when teaching a drummer a new groove, too. If you had fun playing with some of the drum machines in Soundtrap or BandLab from the previous chapter you understand the TUBS system and how it works. For drummers, it makes a lot of sense and is a steppingstone to other forms of notation they may come across (Figure 5.7).

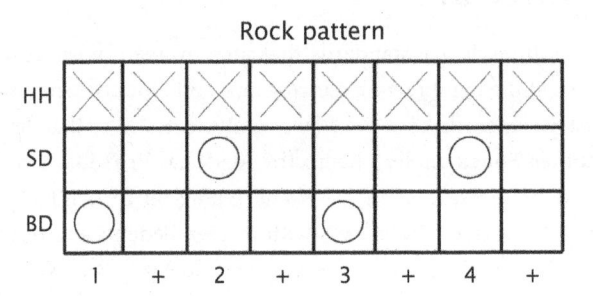

FIGURE 5.7 Rock pattern in TUBS notation

Modern Musicians and Notation

Modern music educators should be versed in these styles of notation. As mentioned in the introduction of this book, just as an English-language learner needs to know all forms of English writing, a music learner needs to know all forms of music notation. The instrument or style that a particular learner is playing may even dictate the notation that is used (or not used). Drummers in rock ensembles, for example (I would argue), may not even need to read any form of notation, since the vast majority of their music making is produced by ear or improvised, as discussed earlier.

Not one notational system is perfect, and no notational system should have superiority over the other. Tab has developed a rather blasphemous reputation among classically trained music educators, but it has a different purpose from that of staff notation. Nashville Numbers resembles figured bass and is used as a form of standardized notation in the country music scene. Rap flow charts and DAWs all focus on different styles and have different benefits, too. This is not an exhaustive list. An entire other book could be written on the standard notational systems that exist; these are simply the most common in North America.

Non-standardized Notational Systems

Many forms of non-standard musical notation systems exist, too, mostly because they can literally be anything. These systems are often used for individuals to help remember a musical idea in a way that only they understand. The following is another non-exhaustive list of some that I've encountered when learners were asked just to write down their ideas without being given a particular system to prescribe to.

Letter notation—Just the note names in order, often with no rhythm or contour indication
Invented notation—Can literally be anything that represents a sound or a duration of a sound
Line Notation—Lines spaced in groups to indicate a rhythm or with a space to indicate a rest
Story notation—A picture to represent the development of a piece of music.

Notation Software

Of course, there are the industry standards that most trained music educators have come across that I like to call the big three: Finale, Sibelius, and Dorico. What is interesting is that many of the industry standards have their own equivalent DAWs that are designed to integrate with one another. For example, Sibelius (by Avid) has ProTools, Dorico (by Steinberg) has Cubase, and, on the flip side, some DAWs have plug-ins for a notation function. There are also free versions of each of these, each with its own benefits and limitations. There are also some useful cloud-based notation programs that integrate well with other software or with other cloud-based apps.

Free Desktop-Based Versions (Staff and Tab)

When discussing desktop-based versions, I mean those softwares that do not exist in the cloud, and can run on your device without being connected to the Internet, much like the industry-standard DAWs from the previous chapter. Even though some features may need an Internet connection to work, there is no website in which they exist. Of course, there would need to be a stand-alone device with notation software like this installed, perhaps the pro versions for facilitators to use but occasionally learners as well. If learners have access to a dedicated lab for desktop computers or a couple of stand-alone desktop computers or even PC/Mac laptops it would be a good idea to have a couple of these programs installed, as you would the industry-standard DAWs.

Finale Notepad

Finale Notepad is likely the most well known of the free big-three software. It is easy to use and the only free version of the big three that does not need a cumbersome license manager application to work. If learners are new to notation software and not overly techy yet, this could be a great choice. There is a bit of a learning curve for this software at first but it is versatile and seems to interpret imported MIDI information smoothly. It has a basic Document Wizard that helps to set up the score for what instruments your work will use and how it will look.

Sibelius First

Since Avid has a number of different pieces of software, including the industry standard, Pro Tools, and various different versions of each of those softwares, Avid uses an account manager application to manage all those in one place. The account manager must be running on the device to be able to use Sibelius First. This account manager can be a bit cumbersome to navigate. My initial reaction to the Sibelius First software is that it is very intuitive and set up quite nicely. The opening page gives options of templates for different ensembles that learners might come across, even one for Orff hand percussion and handbells (Figure 5.8). There are a number of useful features that are easy to apply, like changing the colour of the note, the note

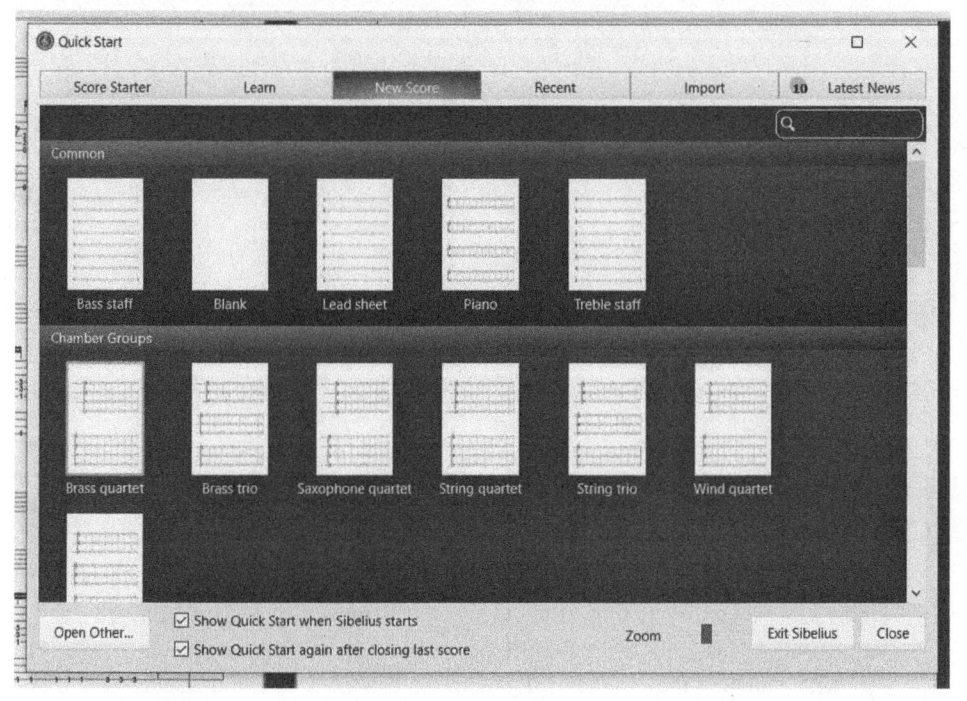

FIGURE 5.8 Sibelius First Quick Start templates

head type, and the number of voices per staff. Learners can easily add parts after the piece has been created, unlike Finale Notepad. Sibelius also released a free version of their software for iPad (Sibelius for Mobile) in the summer of 2021. It functions like the desktop version and is designed to integrate with it.

Interestingly, in the bundle Sibelius First also has a "Score Starter" (Figure 5.9) section, which is a collection of scores spanning multiple genres with beginning material to work with. These files can be stored on the stand-alone device (perhaps the facilitator's device) and can be exported as MIDI and uploaded and imported as MIDI to another notation software that learners might be engaging with in the cloud if there is only one machine with this software on it.

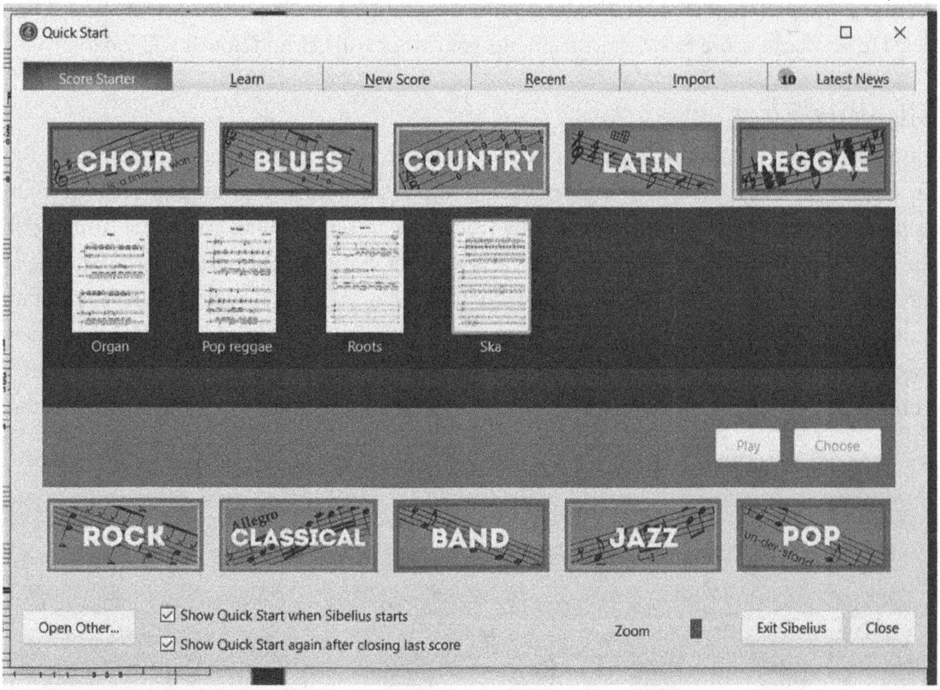

FIGURE 5.9 Sibelius First "Score Starter: screen

Possible Applications

Use the precomposed beginning compositional projects as some inspirational material to get started.

Learners could import the beginning material from Sibelius First to a DAW to continue composing or arranging there, too.

Find MIDI files online to import to Sibelius to rearrange and add harmony to.
Import Music XML files from the Internet to re-compose or rearrange.
Play with changing the assigned MIDI sounds. This exercise could be effective for any grade level.

Dorico SE

Dorico, by Steinberg, uses another account manager to manage all the software the app is responsible for, which includes the DAW Cubase. Dorico SE is the free version of Dorico notation software and for being free there is a lot to it. The sounds must be downloaded separately but are excellent. There is a MIDI piano-roll editor that works alongside the notation sequencer built into it, which is handy. It also has some preset music to work with (which could also be exported as MIDI). It is designed well for film scoring but does have some drawbacks. For example, it's not as user friendly as Sibelius or even Finale. As well, the templates provided with Dorico SE include only one- and two-part pieces (Figure 5.10). Released the same week in 2021 as Sibelius for Mobile is Dorico for iPad, which is incredibly versatile and includes both the note editing and piano roll MIDI editor. It's free with in-app purchases.

FIGURE 5.10 Dorico SE score setup screen

MuseScore (Drive- and Cloud-Based)

MuseScore (Figure 5.11) is a free open-source desktop-based software. It is incredibly versatile for a free software and is capable of many of the functions that the pro versions of the big three possess. Plug-ins are available, too, to help enhance its capabilities. Earlier in the book I mentioned MuseScore's online database of sheet music. This is a valuable resource for creating and arranging. Using this feature, learners can either upload their compositions and arrangements to the site or download someone else's and alter it or use it to find sheet music to play in their ensembles. Learners may notice licensing information on each of the pieces that indicates how the piece of music can be used. This is useful information for facilitator and learners to understand. The online database requires a subscription to access fully, but it is very affordable. These files found on the MuseScore site are all MusicXML files (XML, MXL[MUSICXML]), which are cross-compatible digital-sheet-music file types that the majority of notation software can read. This means if a file from the MuseScore site is downloaded, it can be read, altered, and interpreted in the notation software of the learner's choice.

FIGURE 5.11 MuseScore edit screen

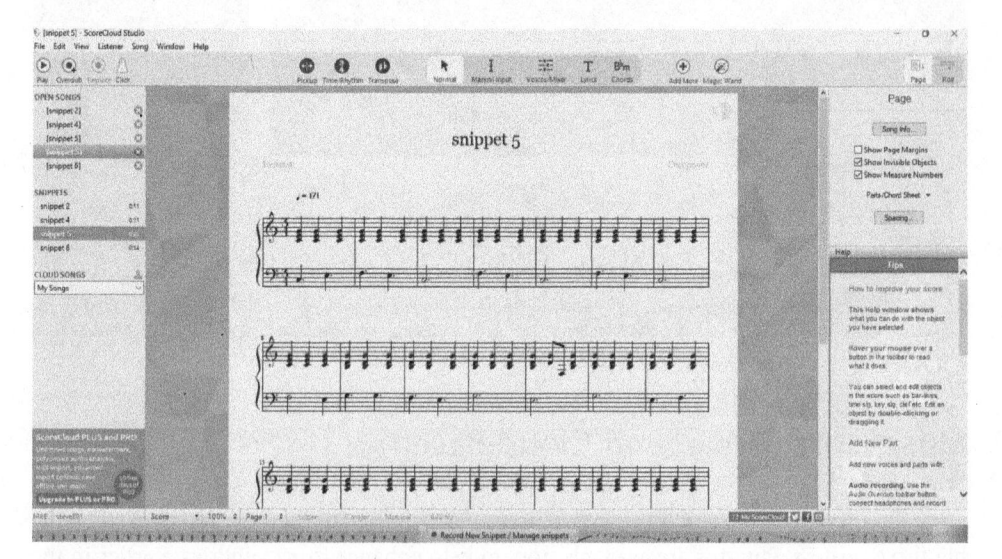

FIGURE 5.12 ScoreCloud transcription from a piece played by a MIDI controller

ScoreCloud

ScoreCloud is a wonderful and shockingly accurate transcription app (Figure 5.12). It has a companion mobile app for iOS. In the free version, the user can play a monophonic piece; ScoreCloud will listen, analyse, and write it down in European staff notation almost flawlessly. The big three aren't even this accurate with MIDI input. This software will even find the time signature for you. There are paid versions of it that can handle polyphonic recordings of an instrument (like an acoustic piano or guitar) and are able to also transcribe *it* in staff notation. It works very similarly to a DAW, but instead of recording in sound waves, it analyses and transcribes musical tones into staff notation, and so the user can track multiple parts just by playing them in with whatever instrument they have.

I could see this software being part of the suite of software-based apps on a stand-alone PC or Mac that can be very useful for

inputting parts just by playing them quickly into the software and printing them out
learners with more complex musical ideas than they can write
learners who are differently abled and need transcription software for music as they would for any writing in their other classes

Cloud-Based

Like the cloud-based DAWs we explored earlier, there are equivalent cloud-based notation softwares perfect for schools and cloud-based devices like Chromebooks. The beauty of the cloud-based softwares (like in the DAW chapter) is that they can be accessed from any device with a good Internet connection. Some even have companion apps for even more easy access. Most cloud-based notation software programs that I come across have a free version and a paid version with more features.

Noteflight

Noteflight's free web-based version has some great features that any beginning user would need. It gives the user the capability to compose or transcribe in staff notation, tablature, or chord symbols (Figure 5.13). Adding instruments to the score and rearranging the order is very easy; it gives learners the ability to import and export MusicXML and MIDI files, making it really quite versatile for a free web-based tool. The premium version, for which the

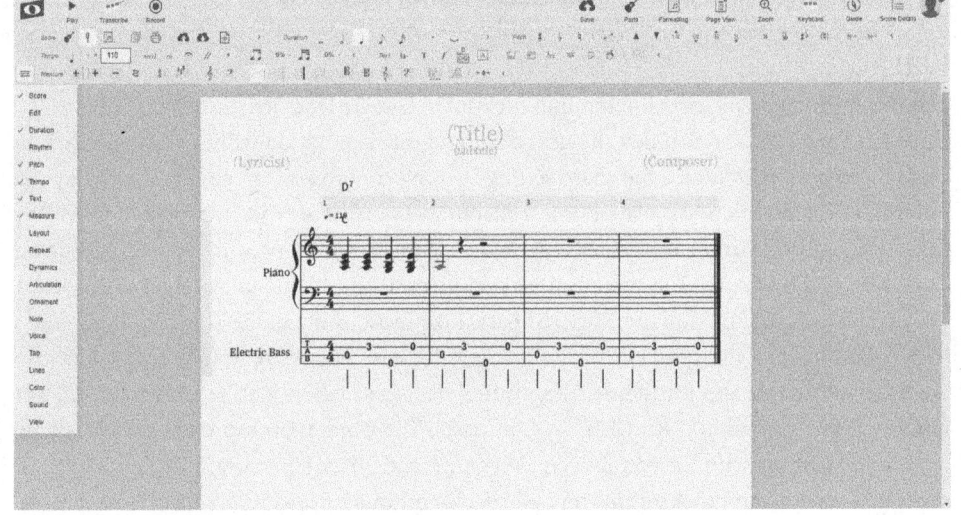

FIGURE 5.13 Noteflight score editor screen

user can pay monthly, yearly, or a flat fee for a lifetime subscription, give users access to MIDI input options, higher-quality sound options, an unlimited number of scores at one time (currently the free version has a limit), and other useful features like colouring notes, and greater access to Noteflight's online community and quick-start scores. Unless you are focusing a large majority of your time and energy with composing or transcribing by using staff notation or tablature, this app might be all learners need access to. Noteflight is also integrated with Soundtrap and included in the "Export" list, among MusicXML, MIDI, PDF, WAV, and MP3. Of course, learners can open these in any DAW of their choice.

Noteflight Learn (COPPA-Compliant)

Like some of the cloud-based DAWs that were mentioned, Noteflight Learn is the paid COPPA-compliant Education version of this web-based app. Noteflight Learn creates a closed network for schools to ensure online safety of learners and integrates with Google Classroom. Even without Google Classroom, it has its own way of setting up an online learning environment where facilitators can assign activities to learners by using activity templates much like BandLab.

One particularly distinguishing feature in Noteflight is the Noteflight Marketplace. It is a great resource for finding standard arrangements of pieces and those of lesser-known arrangers or composers as well. There is music written mostly in staff notation for orchestra, small ensemble, jazz ensemble, concert band, choir, and other large ensembles as well as solo works and various popular music selections. There are lots of pieces that feature tablature as well. Perhaps one of the most intriguing aspects of Noteflight Marketplace is the ability to adapt works purchased on the platform that the user can then resell on the same platform as long as the user doesn't just try to sell the originally purchased piece. As long as the works are marked with "Allowed," they are able to be adapted and resold. The only catch seems to be that users wishing to sell must have a US bank account and be at least 18 years of age. This could be a great way to raise funds for the school by which learners sell works through the school and later adapt their own work again to sell for themselves.

Flat.io

Flat is completely web based and reminds me a lot of Google Docs for music notation. In fact, there is a Docs extension so that the user can input music notation within a Google Doc. In Figure 5.14, you may notice the share settings: young composers can copy a shareable link, publish on Flat online, add collaborators, collaborate in real time, and embed on the web. The free version gives learners the ability to write music in staff notation, chord symbols, Roman numerals, and tablature. The premium version gives access to colour notation, Kodály notation (shape notation), and even figured bass. Like most of these, the ability to input notes with MIDI and the ability to customize hot keys for ease of use are available, too. Flat also has a downloadable app for offline composition. Hot keys you might be used to are CTRL/CMD + C for copy and CTRL/CMD + V for paste. There are many more hot keys for doing just about anything without a mouse. Hot keys are standardized in many DAWs and notation software for easy and quick editing and playback. Common hot keys in most DAWs are "R" for record, "space" for play/pause, and "Enter/Return" for back to the start.

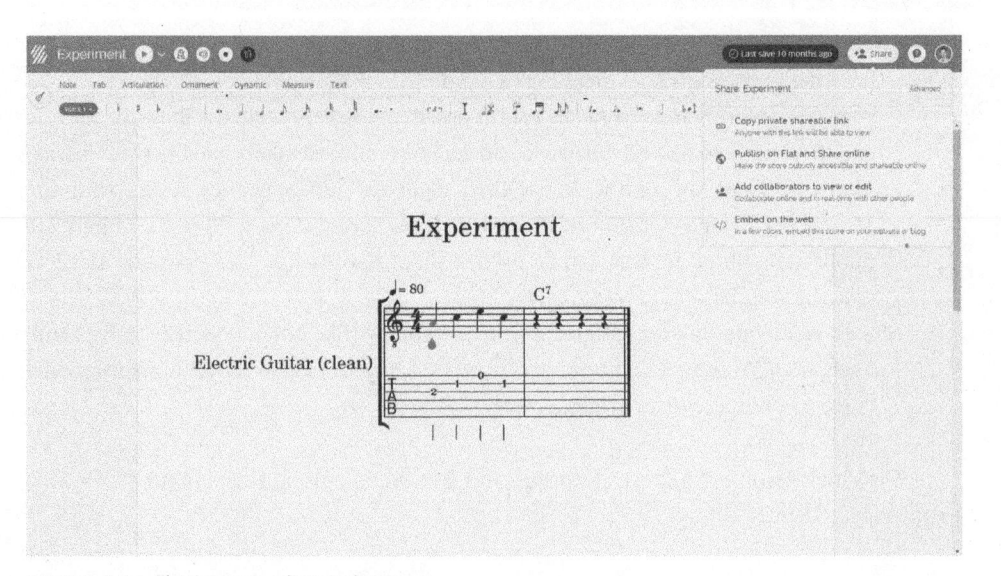

FIGURE 5.14 Flat.io score editor in browser

Flat for Education (COPPA-Compliant)

Flat for Education is the COPPA-compliant version of Flat with education-specific features. It can also integrate with popular Education platforms like Google Classroom, Schoology, and Canvas. As with other cloud-based notation and DAW software, the school would purchase a certain number of seats for their school. In the non-education accounts, there is a database of music that any user can upload to be viewed by any Flat user under the "Discover" tab within Flat. Anyone can comment and it often can become a forum for less-than-desirable language to occur. However, it can be useful for finding arrangements and original pieces of music learners might want to explore.

Possible applications for notation software are the following:

Compose a four-measure AABA melody and add a harmony part or second instrument part to it to compliment.

Compose a short melody in Chrome Music Lab's Song Maker (explored later), export as MIDI, and open in notation software to see what it looks like in staff notation.

Use it as an opportunity to explore how music can be written down and if the learner's intention was to have other musicians play it with their instruments, then it should be easy to read. If it looks really challenging in staff notation, chances are it will be really challenging to play. This could start a discussion about how music is written and the purpose of each kind of notation.

Compose a four-beat melody or rhythm pattern and see if learners can interpret it on their instruments.

Use it to explore staff notation for the first time as a group.

Give out pictures of animals and have the learners compose a short piece about them.

Send learners an MXL (MusicXML) file of precomposed music and have them improve it by adding harmony or another track that they think will enhance the piece.

Find MIDI files online of popular melodies and import to notation software, and then have the learners arrange them into a band piece or ensemble of their choice. Also, if your goal is for them to be fluent in staff notation, learners could use the same melody and then edit it to be easily readable and add expressive elements into the sheet music.

Find music from the online MusicXML database and rearrange it. As with the MuseScore database, many of the works have permissions written in. Others are public-domain pieces that can be used without permission. Use a popular classical piece as your basis for arranging.

Make a video by using a screen recording technology (like Loom or Screencastify) and, using a DAW, record each part and overlay it into the video for a fun instructional video or premiere of an original piece.

Da Vinci Resolve is a great, powerful, and free video editing software for PC or Mac (explored in Chapter 10).

Compare and Contrast Notation Software Chart

See Table 5.1 (next page) for a summary of the notation software discussed in this chapter.

Possible File Types

Aside from MIDI, MP3, and WAV files as explored when learners are using DAWs, there are specific file types that are commonly associated with notation software like this.

MusicXML (MXML, MUSICXML, MXL) are universal sheet-music file types that just about any notation software can interpret. For example, if a file is created in MuseScore and exported as MusicXML, it can be opened, interpreted, and edited in any one of the notation softwares mentioned. The MXL extension is the compressed version of the regular MusicXML file type.

Portable document formats (PDF) are common export files in notation software. It can be used for sharing high-quality print parts and scores across the Internet with the intention of printing them out. They are a universal file format (non-editable in their simplest form) used for many printing needs.

What about the Other Notational Systems?

Earlier in the chapter we discussed all of the standardized notational systems that exist just in North America alone, but these "notation" softwares in this chapter really use only European staff notation, chord charts, and tablature as a real staple of the software packages. Most other notation systems are extras, are part of their premium packages, or don't exist. Sibelius, at the very least, has Nashville Numbers plug-ins available but they are not standard issue. In comes HookTheory's HookPad (Figure 5.15),

TABLE 5.1 Features of Notation Software

Feature	MuseScore	Noteflight/ Noteflight Learn	Flat.io/Flat for Education	ScoreCloud	Dorico SE	Sibelius First	Finale Notepad
Cost	FREE Online database access is cheap	FREE/$	FREE/$	FREE but also a premium version	FREE with options to purchase premium versions	FREE with options to purchase premium versions	FREE
MIDI input	✓	Not in free version	✓	✓	✓	✓	✓
MIDI Import/ Export	✓	✓ import only in free version	✓	Pro only	✓	✓	✓
MusicXML Export/Import	✓	premium or Learn	✓	✓ Import only. Paid version export	✓		✓
PDF Export	✓	premium or Learn	✓	Paid version		✓	
MP3 Export	✓	premium or Learn	✓	✓	✓		
WAV Export	✓	premium or Learn	✓	✓	✓		
Notation covered	Staff, tab, chord, chart. Plug-ins available for a variety of different notations.	Staff, tab, chord symbols, chord charts	Free: staff, tab, Roman numerals, chord symbols, chord charts premium: Kodály, figured bass, colour.	Staff	Staff, shape notation, colour, chord charts	Staff, colour, tab, chord charts, chord symbols, shape notation.	Staff, tab, chord charts
Online Score Database	✓	✓				✓	
COPPA-compliant Educational Version		✓	✓				
Distinguishing Features	Completely free open-source notation software.	Access to SoundCheck performance assessment on Learn site.	There is a Google Docs add-on to insert musical snippets into Google Suite.	Incredibly accurate audio transcription tool. Pro version can import audio files.	MIDI bank sounds are incredible. Includes MIDI piano-roll editing built in.	Full premium version has lots of useful plug-ins available.	Can interpret MIDI information well. No cumbersome account manager.
Desktop-based	✓			✓	✓	✓	✓
Cloud-based		✓	✓				

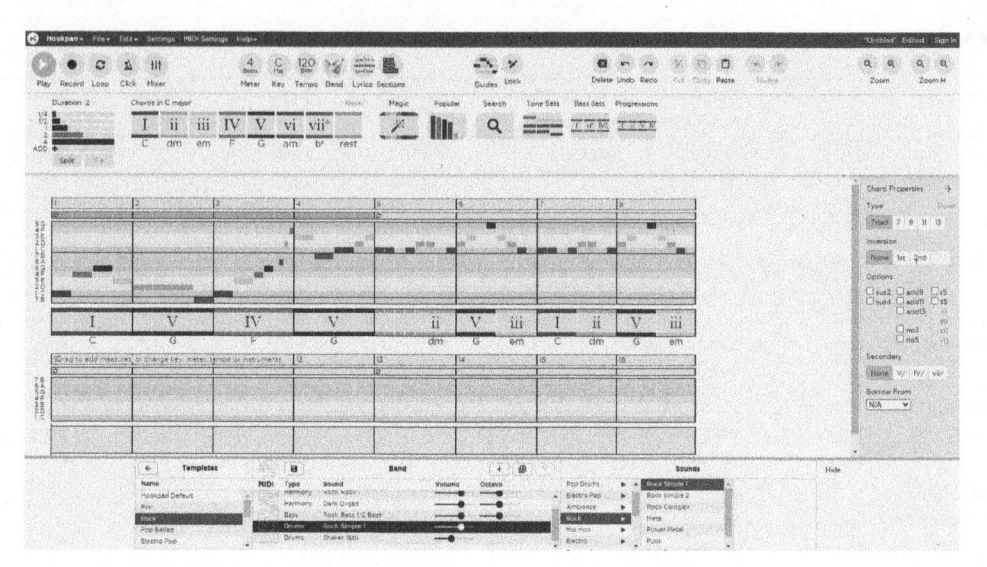

FIGURE 5.15 HookTheory main editing page

HookPad

HookPad from HookTheory takes the features of a DAW and of a notation software and combines them for this versatile cloud-based app. It defaults to MIDI piano-roll and TUBS grid notation by using the Chromatic Colour System, and the paid version can export as a lead sheet, tablature, MIDI, MP3, and WAV. It's designed for writing music in popular styles but can be used for many other genres as well. The free version gives the user the ability to find common chords or progressions, and the music can even be played back in tons of popular styles and transposed into many common modes. The best part is that it is designed in such a way for songwriters to learn theory along the way. The user can save their compositions in the cloud with the free version but will need an account and will be able to save only the chords and melody, none of the other settings. HookPad is designed to be used for teachers in schools with HookTheory's COPPA-compliant HookTheory Classroom. There is a student pay option or a teacher pay option with this version. There is also a database of songs that can be imported to HookPad for analysis and for remixing or rearranging. From what I can tell, though, the free version seems safe for use in schools.

Possible applications include the following:

Explore modes with the transpose feature. Have learners compose a song and then play with the modes to see what changing a mode does to the sound and feel.

Watch a clip of a movie or have multiple pictures available without sound and try to find the mode that evokes the emotion portrayed.

Compose a piece for Boomwhackers and perform it.

Add lyrics to a precomposed melody.

Write a short parody by using the lyrics feature.

Create a short melodic hook and try to find the best combination of chords to fit.

1Chart

1Chart is an app for iOS devices specifically designed for notating in Nashville Numbers.

Chord Sheet Maker

An option for composing in chord charts is ChordSheet.com. It is currently in the beta stage but is good for making clear chord sheets that are easy to read. Learners can easily transpose parts and the company is even working on a Nashville Numbers conversion.

Conclusion

It is important to understand that DAWs and notation software can be used in partnership. It was alluded to throughout this book up until this point, but understanding how certain file types interact with DAWs and Notation Software can be helpful in utilizing each to their potential. Figure 5.16 is a Venn diagram for helping to understand which ones you might need for any particular situation or to help you and your learners understand the differences, similarities, capabilities, and limitations of each type of software, but also how they might interact with one another.

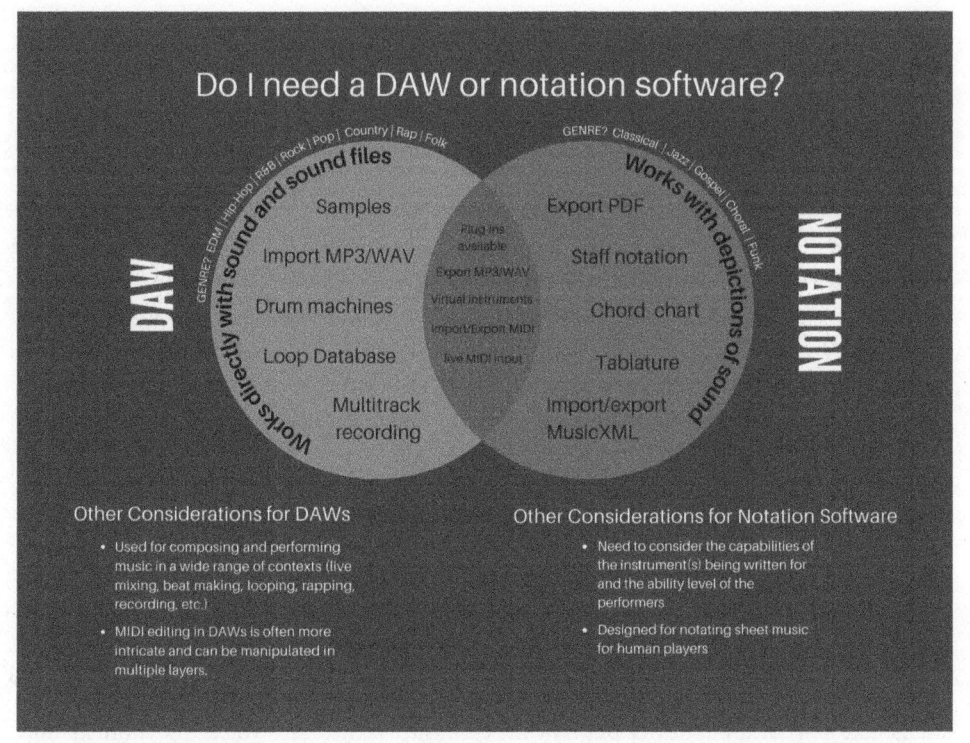

FIGURE 5.16 Venn diagram illustrating the similarities and differences between DAWs and notation software

6

Other Online Tools for Fostering Creativity

The number of online tools can be overwhelming. In this chapter I will give you an overview of some more popular and more useful tools with suggestions for lessons and ideas to help implement them.

Chrome Music Lab

This suite of free apps by Google presents a plethora of cross-curricular connections and is great for introducing basic concepts of electronic music production using virtual instruments, microphone effects, MIDI, drum machines, and oscillators. They can be used for beginners or advanced learners of any grade level from K through 12. The way the interfaces are designed is incredibly helpful for K–6 learners to make music instantly but can certainly be used for 7–12 as well without it feeling childish. If learners haven't begun using Chrome Music Lab, they should. It has some amazingly versatile apps but also some that are just plain fun and can be used to create good music instantly. In this section of the chapter, I will give a quick overview of some of Chrome Music Lab's apps and features and how they can be used in a music classroom. Figure 6.1 shows some of the apps available in Chrome Music Lab.

Song Maker

Find Pitch and Tune

Press the "Mic" button at the bottom of the Song Maker screen and let it access your microphone (Figure 6.2). Once you do, you will see a microphone icon appear at the left side of your screen (Figure 6.3); try singing or playing an instrument to see if it can guess right. It's almost like a MIDI input device but now the controller is the user's voice! The more in tune, the more easily it picks up the sounds. Song Maker also added a "Midi" feature, giving it the ability to connect to a MIDI controller of your choice.

Technology for Unleashing Creativity. Steve Giddings, Oxford University Press. © Oxford University Press 2022. DOI: 10.1093/oso/9780197570739.003.0007

FIGURE 6.1 Chrome Music Lab in-browser interface

FIGURE 6.2 The "Mic" button at the bottom of the Song Maker screen

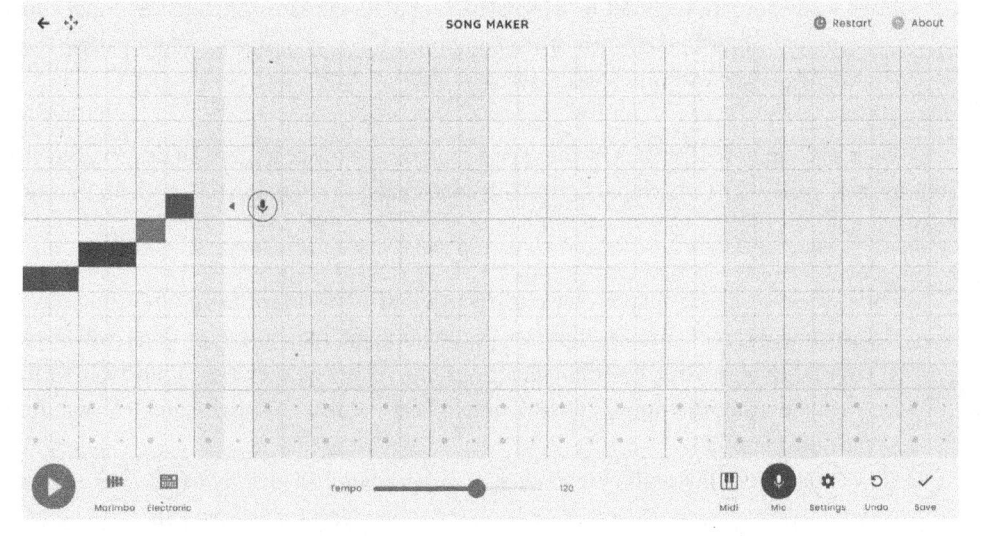

FIGURE 6.3 Song Maker's "Mic" function

Possible Applications

Applications can include the following:

Have learners input notes by using only their voice or an instrument of their choice.

Once they have their choices, play the input back in a loop (it will do this automatically) and figure out an accompaniment that fits while the loop is playing. If learners are working in a particular key, this exercise could work really well for reinforcing that particular key signature.

Help reluctant singers find their pitch by seeing if they can make one of the colours light up.

This function is much more sensitive if the notes played are in tune and audible. It could work for helping singers stay on pitch or for pitch training. It's a similar concept to how Auto-Tune functions by giving the opportunity to experience unhindered creativity. Being able to write down what they sing could be their creative hook. Using a condenser microphone (discussed later) and headphones will help them to feel more confident with this exercise.

Have learners sing or play a simple melody to see if the app will catch the notes, and then have the learner arrange the rhythm to fit.

Learners can use the arrow keys on their QWERTY keyboard to specify which block on the grid the pitch will be sung into.

Have your group of recorder or wind players playing the same pitch to see if they can keep their notes in the centre. Then compose a piece of music together by using the "Mic" function with the notes they know.

With a group of K–2 singers, it could be a fun exercise to see if they can sing in pitch as a group, and if they can't match pitch, take the notes that *it* decides on and use them in your composition.

For ukulele or guitar players, have learners input notes into the app by using their instruments, then find a chordal accompaniment that fits, beginning with two chords. They can begin with open strings or a scale that they are comfortable with. After inputting the notes, create a simple beat to go with it that complements the melodic material.

Have a prepared link with part of an easy or very familiar melody for the learners to complete or alter to make correct to practice their learning by ear skills

Katie Wardrobe of Midnight Music Technology has a fantastic Star Wars lesson plan for finishing the melody for various grade levels. When they are finished, they can rearrange and remix the melody. When they are doing the remixing, I tell them that the original song still has to be recognizable.

Export as MIDI to a Notation Software

All notation software has the capability to read MIDI, but they all interpret them differently. Finale, for the most part, is pretty good at what was intended.

To export from Song Maker, start by clicking on the "Save" Button to see the options (Figure 6.4).

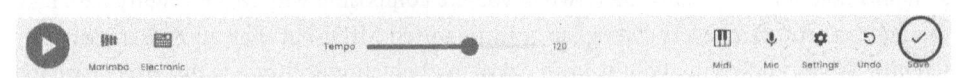

FIGURE 6.4 Click "Save" at the bottom of the Song Maker screen

When learners click "DOWNLOAD MIDI," it will begin to download the file in MIDI format to their device's drive (or to the Google Drive on Chromebooks) (Figure 6.5). When learners go to their notation software, click on "import" and then "import MIDI." Every notation software deals with this function differently. Learners may be able to select the file type from the "open" menu or there may be a dedicated MIDI import option. Once it has opened in a notation software, it will be rendered in European staff notation and can be manipulated and arranged from there. Many times, it will be rendered in two tracks (rhythm and melody).

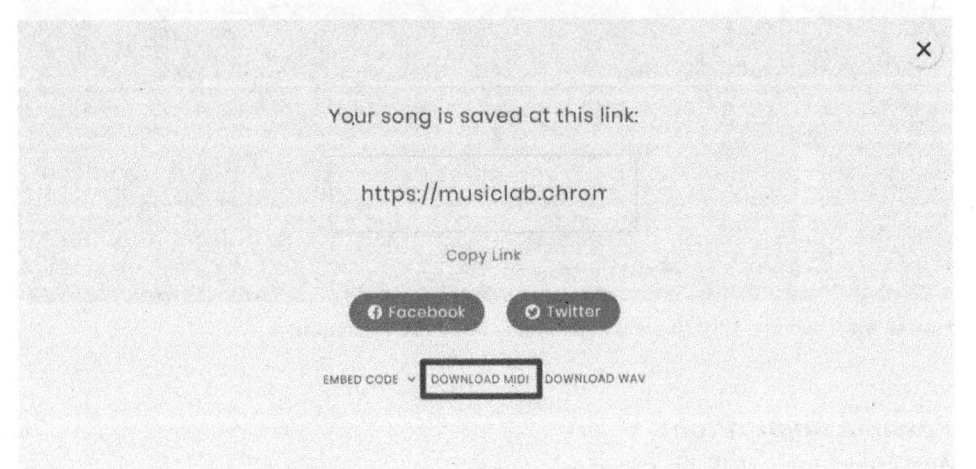

FIGURE 6.5 Click on "DOWNLOAD MIDI"

Possible Applications

Applications can include the following:

After learners compose a melody, import it to notation software and add another part to complement the original.

If learners are working on particular scale concepts, have them set those parameters in Song Maker, compose within those parameters, and export to a notation software.

Song Maker can be used as a really good introduction to how MIDI works or how European staff notation works. For younger learners, simply having them go through the process of exporting then importing is a useful musical technology skill.

Export as MIDI to a DAW

Song Maker uses MIDI piano-roll notation with the Chromatic Colour System, which is a standard notation within any DAW when you are composing with MIDI (Figure 6.6). Like the notation software, every DAW can read imported MIDI but they all render them differently. What is different about using a DAW over notation software is that users have the ability to add loops, other MIDI instruments, and beats to the melody/riff. A riff is what is commonly referred to as an ostinato.

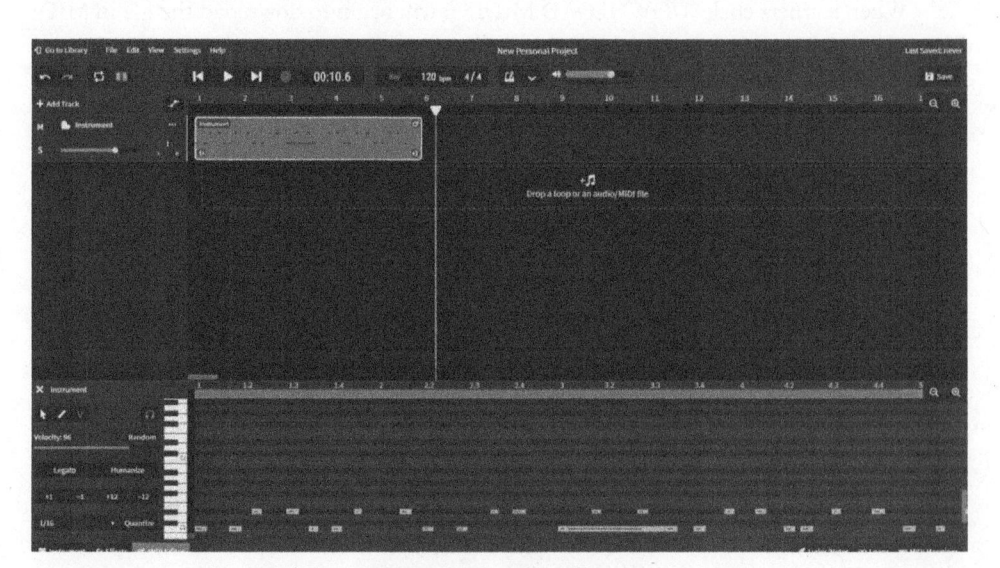

FIGURE 6.6 Importing MIDI composed in Chrome Music Lab to BandLab

Possible Applications

Applications can include the following:

Learners can also change the original melody within the MIDI Editor on most DAWs.
Learners can be asked to create a melody in Song Maker and then asked to add a beat to it in a DAW.
Learners can add loops to the MIDI part and try to match tempos.

Learners can create a MIDI part that complements the imported track by using a MIDI controller or virtual instrument within the DAW.

Learners can import a MIDI file and change the sound.

Generate a Link and Share

After the user clicks on "Copy Link" (Figure 6.7) the link will automatically be saved to your device's clipboard; all you have to do to release it is select where you want it to go and then paste it (CTRL + V on a PC and most laptop devices; CMD + V on a Mac).

Learners can paste it anywhere: for example, in an email, in a text message, on social media, or in a Google Doc. Anyone who can view their composition can edit it, too, so they could pass it back and forth with different versions each time.

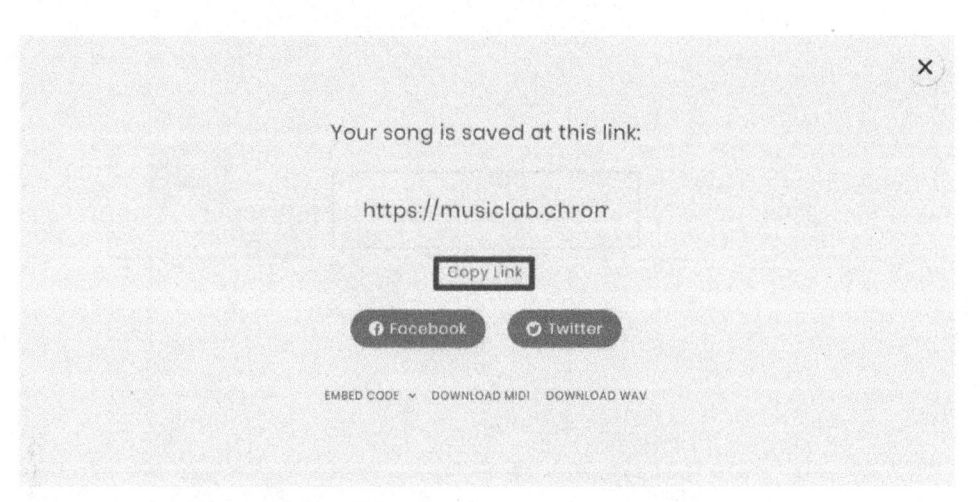

FIGURE 6.7 Click "Copy Link" after clicking "Save"

Possible Applications

Applications can include the following:

Ask learners to create an A section and someone else to create a B section by sending it through email or another method.

Ask learners to create an entire ABA piece, send it to someone, and ask them to change one thing to enhance the composition.

Ask learners to create a melody or harmony part and send it to someone else to add a rhythm part.

Ask learners to save their music to a particular platform as a type of creative portfolio.

Every piece of music ever composed on Song Maker has its own unique URL, so as long as learners have the link, they can always go back to it. Users can save them in a portfolio on Google Doc or a Google Site (discussed in Chapter 10). Learners can save the screen to their clipboard by pressing "PrtScn" key on the keyboard. (CTRL/CMD + V releases or "Pastes" it). They could even record your screen by using Loom or Screencastify.

Uses of the Chromatic Colour System

The Chromatic Colour System (mentioned earlier) (Figure 6.8) is a legitimate standardized notation system first theorized by Isaac Newton in 1702 and adapted by many. Think about how many other instruments or notation systems use these same colours.

Of course, this is useful knowledge because learners can now compose music for Boomwhackers and a plethora of other instruments. And if they memorize the colours, they can translate their music to any instrument at all without having to export it to notation software.

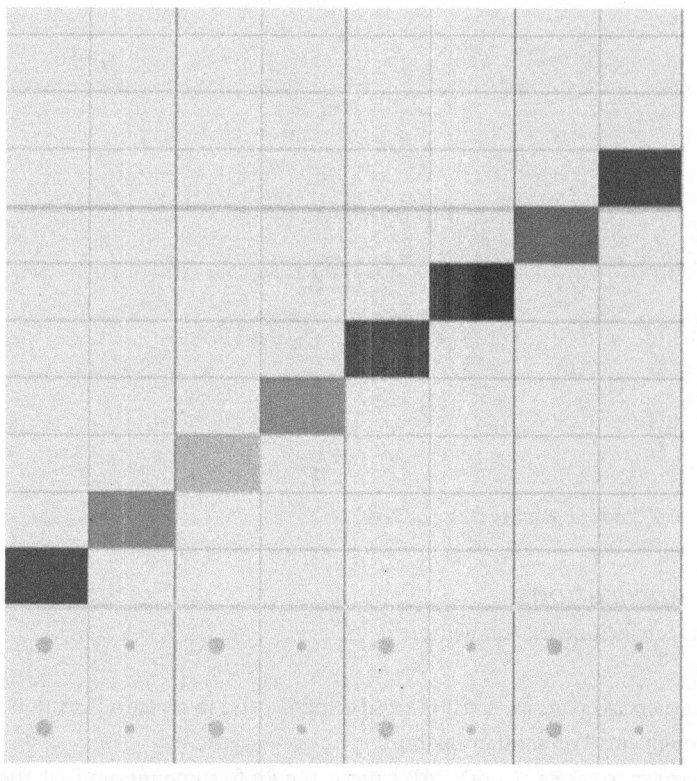

FIGURE 6.8 Chromatic Colour System in Chrome Music Lab

Change Key, Number of Bars, Metre, and Scales

Clicking on the "Settings" button at the bottom will present learners with some options (Figure 6.9). See Figure 6.10 for the parameters learners can work with.

FIGURE 6.9 Click the "Settings" button on the bottom of the Song Maker screen

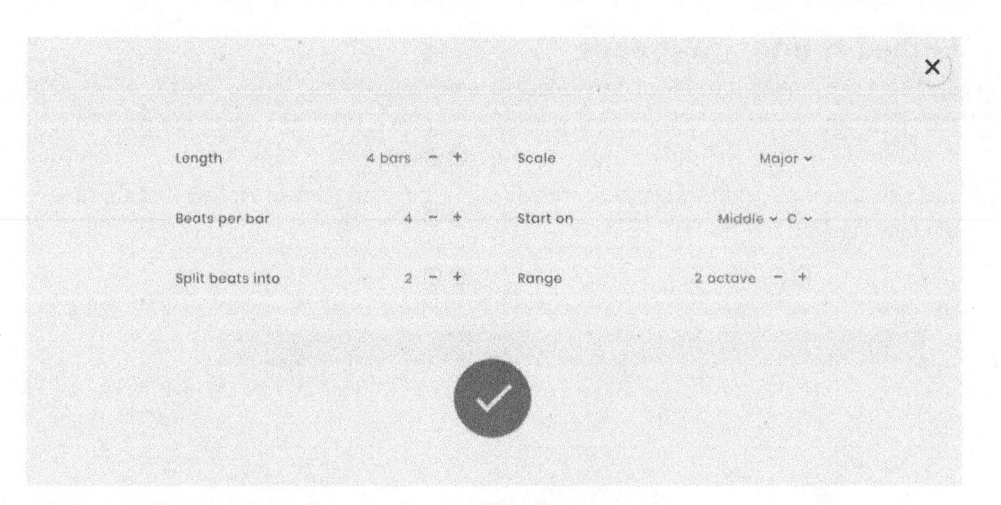

FIGURE 6.10 The parameters for composing under the "Settings" tab

K–3 Snowflake Project

This project begins by making snowflakes from circle-shaped paper that are folded first in half, then into a right-angle triangle, and finally isosceles. Once they have been folded, proceed to make cuts by using scissors to produce interesting shapes and unfold the triangle paper to reveal an intricate snowflake pattern. Then project Chrome Music Lab's Song Maker onto the dry-erase board, set it to pentatonic, and attach a snowflake to the board with a magnet over the Song Maker grid. Proceed to fill in negative spaces on the snowflake that was chosen with colour from Song Maker. Play it back and repeat until you have a finished piece. Figure 6.11 shows an example of a section of a "Snowflake Song" from a Grade 1 class. Notice the snowflake patterns in the grid.

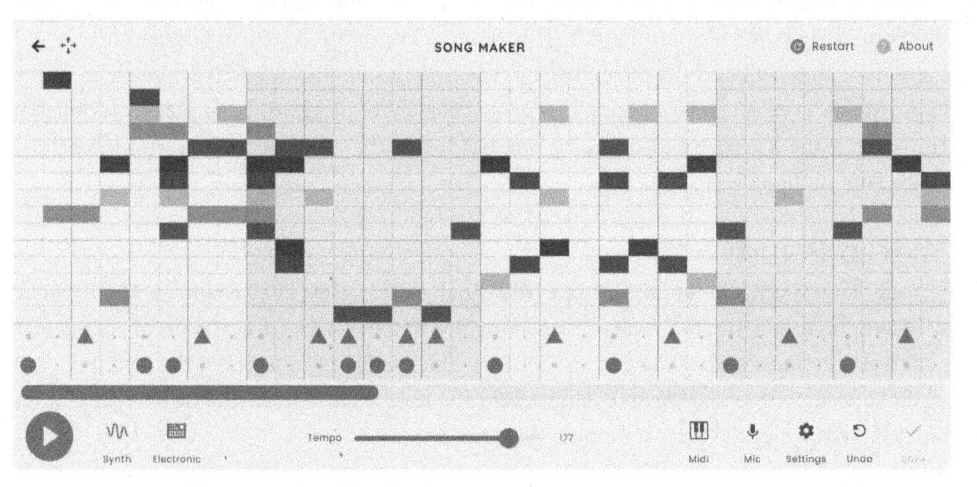

FIGURE 6.11 "Snowflake Song" in Song Maker

Embed It Into a Webpage

Learners can embed the snowflake project to a web page like a Google Site to collect all of the compositions in one place like a portfolio (Figure 6.12). Then when the page is published it will appear right there and you will be able to play it from within the web page and edit it as you see fit. If learners are editing it they will have to embed it again to save the new version.

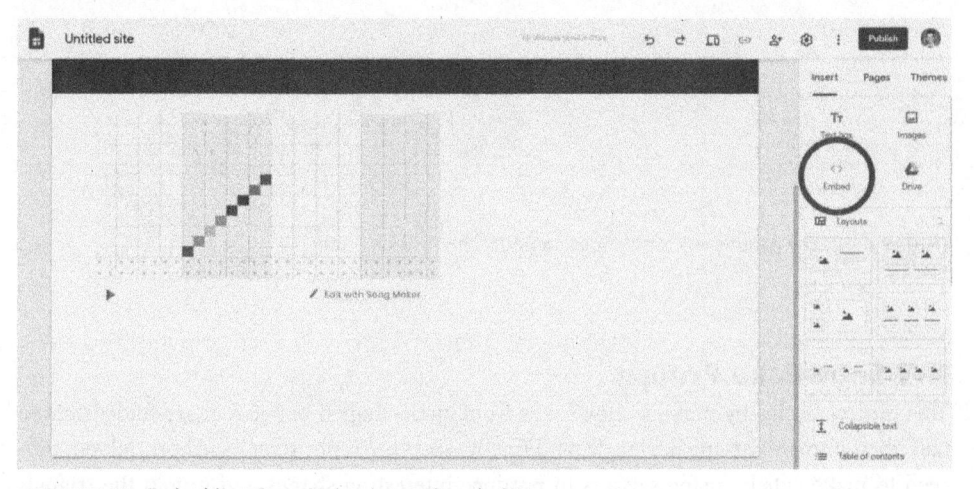

FIGURE 6.12 Embedding Song Maker into a Google Site

Summary of Song Maker

There are a lot of creative possibilities using this simple app. And this is just one app within the Chrome Music Lab suite of apps. There are so many meaningful musical learning opportunities to be had here. From exporting MIDI, to pitch, and standardized colour notation systems, this app has something for everybody.

It is important to mention that there are databases of songs composed or transcribed into Song Maker. There are also videos and JPEGs of composed or transcribed music that use Song Maker all over the Internet. This point is important because learners know about them, too. They will find the databases and use them when they are first exploring this app. Knowing these exist can be a practical way to speak about plagiarism and academic honesty. However, if the learners end up using one of these, turn it into a positive and have them create something new from it.

Shared Piano

Shared Piano was added to the Chrome Music Lab roster in late 2020 (Figure 6.13). It can be used as a stand-alone virtual instrument connected to the QWERTY keyboard of your device or can also connect a MIDI device. In "Settings" it is possible to customize the layout of your virtual instrument to display note names, how the note trails behave, and how many octaves are displayed, among other parameters (Figure 6.14).

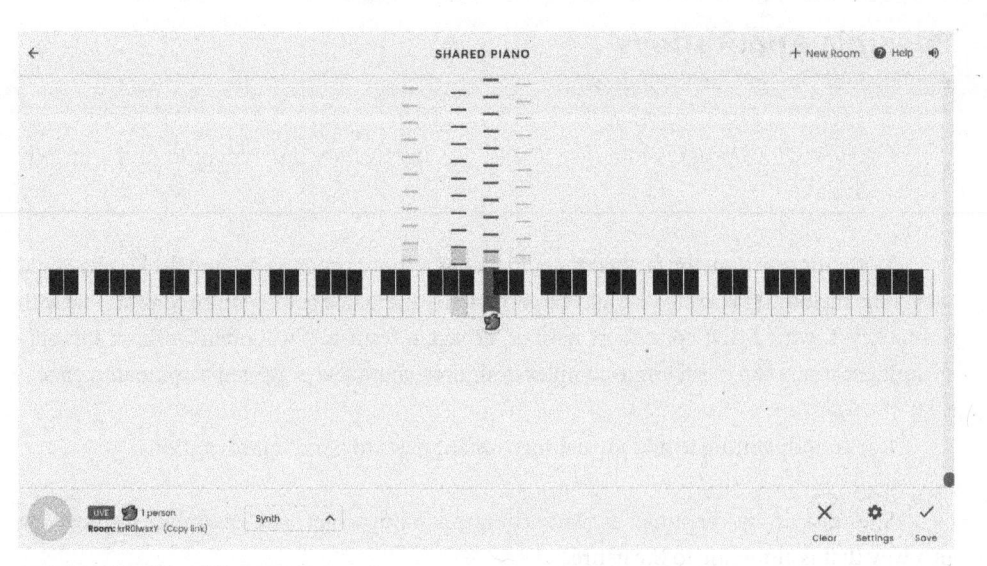

FIGURE 6.13 Shared Piano main screen

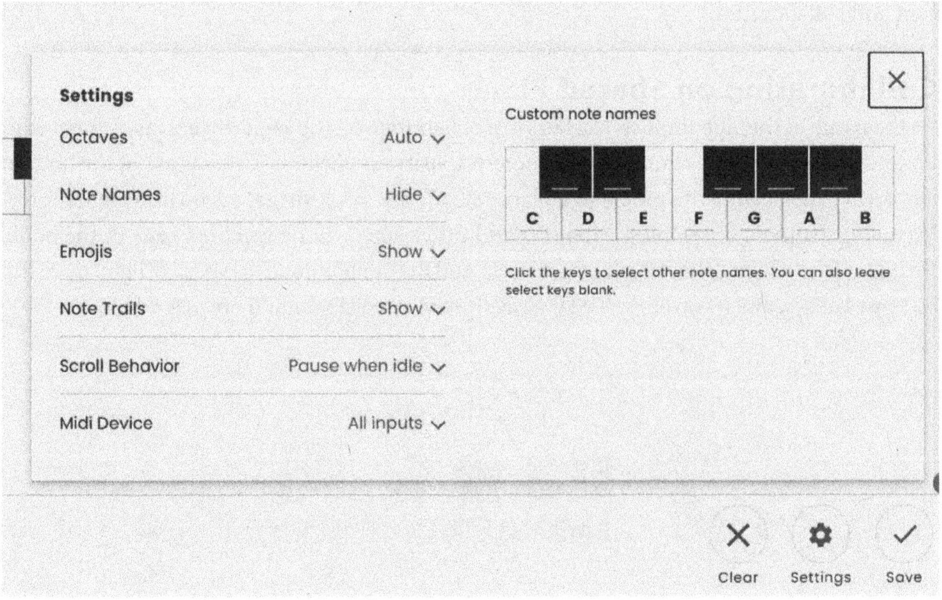

FIGURE 6.14 Shared Piano parameters screen

By clicking on "Save," you generate a link that has already recorded everything that was played. It can be used for playback, but a unique feature of this function is that learners can continue to play over the recording once it is playing. Melody and accompaniment can be practiced separately. The link works the same as a Song Maker link: anyone who has it can access it and interact with it.

Possible Applications

Applications can include the following:

> Create a chord progression, save it, and use any melody instrument to find a melody to fit.

With this function, the facilitator could record a chord progression, and the learner could create the melody. This exercise could be particularly useful for getting more comfortable with a new key. If your MIDI controllers have an arpeggio feature, it will often work on this app, meaning learners can create more complex-sounding chordal arpeggiated accompaniments.

> Use soundpainting to add virtual instrument parts to band improvisations.

Soundpainting is explored in a later chapter as a way to get large ensembles improvising in a way that is authentic to the genre.

Shared Piano is useful for exploring creativity on the piano (many digital pianos and keyboards have MIDI capability). This app has huge implications for online piano composition and collaboration.

Collaborating on Shared Piano

As the name of this app implies, learners can collaborate on the same virtual instrument with up to nine other people at one time, remotely. If learners click on "Copy Link" at the bottom left corner they can invite others to collaborate on the same virtual keyboard (Figure 6.15)! Virtual instrument ensembles using this and other apps will be explored later in the book. Because of the nature of how the Internet works and the limitations of the speed of light, there will be some latency, and if you are really far away from your collaborator there may be more.

FIGURE 6.15 Room code and player avatars

Possible Applications

Applications can include the following:

> Have your piano classes jam together to a simple tune. One person plays a simple repeating pattern or riff, and another plays a melody, while another plays a drum pattern by using the drum-kit or drum-machine feature.

If latency is too great, hindering the ability to play in time together, call-and-response improv activities can be really effective for any grade.

If learners don't have access to a keyboard lab, a keyboard lab facilitator who is using keyboard MIDI controllers and headphones can create groups for learners to join on Shared Piano and will replace the need for a central headphone amplifier hub. MIDI controllers are much cheaper than full keyboards. Also, if you have a few digital pianos in your room, hooking up to a device is simple with a USB cable or a five-pin MIDI-to-USB interface cable.

This exercise can work on a touch screen, too, and would be very effective for younger learners.

> Play an A section and have learners create a B section (moshed or one at a time) and then play the A section again.

Moshing is when everyone improvises a melody over the same chord source so that they can create melodies and harmonies without being put on the spot.

Rhythm

This app has some clever features to it as well. There are four metres to choose from: $\frac{3}{4}$, $\frac{4}{4}$, $\frac{5}{4}$, and $\frac{6}{8}$ and each has a different flavour, so to speak. The second one (in $\frac{4}{4}$) (Figure 6.16) has a distinct drum-set or rock/popular feel to it while the fourth one (in $\frac{6}{8}$) has a very Latinesque flavour to it. The beats are also subdivided into eighth notes.

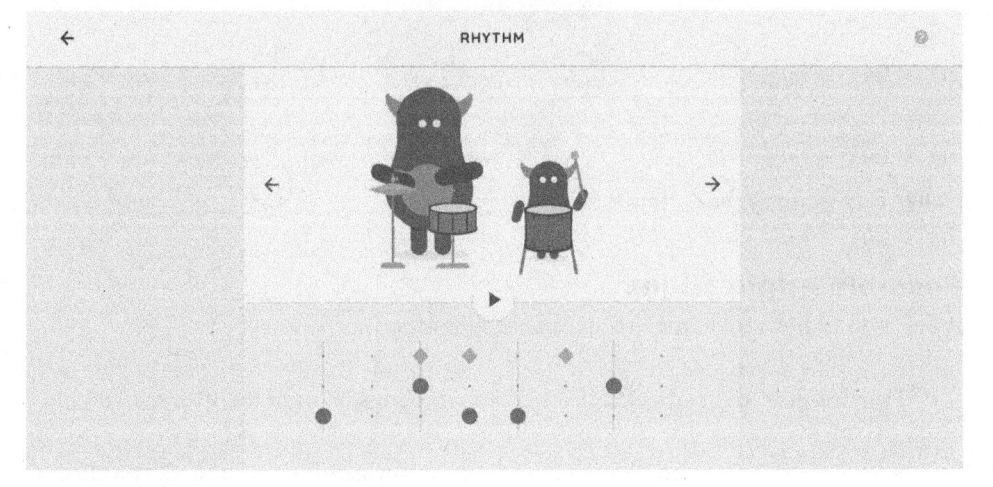

FIGURE 6.16 Rhythm app in Chrome Music Lab

Possible Applications

Here are some ways to utilize this app:

> Create a rhythm pattern and a live instrument melody to go with it.
> Create a pattern and write it down in a notation of the learner's choice.

Create a topline by using the Rhythm app as the beat.

Have learners create a two- or four-beat pattern to reinforce rhythmic knowledge. Have other learners figure out what rhythm it is.

Arpeggios

This app is similar to the Smart Piano and Smart Guitar functions in GarageBand. Instead, there is no set key. Closely related chords are close together (Figure 6.17). There are no diminished chords, because they don't sound good and are rarely used. One of the most intriguing features about this app is that learners can experiment easily with borrowed chords because if they don't stray too far from the area in which they started, the progression will still work really well. Borrowed chords are completely fine, especially if they sound good—there are no real "rules" per se. Like the GarageBand app, it will autoplay a few preset patterns. Learning an instrument doesn't get in the way of creativity.

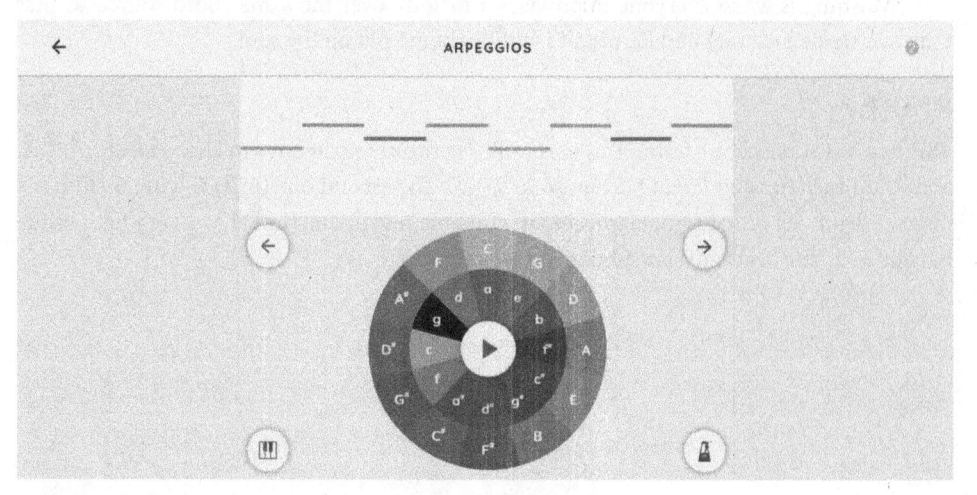

FIGURE 6.17 Arpeggios on Chrome Music Lab

Possible Applications

A few ways learners could use this app are the following:

Have learners go in pairs. One creates a chord progression while the other solos over top.

Keep in mind that improvisation can happen in any genre, even classical. For this one, you might have to give a few parameters, like what three chords to use, or they can use only one closely related chord, especially if they are beginning improvisers. More experienced learners may be able to hear the changes. You could limit the exercise to two notes to adapt this for beginners or younger learners.

Create a chord progression and compose a melody to go along with it.

Create a pop song that has lyrics and a chord progression.

Use the app for group jamming. Have the facilitator in charge of the chords and then have learners improvise over it in a mosh style of improvising. Or, in a popular ensemble setting it could be used as a way to get ideas out to see how the progression sounds before using it in a song.

Have one learner create a chord progression in Arpeggios, and a melody to go with it in Melody Maker and see if they can get it to sync up.

Explore high and low by scrolling through the patterns and figuring out which pitches are higher or lower.

Kandinsky

Based on the abstract artistic style of painter, Wassily Kandinsky, this app lets the learner create digital art that becomes music (Figure 6.18). Any scribble becomes the default sound. Drawing a triangle creates a percussion sound and a circle turns into a singing voice. The rhythm is chosen by the app. Learners can change sounds by selecting the two-colour circle at the bottom centre of the screen.

FIGURE 6.18 Kandinsky app from Chrome Music Lab

Possible Applications

Applications could include the following:

Have learners draw their names with some decorations to see how it sounds, as I did with my name in Figure 6.18.

Explore high and low by drawing circles to become faces. The pitch goes up if the drawings are at the top of the screen.

Add a complementary part to it by using acoustic instruments or rhythm tracks.

Have learners draw a scene of their own homes and see how it sounds.

Incredibox

This is an online DJ/hip-hop beatboxing composition app found at Incredibox.com. It's intuitive and can quickly make anyone seem to know what they're doing. It functions very much like a looper (discussed in Chapter 10). With the correct combination of voices, a user can unlock new mixes or composition material to add to their work. Learners can also record, save, and share on social media. It can be an amazing thing if learners have access to these functionalities at school. There are four free versions of this musical composition game and currently three paid versions. Something interesting about this app is that when you add a layer, it is quantized to every four measures, meaning it waits until the phrase is finished before adding it in and plays a fill to set it up. Figure 6.19 shows the interface on the web app for Incredibox wherein learners pick clothing and drag it to the person to start the loop.

FIGURE 6.19 Incredibox web app main gameplay screen

Possible Applications

Applications could include the following:

Create compositions and present them to the class.

Create a composition on Incredibox that becomes the backing track for a rap song wherein the beat is recorded while other learners create a flow (see the rap flow chart in Figure 5.5) as a topline.

More advanced learners could preserve these compositions in a DAW by using a virtual audio device like VoiceMeeter or using Chrome Audio Recorder to record into WAV or MP3 format.

Compose a track and play a simple melodic or harmonic topline on an instrument of their choice. Learners would need to find the key of the jam first, in practice for a useful skill.

Use it as a backing track for rhythm activities or rhythm improvisations. There are some combinations that are fun to jam to on pitched instruments as well.

Create a pattern and use it to chant or rap words over in a call-and-response manner.

Some Other Useful Features

Incredibox has a couple of useful features like "Reset," "Auto," and "Rec[ord]" (Figure 6.20). Reset, of course, clears the canvas and starts over. "Auto" automatically generates beats and variations as it goes. It could be a really useful feature for an organic backing track or a way to get started with creating a good beat. Using the "Rec" feature will let users record a mix as it is performed. Figure 6.21 shows what comes up once learners have saved a mix,

FIGURE 6.20 Other Incredibox features

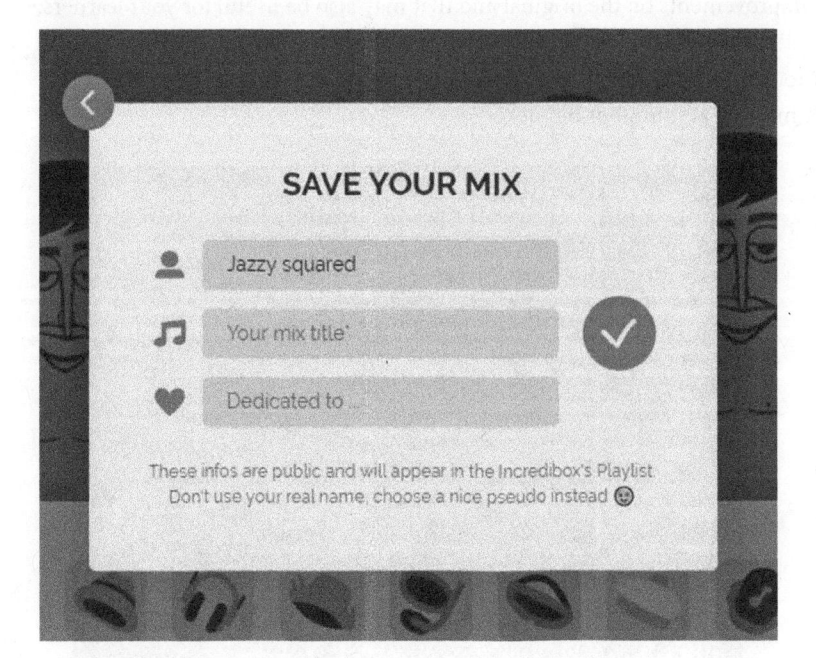

FIGURE 6.21 Saving options in Incredibox

Sequencers

MIDI grid and piano-roll editors are a type of step sequencer. There are lots of different types of sequencers that all have different purposes but the most common are step sequencers. Song Maker, Rhythm, and Melody Maker from Chrome Music Lab are all step sequencers. Notation software is also a type of step sequencer because the apps read left to right and interpret instructions one step at a time. This next section of the chapter explores some useful MIDI and drum-machine step sequencers that can be used in creative projects.

BeepBox

BeepBox (Figure 6.22) is an in-browser MIDI editor similar to Chrome's Song Maker. It uses MIDI notation with tons of MIDI and synthesizer sounds and has many more capabilities than Song Maker. Figure 6.23 shows just some of the parameters learners can work with in this online app.

A couple of distinguishing features of this app are that learners can bend pitch and glissando, but also have the ability to export and import from other sources, too. To share, it works much like Song Maker: all learners need is the link from the browser and anyone who has the link can manipulate it. It is pretty common to share compositions made in this app on social media, although in a school setting, this is likely not possible in many situations.

BeepBox provides the source code for the app at the bottom of its page. This means that those good at coding can add upgrades or modifications to the original code and relaunch it. These modifications use the source code of the original and are altered in programming sites like GitHub or BitBucket. There are at least two "modded" BeepBox sites that have made useful improvements on the original and that may also be useful for your learners:

ModBox at moddedbeepbox.github.io
JummBox at jummbus.bitbucket.io

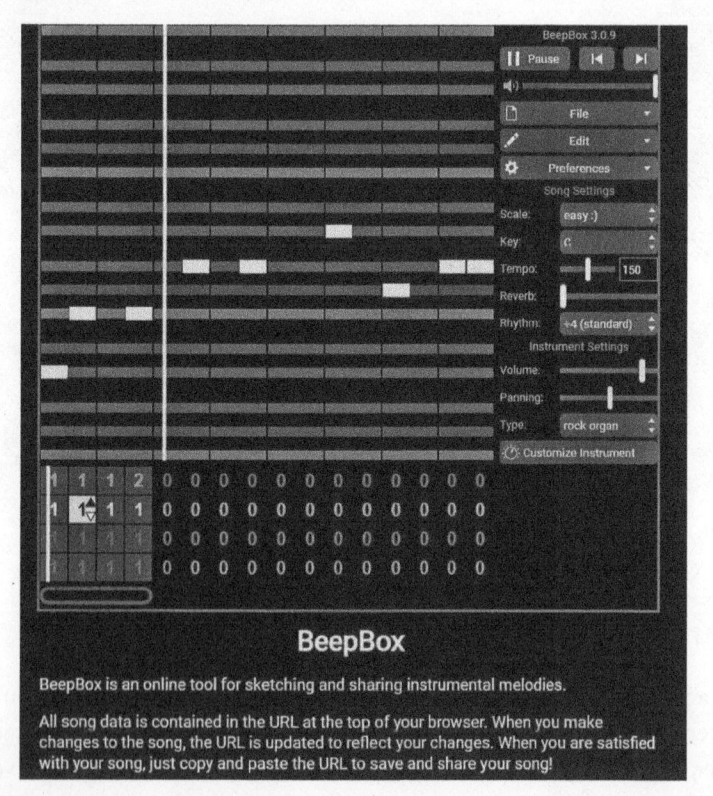

FIGURE 6.22 BeepBox main interface screen

FIGURE 6.23 Some more features and functions of BeepBox

Possible Applications

Applications can include the following:

> Create music for a retro video game by using some of the retro synth sounds that are included.
>
> Search for precomposed MIDI files on BitMidi or Midiworld to upload to BeepBox to rearrange or change the sounds.

Once learners have composed a piece of music in BeepBox, they can export it as a MIDI file and import it to any DAW or notation software to then edit further in that software.

> Use the file to compose a backing track.
>
> Create a video game character and theme music to go with it.

Paint Composer

Those of my vintage would remember Nintendo's "Mario Paint" for the Super Nintendo Entertainment System (SNES). Within that game cartridge contained a creative suite of Mario-inspired activities. It came with a mouse. It was one of a kind and ahead of its time in a lot of ways. One of the "apps" within that suite was Mario Paint Composer. Learners can play with the original Mario Paint Composer with this online emulator (also created on GitHub): https://minghai.github.io/MarioSequencer (Figure 6.24).

Danielx.net has created an updated version of Mario Paint Composer with more features but with the retro feel with similar graphics, gameplay, and all the same sounds as the original (Figure 6.25).

Under the "Save/Load" feature, there are a number of ways to import, export, and interact with the app (Figure 6.26).

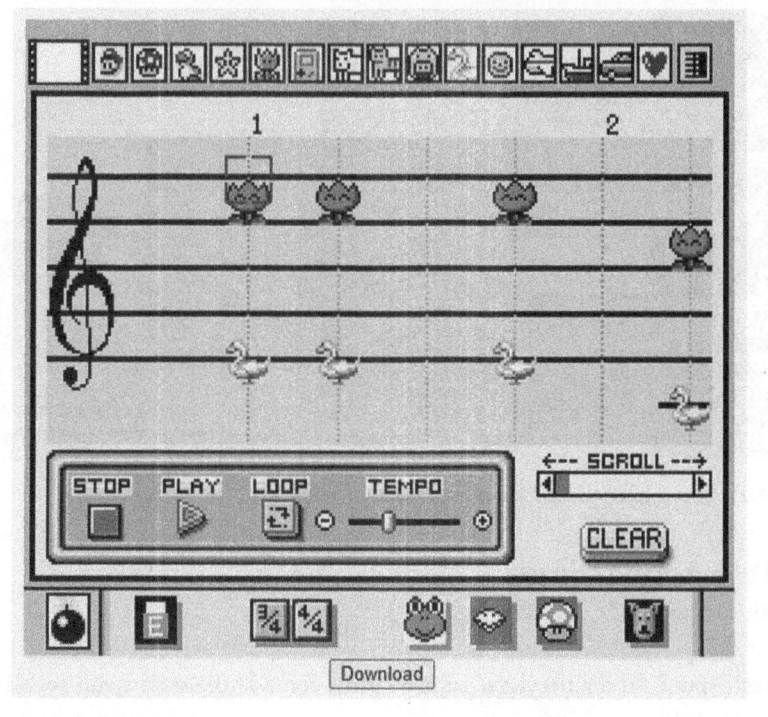

FIGURE 6.24 Mario Paint emulator

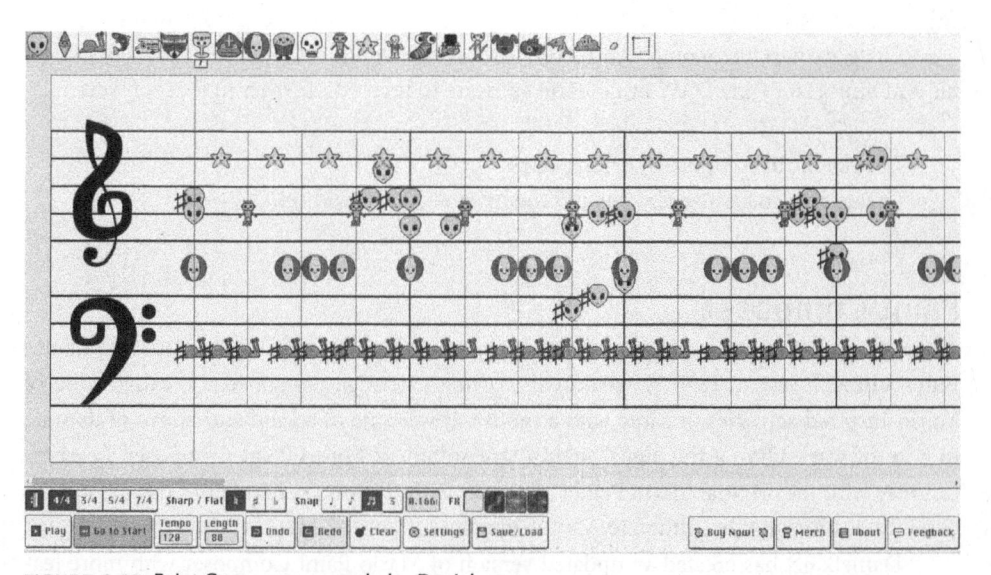

FIGURE 6.25 Paint Composer upgrade by Danielx.net

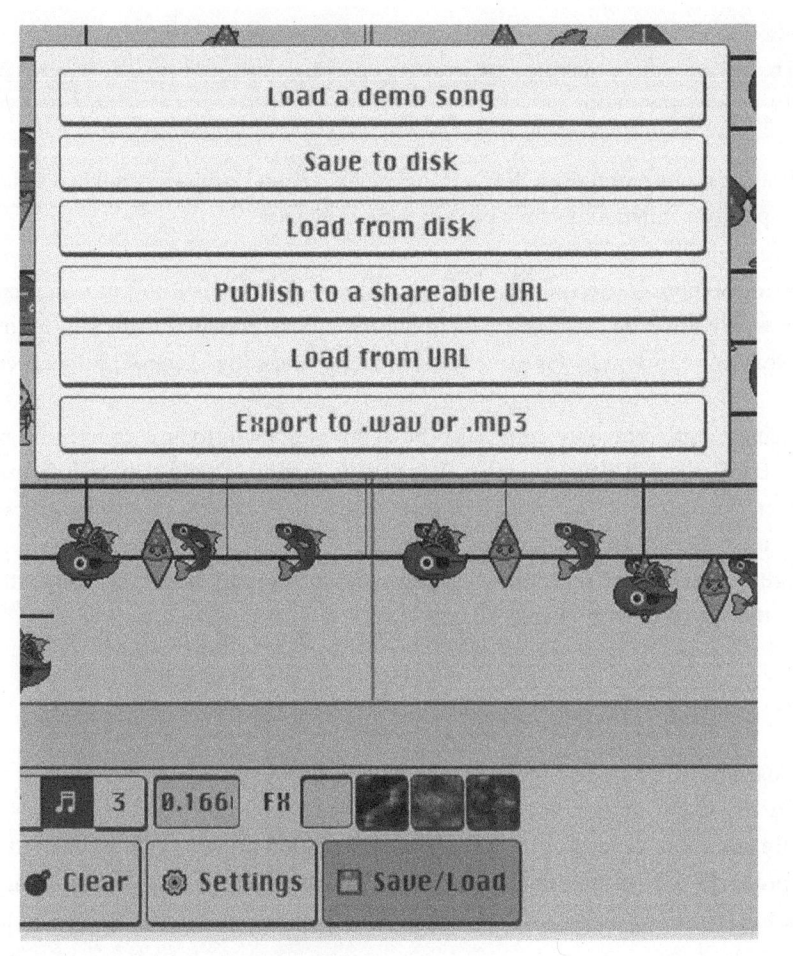

FIGURE 6.26 Paint Composer by Danielx.net features

Possible Applications

Applications can include the following:

Input an existing piece of music into Paint Composer to see how all the new sounds effect the piece.

Use one of the demo songs as a starting point and have learners add or remove one element at a time. Perhaps they are asked to add a harmony part to one, or perhaps they are to remove the bassline and add in a new one.

If it is a band, orchestra, or choir (BOC) class, input all the parts to Paint Composer to see all the different ways in which the piece that the learners are working on could sound.

The reduced scores would likely be a better choice than full ones, or it could be used as a way to rearrange a piece that they are working on as a group into a smaller score that sounds a lot like video game music.

> Learners could compose a BOC arrangement in Paint Composer and then write out the parts for instruments they have in their ensembles.

Paint Composer currently has no way to download as MIDI, so this would create another possibly unneeded step in transcribing for a BOC ensemble; however, it could be a worthwhile and fun activity for some learners to gain meaningful transcribing experience.

> Using Paint Composer could also be a fun way to introduce composing music in European staff notation, as a staff is used to input pitch and rhythm information.
> Your youngest learners could find sounds they like and make a short piece with it by using a couple of staff lines or spaces.
> Create a game level scene by using pencil and paper, and then music to suit the world that was created by using this app.

Drum Machines

Drum machines are a type of step sequencer that emulates sounds of a drummer or use samples of actual drum sounds. Some iconic drum machines, like the Roland TR-808, with its signature electronic drum sound, became the foundation of much of hip-hop and modern music production. Here are a few different drum machines and step sequencers that learners can use to explore beatmaking and that can be used for various other creative activities.

GroovePizza

GroovePizza is created by NYU Music Ed Labs. It is a mathematical and theoretical approach to the traditional drum machine. Your math and computer science teachers will love it, too, for its clear cross-curricular connection to fractions and programming. It is a unique drum machine because it is easy to create a really good-sounding beat by using shapes and lines instead of only programming in a traditional drum grid sequencer (TUBS grid) (Figure 6.27). In my experience with the app, this "pizza grid" facilitates creativity of a good-sounding beat by having the user find interesting combinations of abstract shapes within the pizza. The more interesting the geometry, the more interesting the beat sounds. If a learner is having a difficult time in coming up with a rhythm track that they like, GroovePizza is a wonderful place to begin for generating ideas. An interesting feature of this app is that users can play with the number of slices (subdivisions) in the pizza as well as the bpm and amount of swing to the rhythm. There are some other features that make this app very versatile for composing and creating original music (Figure 6.28).

As with Chrome Music Lab's Song Maker and BeepBox, grooves composed in GroovePizza can be shared through a link, but this app also easily integrates with Soundtrap. A rhythm track

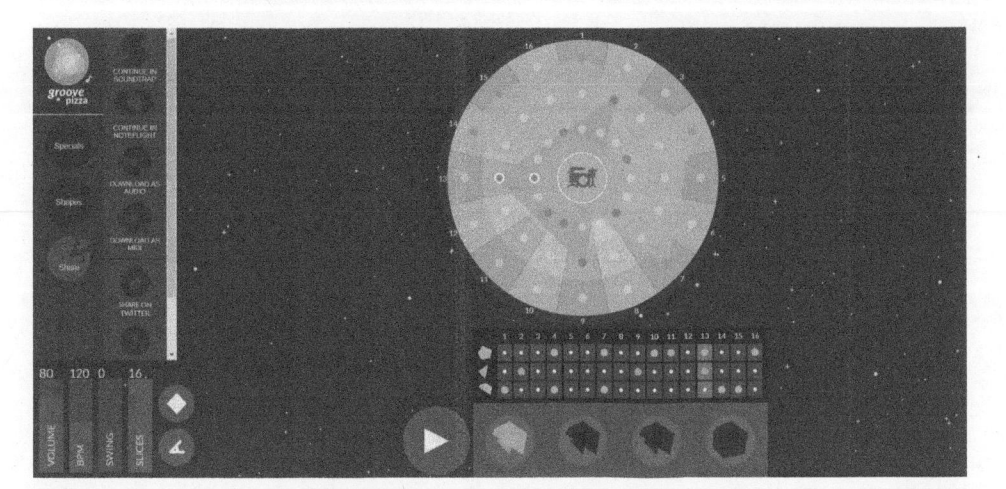

FIGURE 6.27 GroovePizza main screen

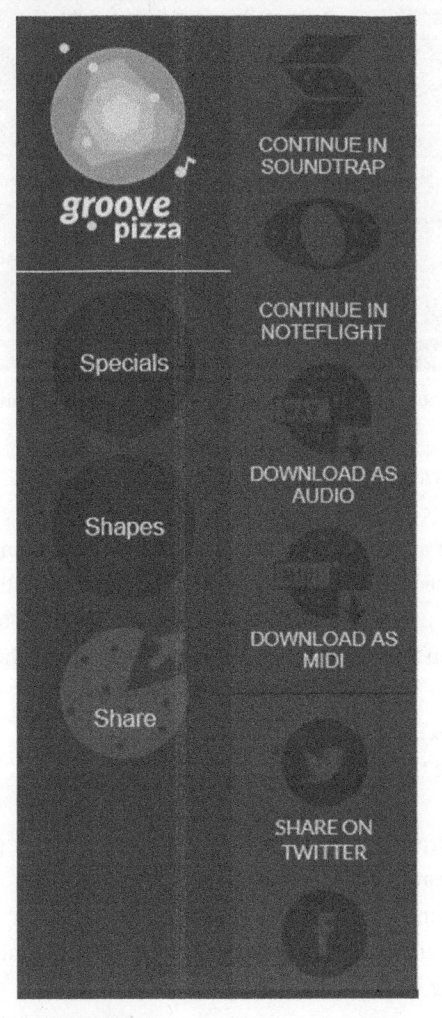

FIGURE 6.28 Some features in GroovePizza

composed in GroovePizza can be continued in Soundtrap without reformatting. It can also be transferred over to Noteflight and continued in that notation software as well. Currently, there are no other platforms where it transfers as seamlessly; however, it can be transferred to pretty much any DAW with a few tweaks. For a DAW like BandLab, learners could download files as WAV or as MIDI but they would interact differently. If exported from GroovePizza as WAV it becomes an audio file that cannot be altered once it has been imported to a track in your DAW. If the groove is exported as MIDI, it can be imported as a MIDI file in the DAW but will not be transferred to the drum sounds automatically. Instead, it will default to a grand piano sound as a traditional MIDI file and interpreted as pitch. To get the appropriate sound, click the piano icon to the left of the track (a virtual instrument will pop up) and select a drum-pad instrument from the drop-down menu, and then the type of kit. At this point, users can alter it like a regular MIDI file by selecting the "MIDI Editor" and altering pitches in the piano roll (Figure 6.29).

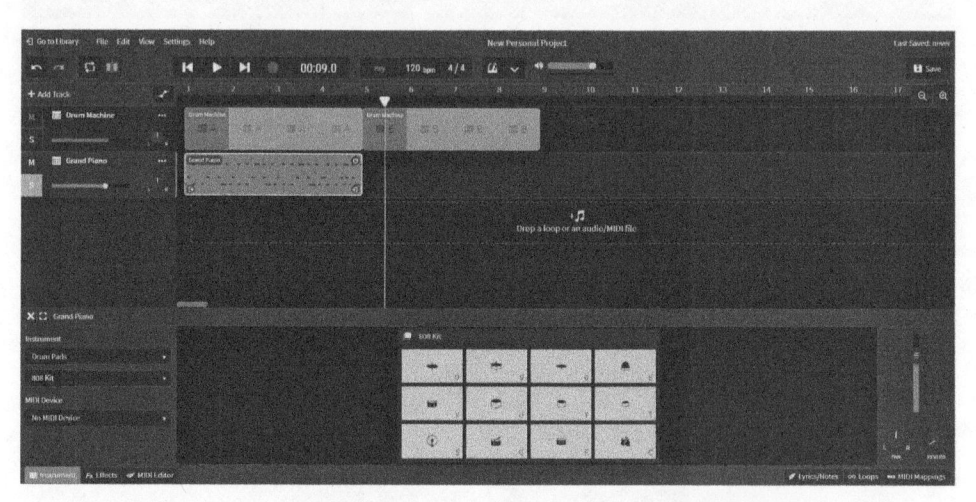

FIGURE 6.29 Drum Pad virtual instrument view in BandLab with an imported GroovePizza track

In a notation software other than Noteflight, the MIDI file defaults to grand piano much like in a DAW, but changing the sound in a notation software after the sound has been assigned is a bit more of a challenge than it is in a DAW, depending on the software. To get close to what was intended, users would have to import as MIDI, then highlight, copy (with CTRL/CMD + C), open up a new document and assign drum set to it, and then paste (with CTRL/CMD + V). It won't be perfect, but at least it will be the right instrument.

Possible Applications

Applications can include the following:

Create a rhythm track for learners to chant to while they pat to the beat. Or have learners help create a rhythm track to use.
Use the app for a fun metronome for traditional ensembles.
Collaborate with learners to help create a rhythm track that might fit with the repertoire they are working on.

See how some basic shapes sound and try to replicate them on an instrument.

Have younger learners decide on a pattern and use it to play or sing over with notes of their choice.

Create a four-bar phrase with a fill in the fourth bar.

Create or borrow a chant and compose a drum-machine pattern to go with it with learners.

Drumbit

The Drumbit app is a versatile, free, web-based drum sequencer (Figure 6.30). There are lots of preset rhythm (beat) patterns to choose from and many different effects, too. It allows learners to program four four-beat patterns to complete a phrase. The swing and bpm can be adjusted overall, as well as the pitch and volume for each track. These capabilities mean each instrument track can be customized to find that perfect sound. "Keys Mode" allows the user to manipulate the machine's rhythm blocks with their computer's QWERTY keyboard. Projects can be saved in JSON format, a web file that can be downloaded to a hard drive and then uploaded to "load" the saved project. Drumbit currently does not have the ability to export files to a more widely recognizable file type, but it isn't needed, because any composition can be saved as a Drumbit project file and loaded to the drum machine whenever needed. Although using a virtual audio router, screen recorder, or Chrome Audio Capture (GitHub version), users could record a drumbit pattern into a DAW.

Amazingly, the paid version is only $1.99 CAD in the Chrome Web Store and saves as a web app within Google Chrome; meaning it will work with Chromebooks (Figure 6.31). And for that cheap price learners get many more convenient features that include velocity

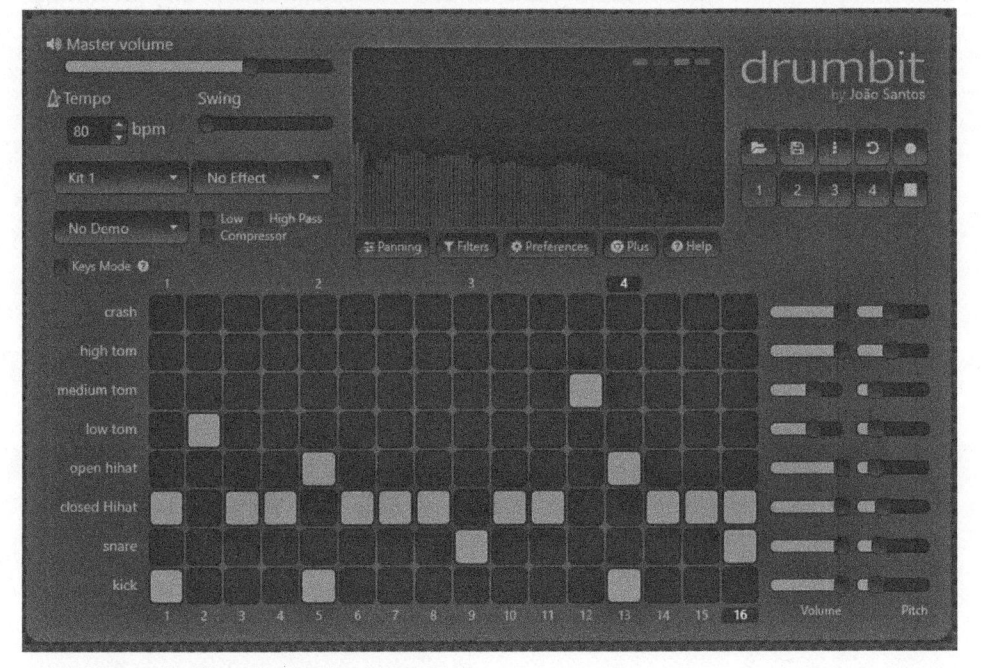

FIGURE 6.30 Drumbit main sequencer screen

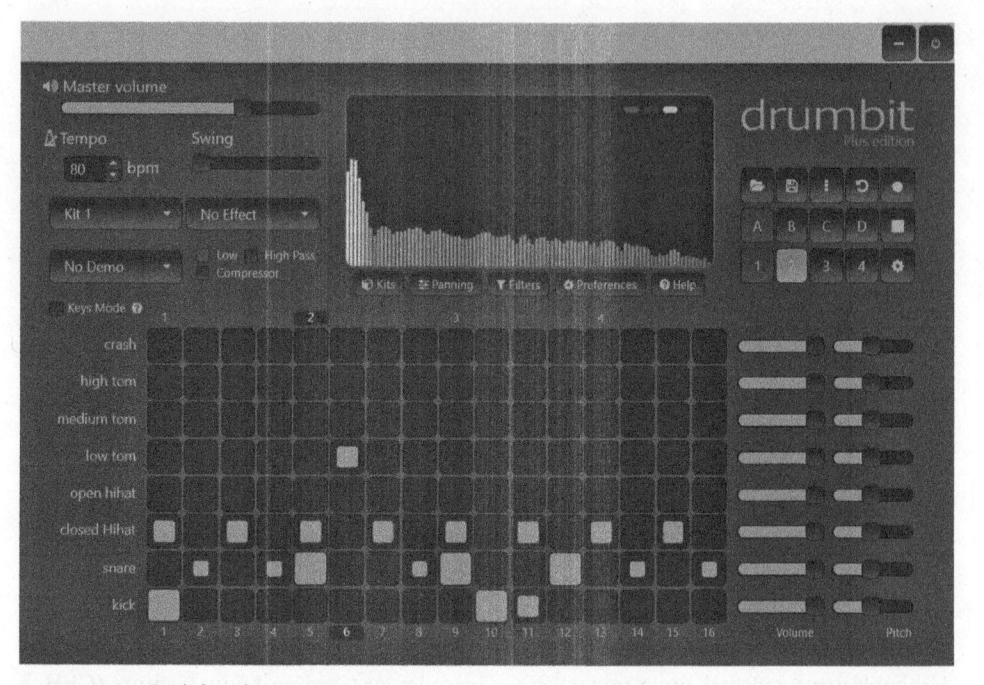

FIGURE 6.31 Paid drumbit app main screen

variance of each block, the ability to save up to four separate phrases (banks) of beats (A, B, C, D), more effects, more kits, and more preset patterns, as well as the ability to customize each kit sound with the built-in samples. In addition, the app can also be used to upload "User Samples" to play with, meaning that the user can upload sounds they recorded or sample packs they might have found online. Just select the folder on the device that contains the sample to add it to the sequencer and it will appear as a custom kit and be given a place on the sequencer screen (Figure 6.32).

Possible Applications

Applications can include the following:

Create a rap with learners and use drumbit to find a "beat" for a backing track. Have the learners choose between the presets and effects or compose one together.

Use the app as a fun metronome.

Have learners create a drum pattern to accompany their long-tone exercises or to accompany their scale patterns for BOC groups.

Have learners compose a piece or lift a piece of music by ear and compose a drum pattern to go along with it in addition to their skills homework.

Compose a beat together to help your choir groove on your pop arrangements.

Use Audacity, Chrome Audio Capture, or a virtual audio router to record system sound so that learners can record a topline over it.

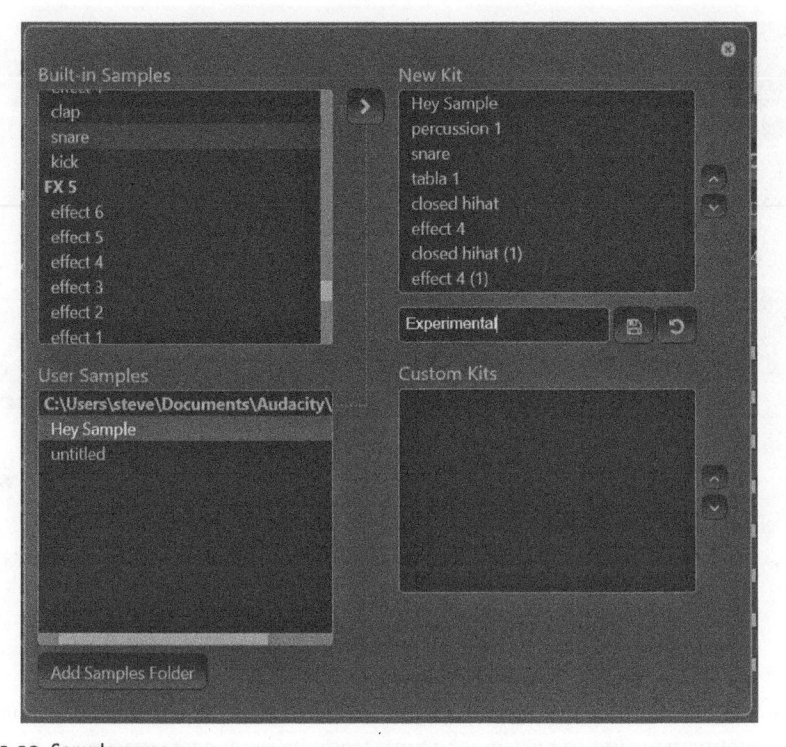

FIGURE 6.32 Sample screen

808303.studio

This cool drum-machine site became a thing in late 2020. It is a virtual musical instrument emulating the sound of the original TR-808 iconic drum machine and the—also iconic—TB-303 bass synthesizer. They are automatically synchronized on the site (Figure 6.33). As mentioned earlier, the Roland TR-808 and its drum-machine sound became very popular in the early hip-hop scenes and is still widely in use today as a backing track for lots of songs. This site gives the user the ability to compose a piece of music for a track in real time by using these two step sequencers. At this time, it gives the user only two minutes to record a song but allows the user to download the file as an MP4 video file to the hard drive, as well as the ability to share directly to social media once the song is complete. These step sequencers have features that let the composer/producer create a great-sounding track easily.

Possible Applications

Applications can include the following:

> Use 808303.studio to compose a semi-improvised two-minute piece of music.
> Check the video of "A Guy Called Gerald" within the site and take his advice for composing a track beginning with few sounds and building to the middle and then "working it down" to the end.

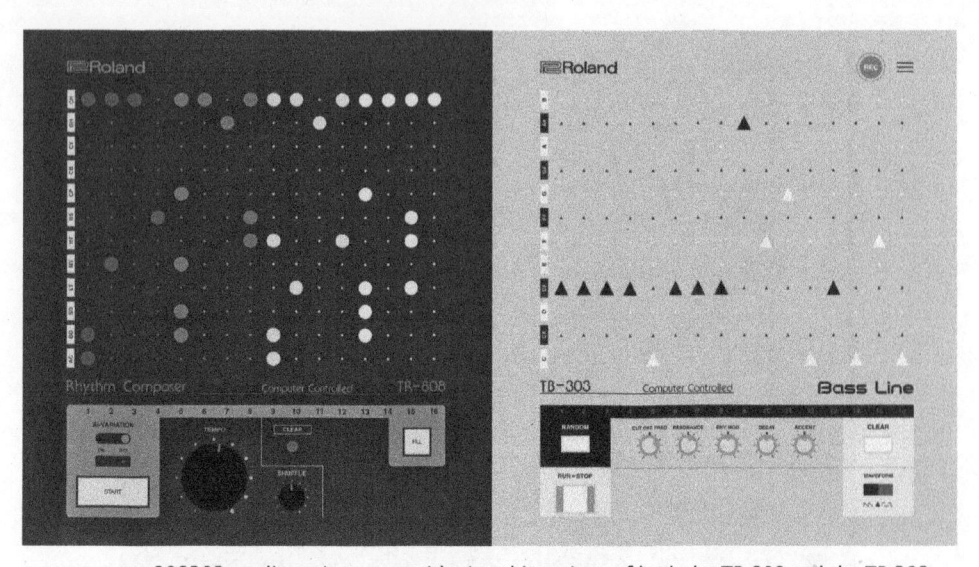

FIGURE 6.33 808303.studio main screen with virtual iterations of both the TR-808 and the TB-303

Record or improvise a beat to accompany a cypher.

For a notation exercise, create a bassline in the TB-303 emulator and write it out in the notation you choose by using the hints from the sequencer's screen.

Use Chrome Audio Capture or Audacity's loopback feature to record system sound or tab sound to create a longer composition that's in an audio format that can be imported to any DAW.

To capture both the microphone and the system audio at the same time, you must use a virtual audio device called VoiceMeeter (PC) or LoopBack (Mac) and Audacity to record both the microphone and the system sound at the same time. You could also use BandLab, or Soundtrap for this if you have a virtual audio device like VoiceMeeter.

If your device uses the cloud for storage only (Chromebooks), record tab audio only by using Loom or Screencastify or use Chrome Audio Capture.

Conclusion

These apps have the potential to give a really good overview and introduction to electronic music and composing music by using technology. I'm hoping you are able to find some ideas and work-arounds to help facilitate authentic creative endeavours in your classroom.

7

Makey Makey and Coding for Creativity

Coding and programming have become exponentially more accessible since 2010. And with block-coding sites like Scratch, or MakeCode, and an invention kit like the Makey Makey, learners can literally program an apple to say, "How are you today?" and play a rendition of the "Moonlight Sonata" while it lights up to emulate moonlight.

Outside of a physical presence of an invention kit or a controller, coding sites can be used to create musical games, online virtual instruments, and musical activities that facilitate real-life, authentic musical programming skills. And if you think these uses are moving too far from music education and more into computer science education, sequencers (virtual or not) are preprogrammed musical instruments that can be then programmed on the user's end to make music, too. So computer science and programming are not a far stretch from music making—they are completely integrated and intertwined and, in many respects, one and the same.

Makey Makey

The Makey Makey is an invention kit by JoyLabz designed as a STEAM (science, technology, engineering, arts, and mathematics) facilitating device. STEAM approaches promote the integration of these five subject areas through meaningful interactions and inquiry-based learning. A Makey Makey kit can be programmed with the help of a computer device like a laptop or a phone to do many different things, but namely, it can be programmed to produce sounds and act as a MIDI controller of sorts. It facilitates the use of alligator clips to connect to conductive material (fruit, Play-Doh, copper tape, etc) to the device that can be activated just by touch (Figure 7.1).

Makey Makey claims that "extended usage may result in creative confidence."[1] Confidence is an important factor in a learner's creative self-perception. Everyone is creative in some regard

1. "Makey Makey," Joylabz Official Makey Makey Store. Accessed December 3, 2021. https://makeymakey.com/.

Technology for Unleashing Creativity. Steve Giddings, Oxford University Press. © Oxford University Press 2022.
DOI: 10.1093/oso/9780197570739.003.0008

FIGURE 7.1 Makey Makey hooked up to Play-Doh to produce sounds with an online virtual instrument

and the Makey Makey kits help to unlock that creativity that learners inherently possess, giving them confidence as creators and inventors. On Makey Makey's own website (makeymakey. com) there are preset virtual instruments designed for use with Makey Makey. There are also a few suggested virtual instruments that integrate well with Makey Makey or designed through Scratch to work with a Makey Makey kit. These can be found on makeymakey.com/blogs/how-to-instructions/apps-for-plug-and-play. There, learners can find a piano, bongos, samplers, synthesizers, and the like that can all be hooked up to a Makey Makey. And really, anything that runs on your computer can be hooked up to a Makey Makey because the invention kit is, in essence, an extension for your computer's QWERTY keyboard. It can even be used as a video game controller for any cloud-based game learners might be into. The Makey Makey can also be remapped so that the user can specify which key does what.

It seems pretty simple in concept, but where this gets interesting is when the learner hooks the provided alligator clips onto conductive material like bananas, pencil lead, copper tape, water, other people, Play-Doh, a trombone bell, or any other possibly conductive material with the virtual instruments, the possibilities become endless. Learners can build and design their own instruments or MIDI controllers and sample triggers. And using programming or coding languages, learners can not only design but also program their own virtual and digital instruments from "scratch" (both literally and figuratively). They can even record their own sounds into Scratch and use Makey Makey inventions to trigger the sounds.

JoyLabz also has a smaller, USB-stick-style Makey Makey called the Makey Makey Go, a much more portable, plug-and-play version of the original invention kit.

Coding Language

There are lots of different types of programming languages. Each one can tell a computer or website to render pretty much anything. Some are easier to use than others; some are better suited for gaming while others for web design, or interactive web content. You've probably come across some different programming languages just through using the Internet. HTML and JavaScript have been incredibly common web-design languages and for a very long time, Adobe Flash Player was needed as a plug-in to interpret interactive websites written in ActionScript. In 2020 it was made public that Chrome and many other web browsers were no longer supporting Flash and that it would be discontinuing its use after December 2020. Most interactive sites that wanted to stick around or not fade into obscurity in 2021 were anticipating this switch and began reprogramming their interactive sites in HTML5 or other programming language; hence, most of the sites mentioned in Chapter 6 run on HTML5 programming. Of course, learning how to code can be confusing at times and difficult unless learners know their options. Thankfully, there are block-coding sites like Scratch that help to simplify coding.

Block Coding and Scratch

Block-coding sites contain preset blocks of code that can be mixed and matched to program a game on a screen or a piece of hardware like a Makey Makey or Micro:bit (discussed later). Figure 7.2 shows an example of what coding looks like in Scratch.

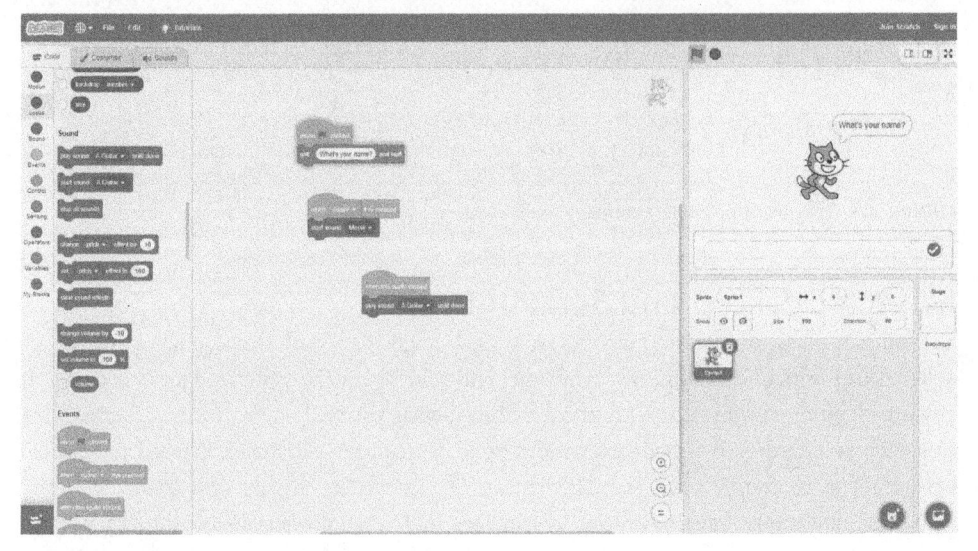

FIGURE 7.2 Example block code in Scratch

Some ways to use this versatile coding app include the following:

Record the learner's own sounds and insert them into the code.
Make original interactive music games.
Make virtual instruments (great for teaching music online).
Program a Makey Makey or another invention kit to make musical sounds.
Use Makey Makey and some craft supplies, to build your own working musical instrument controller.
Tell a sound story with moving pictures and words.

Learners can use Scratch without an account and can also save their code for future use. If learners save the project to their computer, it saves as an SB3 project file that can be uploaded at any time to rework, much as the way Drumbit (Chapter 6) works for saving files for an online app without an account. Another similar site for block coding is called MakeCode. There are also lots of sites that use traditional text-based coding for more advanced programmers as well with sites like Python.

Also, Scratch has a fully integrated Makey Makey extension enabled by clicking on the "Add Extension" tool at the bottom left corner of the coding screen along with a number of other extensions (Figure 7.3).

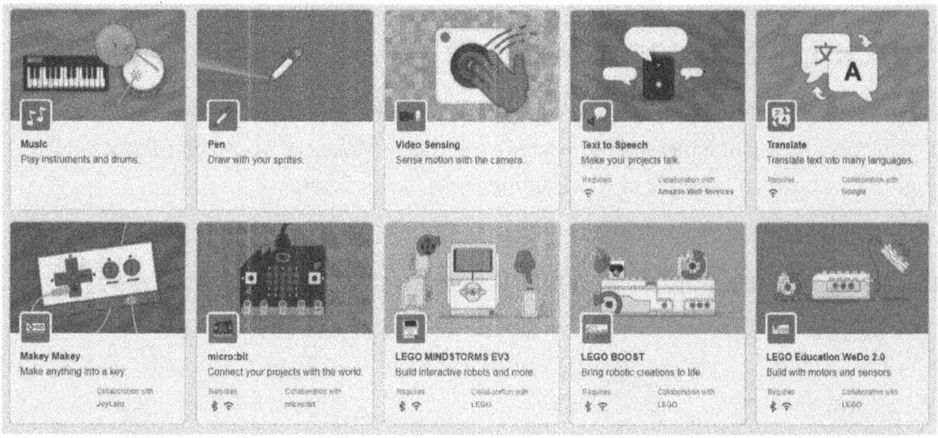

FIGURE 7.3 Options of possible extensions in Scratch

Scratch Desktop and ScratchJr

Scratch is available on Android devices from the Google Play Store and also has a downloadable desktop version for Windows, Chrome, and Mac operating systems. Please note that if you are plugging any invention kit into a mobile device, you will likely need an adapter cable to switch standard USB to whatever input your device uses. Scratch is catered to learners aged eight to 16 and also has ScratchJr catering to five-to-seven-year-olds available on the App Store and the Google Play Store. This means that ScratchJr is available for Apple products and Android-powered devices. There is currently no web-based app for ScratchJr. The touch-screen interface means that young learners can easily drag and drop their code into the space at the bottom and tap it to see what happens. Figures 7.4 and 7.5 show the recording features of this app wherein learners could record themselves playing a number of patterns and be able to arrange them easily into where they would like them to go. They can also design a character or a picture to go with their composition—a great way to introduce arranging, recording, and composing. They could also create a character and record a short motif or theme music to go with it. They could even choreograph a dance to go with the music.

FIGURE 7.4 ScratchJr coding screen

FIGURE 7.5 ScratchJr recording screen

GitHub and BitBucket

Both GitHub and BitBucket are sites where many software developers write code for a variety of different open-source apps and software. The modifications for BeepBox (ModBox and others) were written in GitHub. You may also notice that the Mario Paint Sequencer was written in GitHub, too. Audacity has open-source code on GitHub as well. GitHub in particular has a learning section called GitHub Education designed for schools with access to the premium features.

Micro:bit

The Micro:bit by BBC is another—more advanced—invention kit similar to the Makey Makey except it has a tiny microchip, a sound processor, an accelerometer, a small LED display, and Bluetooth capability. Scratch has a devoted Micro:bit extension, too, but Microsoft's MakeCode seems to integrate more smoothly with it. Learners can attach speakers to the Micro:bit to hear the sounds that are programmed into it. Code for the Micro:bit has to be downloaded to the Micro:bit itself. As with Scratch, there is a simulator screen on the side to see what the code is supposed to do (Figure 7.6).

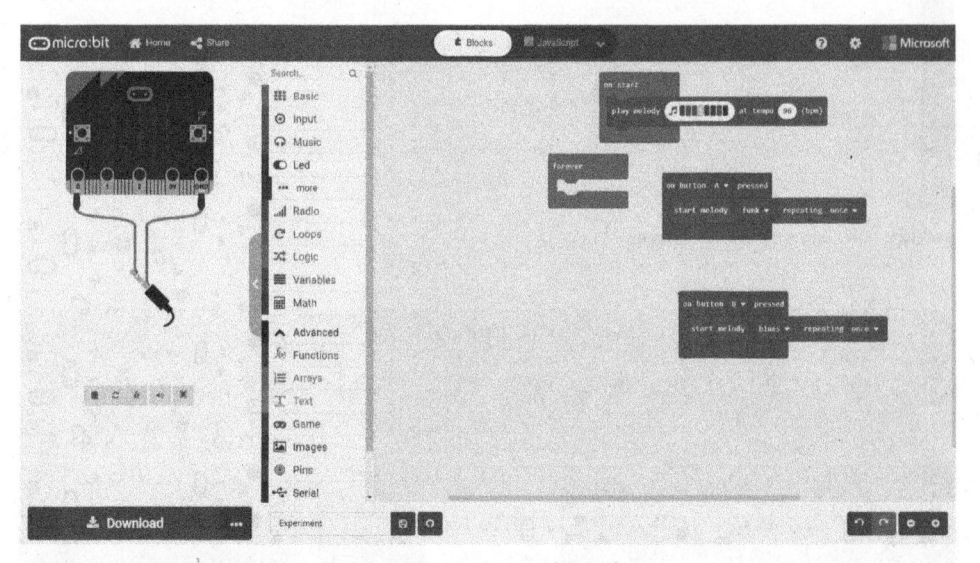

FIGURE 7.6 MakeCode screen with Micro:bit simulator on the left

An interesting feature of MakeCode is that learners have the option of rendering blocks in JavaScript or Python or sticking with the blocks. There doesn't seem to be a way to upload sounds, but users can manipulate melodic material within the Micro:bit itself. This capability is great for creating loops and similar creative material.

Playtron

Playtron is a similar idea to the Makey Makey, but has the possibility to program up to 16 triggers at one time. It is designed to be a programmable MIDI controller and with 16 triggers, meaning learners could have access to a little over an octave of chromatic pitches.

Of course, if many of those chromatic notes aren't needed, those other available triggers can be used for other purposes, like samples or loops, or can remain unused. Unlike the Makey Makey, Playtron is programmed automatically to use USB MIDI protocol, so it works exactly like a MIDI controller without any further programming. Learners could plug it into their favourite DAW with virtual instruments and use those sounds. Much like Makey Makey, though, it is essentially an extension of learners' QWERTY keyboard and all it needs is a completed circuit and any conductive object to make a sound. Using adapters for a particular device, learners can hook these objects into anything.

TouchMe

TouchMe is another MIDI controller from Playtronica designed to explore music through human touch. Once it has been connected to a virtual instrument, one person holds on to one end, and another holds on to the other end. To complete the circuit (make the sound), each person needs to make skin contact. The virtual synths on playtronica.com have specific sounds designed for this particular MIDI controller. This one is also touch sensitive (go figure), so the softer the touch, the quieter the sound. It can be set to play a particular scale, too. Learn more about these two devices from Playtronica at playtronica.com.

The company is currently working on a new product called the Orbita, which is a rotational drum sequencer like GroovePizza, but designed like a customizable record turntable in physical form instead.

Other Coding Sites and Kits
Sites

Blockly

Blockly is less a coding site and more a code-training site. There is a specific music code training section to it. Each section has the user solve a series of puzzles to learn the coding language by using block coding.

EarSketch

EarSketch is a music coding site that uses text-based coding languages to input code into a DAW on the simulation screen.

Sonic Pi

Sonic Pi is a site similar to EarSketch but where the music is generated and inputted completely through text-based programming. There is no visual simulation other than when it runs the code.

Kits

Korg LittleBits Synth Kit

The LittleBits Synth Kit is a modular synth kit for building and creating analog synthesizers. Each unit has a separate specific function and can be mixed and matched very much like block coding, but with actual physical blocks. Each unit affects the synth differently, so the possibilities of sounds that can be produced are vast.

Pocket Operator

Teenage Engineering's Pocket Operators are small, handheld DAWs that resemble a large Micro:bit with more buttons. There are a range of different ones that all have unique features. It doesn't teach coding specifically but it's completely programmable.

Possible Applications for Large Ensembles

Coding a Makey Makey with Scratch can be a very effective tool for differently abled learners. I envision melodies, chord progressions, loops, or specific notes being programmed and attached to the metal strings on a violin, or using an external Play-Doh controller programmed with MIDI sounds or samples that resemble the instrument being played. One learner could be in charge of creating this for the other, or it can be done in partnership with the differently abled learner.

Other applications include the following:

> Learners can code a loop that was prerecorded on their instrument and improvise/compose a part that goes with it.
>
> Using soundpainting gestures, create a loop or new sound and have learners create a sample pad controller to be included in soundpainting compositions.

In soundpainting language, this is typically called a palette. Soundpainting is explored in more depth in Chapter 8.

> Have learners create a warm-up and program a drum loop to act as a metronome, or a bass drone for long-tone exercises. They can improvise long tones over the bass drone.
>
> The guitar player in the jazz band doesn't have a footswitch? Build one with a Makey Makey by using amp models in GarageBand, Soundtrap, or BandLab. Hover over the added effect and program the click to turn the effects on and off.
>
> Use Makey Makey to create a recording footswitch for band and orchestral instruments. Wire the Makey Makey to the recording hot keys that exist (space for play, "R" for record, etc). They occasionally vary but most are standardized.
>
> Use Micro:bit to program accompaniment loops and improvise a melody over them in the specified key.

Compose a melody by using Micro:bit and MakeCode, learn it on their primary instrument, and transcribe it by using a notation of their choice (Figure 7.7).

Notice the term ¼ and ½ beat are used for 16th and eighth notes, respectively. This is where the "M" of the STEAM approach appears.

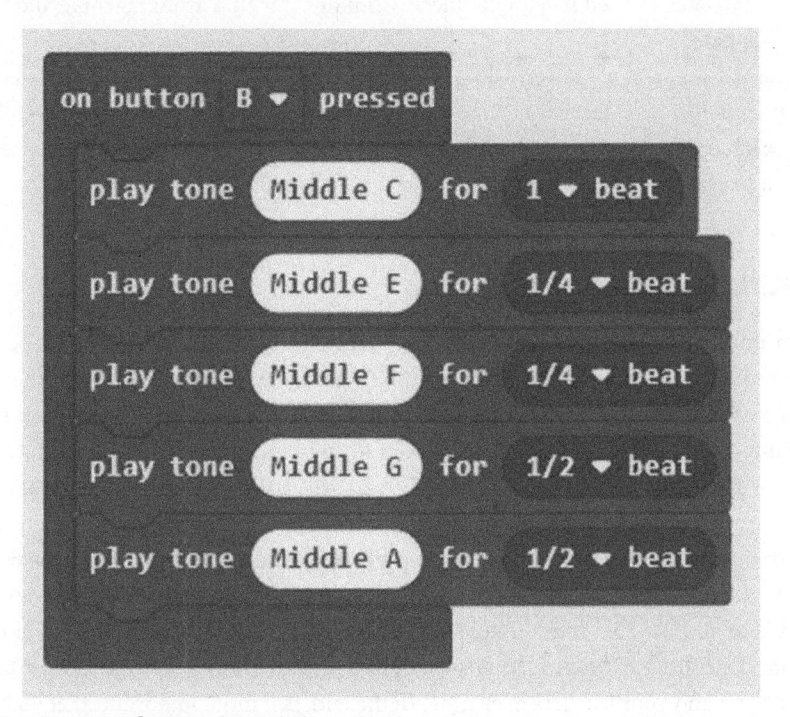

FIGURE 7.7 Example of a Micro:bit melody

Possible Applications for General Music Classes

Possible applications include the following:

- Design a game character by using the sprites provided with Scratch or ScratchJr and create theme music for it with the prerecorded sounds or record your own sounds and samples. Younger learners might want to use paper and a pencil to create their character.
- Using Makey Makey, design a controller and then create a soundscape by assigning different found sounds that were captured to each trigger.
- Using conductive materials and Makey Makey, create a working musical instrument that actually makes sounds.
- Create a recording footswitch by using a Makey Makey, as in the previous section.
- Have learners record themselves playing a chord into Scratch and assign different chords to each trigger.

Make music by using a Makey Makey and a row of people in the class. Learners can literally become the notes.

Record single-note sounds of a recorder or xylophone and arrange Makey Makey triggers to create a catchy melody.

Use Micro:bit and MakeCode to compose a short melody to see how it sounds. Perhaps it can later be used in a longer piece. Combine it with a drum machine and see what happens!

Create a sound story by recording voice and sound effects in Scratch or ScratchJr.

In ScratchJr, have learners create two- or four-beat melodies or rhythms and record each one by using the microphone block and then arrange the music and rearrange it to create a two- or four-bar phrase.

Conclusion

Modern music creation often relies on some form of programming; whether it be a drum machine, or writing code to make music, they are all ways that programming has shaped musical creativity. I'm hoping that the descriptions and ideas here can work for your learners. What's important is that you don't really need to fully understand it at this point, because learners will come to understand it quickly and will come up with some amazing ideas through experimentation and play by using the informal learning approach. As mentioned earlier in this book it is important that the right amount of time is budgeted for this experience to work and to let learners explore. A good rule of thumb for learner-driven creative projects is to add 20–25% more time than you would normally budget. There will be some variation, depending on your learners, though, and you will find the amount of time that works for you and your learners over time. In the end, is it more important that you have 10 pieces of music written by people you've never met or half the number of tunes written and arranged by the learners in front of you?

8

Electronic, Digital, and Virtual Instruments

Earlier in this book we discussed analog and digital technologies and how they differ. Virtual instruments have been mentioned, but not really explored in depth. Whereas analog and mechanical instruments have a completely physical existence, and digital instruments also have a physical presence but mainly use a computer to function, virtual instruments exist entirely on a computer and can be accessed only with software or an Internet connection. An example of a virtual instrument is Chrome Music Lab's Shared Piano, or the virtual piano included with GarageBand. There are more discrete virtual music instruments, too, that have specific functions and may not even look like a traditional instrument. Touchscreens make virtual instruments much more accessible and give them almost a physical presence that can greatly enhance their playability and usability. Without a touchscreen or a MIDI controller, virtual instruments often turn learner QWERTY computer keyboards into a usable instrument. Throughout this chapter we will be exploring different kinds of electronic instruments, digital instruments, and virtual instruments that could be used to enhance creativity in classrooms. Ways to use virtual instruments in practical and meaningful ways will also be explored here.

Most Western instruments have an electric version or have a piece of technology that gives them electronic features. Each can be hooked up to a digital guitar amplifier or other amplifier with effect pedals, which will be discussed further in Chapter 9.

Stringed instruments are commonly made into electronic instruments. The metal strings can easily be transferred into electronic signals by using built-in amplifiers or magnetic pickups. Electronic wind bands and orchestras playing classic orchestral and band repertoire are underutilized. Imagine how your large ensembles could sound by simply adding electronics to them. It could be playing the same music but on electronic instruments to help enhance the creative ideas of your ensemble members—a major interpretation of sorts. It could be done as a creative exercise or as a performance. Or learners could use a classic band or orchestra piece to rearrange to utilize electronic instruments. It could be a large project for more advanced learners or a more basic arrangement with electronic elements added in.

Technology for Unleashing Creativity. Steve Giddings, Oxford University Press. © Oxford University Press 2022.
DOI: 10.1093/oso/9780197570739.003.0009

It may be considered inauthentic to just play what was written with cool effects, but it would be more authentic if it was rearranged to better facilitate electronics. Here are some electronic stringed instruments to consider:

electric guitar
electric ukulele
electric bass
electric violin
electric cello

Even investing in a few (often cheaper) pickups for stringed instruments can greatly increase the possibilities.

What about Electronic Wind Instruments?

Silent Brass systems are devices manufactured by Yamaha that act like mutes for Brass instruments and can be hooked up to headphones, processing units, amplifiers, or pedals for a plethora of different sounds and abilities. There are silent Brass units for all typical orchestral Brass instruments.

Aerophone by Roland is a digital wind instrument that uses Roland's advanced modelling technology. It feels like an acoustic saxophone and has all the same fingerings, but also models the breath fluctuations. It is actually surprising how natural it sounds. It has the ability to model the sound and characteristics of any wind and orchestral instrument as well as some other synthesizer sounds, too. It can even stand alone without external amplification because of being a digital instrument with battery, and even has wired and wireless MIDI capabilities, opening up a whole new realm of creative possibilities for learners. There are multiple tiers of these wind instruments tailored for beginners or professionals. They each have apps that work with them, too.

There are other digital wind instruments from other companies, too, but the Roland Aerophone and the Yamaha WX series both do a good job of emulating that iconic sound and feel of an acoustic sax. They can also make clarinet and flute sounds easily. All the higher-end Roland, AKAI, and Yamaha models have bite sensitivity and wind velocity sensitivity of the lower models, meaning expressive elements like vibrato can be added.

Even having a couple of these systems (Aerophones, Silent Brass, electric strings) can be helpful in giving learners the opportunity to explore their creativity in new ways.

Electric Drums

There are lots of different types of electronic drums, from drum pads to full electronic kits, and the sounds are pretty endless. Roland, the leader in digital and electronic instruments, has a wide array of choices for electronic percussion instruments. Timpani sounds are common and many newer models have the ability to let the user upload sounds, too.

Possible Applications

Possible applications for electronic instruments include the following:

> Using arrangements for chamber ensembles, have learners find the best sounds on their electronic/digital instruments to reproduce the piece with a new flair.
>
> If learners have access to enough of these electronic or digital instruments, give each learner in your ensemble one of these and together they can rearrange a classic band and orchestra piece to include electronics. If there are not enough for every section, add a couple in each and find ways to feature the sound.
>
> Give learners a preloaded melody in a DAW and have them add harmony parts with their respective electronic instruments.
>
> Assign learners' solo works that they can adapt to include electronic sounds by using these instruments.
>
> Have learners learn the guitar solo or another iconic solo in popular music and have them mimic the sound as closely as they can with the electronic or digital instrument they have. Then add a backing track (beat) to it and rearrange it in a DAW.
>
> Use looper pedals (explored in Chapter 10) to create a short riff and experiment with harmony parts that work. Once they have some that work, have them reproduce it in a short performance. Use the data as a backing track (beat) for a song in a DAW or write it out in staff notation in a notation software.
>
> Learn pop melodies on their instruments and make simple arrangements.
>
> For vocal groups, exploring vocoders and live looping of vocal parts and beatbox patterns would be useful.

Vocoders are synthesizers that turn a vocal signal into a synthesizer sound. Learners could explore rearranging popular tunes or classical tunes with beatbox patterns and vocoder parts, with all sounds reproduced creatively through vocal sounds only. For a great demo of vocoder and rearranging music with just vocal sounds check out DoctorMix on YouTube, specifically this video: https://www.youtube.com/watch?v=0kEHP2aUItA&ab_channel= DoctorMix (10 Most Famous Vocoder Songs).

Virtual Instruments

Virtual instruments exist all over the Internet, in DAW software, notation software, and mobile apps. They have no physical presence until played on your QWERTY keyboard or connected to a MIDI device. Many times, MIDI controllers enable more features that the virtual instrument itself does not (repeat note, velocity sensitivity, arpeggiator). Most MIDI controllers can be connected to any mobile device with the proper adapters. It is a good idea to have a plethora of adapters for different mobile devices on hand. I personally keep every cable and adapter I've ever owned and I find myself going to that container more often than you would think.

Ports on mobile devices are updating constantly, but the basic principle of the USB port on laptop-style devices remains the same. They all come in various sizes and shapes but all have a variation on a particular logo. Figure 8.1 shows the basic logo that all USB port devices are based on.

FIGURE 8.1 USB port logo

Virtual Instrument Bands

iBands, vBands, or eBands have been growing in popularity and are completely possible with a class set of Chromebooks, iPads, or Android devices using a device's QWERTY keyboard or a touchscreen interface. These apps are also great for when learners can bring their own devices. And a mix of electric guitars and USB vocal microphones can make this experience even more fun by using vocal effects and the guitar amp simulators built in to apps like GarageBand (iOS) and BandLab (Android and iOS). With some of the settings for pentatonic or blues built into GarageBand, learning the instrument itself doesn't get in the way of the creativity (Figure 8.2).

If your school already has a class set of Chromebooks, iPads, or a BYOD (bring your own device) policy, there are no additional instruments or amplifiers learners would need besides some extra cables, adapters, and a speaker or two. This set-up can even be done without extra cables in smaller groups, but making sure everyone can hear one another clearly is important. The devices that learners have access to will depend on what adapters or hubs they would need.

There are a number of ways to play together on virtual instruments. The most "low tech" way would be to get five-way 3.5mm (⅛") input hub with enough male-to-male 3.5mm cables to connect from your device to the hub and then to a speaker. If learners are connecting to a

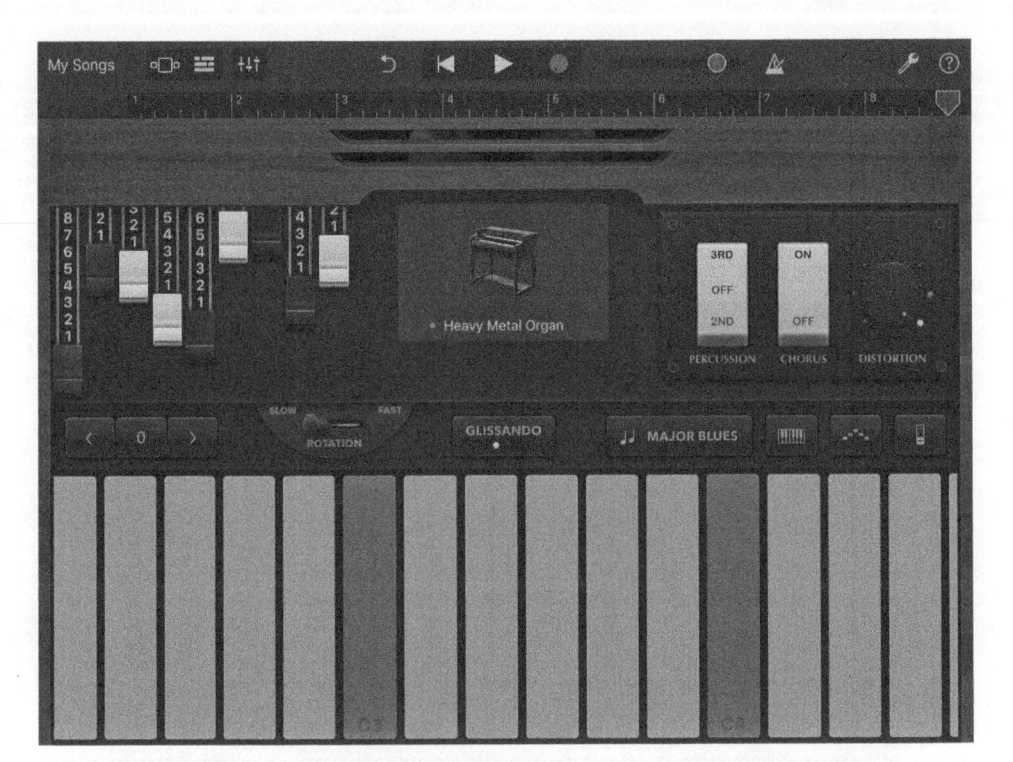

FIGURE 8.2 Virtual "Heavy Metal Organ" in GarageBand for iOS set to major blues tonality

large speaker, a 3.5mm to ¼″ adapter will definitely be useful. For a live performance, each device with its own speaker and direct input box (DI) to send to the board would be ideal (much of this required gear will be discussed in the next chapter). When you are dealing with live or recorded sound and a number of devices like these, wired is best. Bluetooth can often be glitchy and has natural latency but also cannot layer multiple Bluetooth sends over one another at this time. Wired systems or local area networks (LANs) are much more predictable. Many newer devices are foregoing the 3.5mm jack so having the proper adapters will be handy. For some adapter end types you may need, please refer to Figure 9.18 in Chapter 9.

Ableton Link

Using Ableton Live (even the Lite version), learners have the ability to set up a LAN that automatically syncs any virtual instruments connected to it. There are a number of apps for iOS, Android, Linux, macOS, and Windows that are Ableton Link enabled. Go to Ableton.com to find out more. All versions of Ableton have this ability as long as the ASIO drivers are enabled in the preferences. Often, a key code for Ableton Live Lite—which is also Link enabled—comes with the purchase of many recording hardware devices like a Focusrite 2i2 audio interface and others, meaning a school could purchase multiple interfaces and get multiple key codes for Ableton Live Lite for multiple devices. With Ableton Link, a mix of devices can sync together over the LAN to jam together and add to one another's beats and melodies by using loops and samples in real time. Each musician would need their own speaker and device, and then they turn on Link on their Link-enabled device. As long as one device (such as a stand-alone computer or teacher laptop) has Ableton Live Link enabled, this connection is possible. If learners have access to Ableton Live, make sure that under "Link MIDI," "Show Link Toggle" is set to "Show" in the preferences (Figure 8.3).

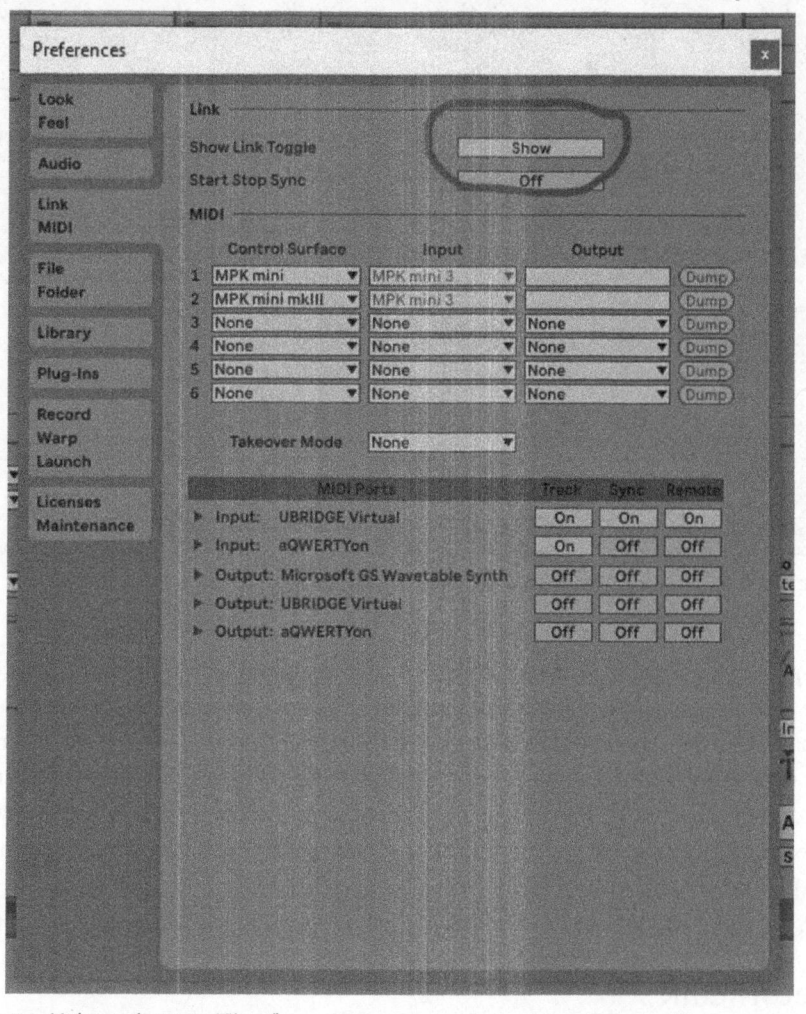

FIGURE 8.3 Link toggle set to "Show"

Then, back at the main screen, click the "Link" button that will appear at the top left corner. Once learners have a Link-enabled app, go into the settings of those apps and make sure that Ableton Link is enabled. As soon as it is, the Ableton Link button in Ableton Live will show the number of links on the network and the loops will automatically line up with little to no hassle (Figure 8.4). The main tempo can be controlled from any device connected to the Link

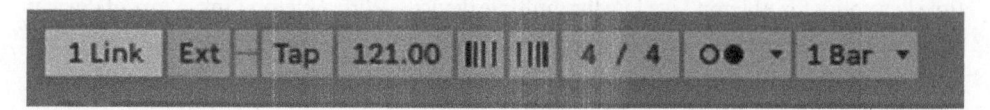

FIGURE 8.4 Ableton Link button showing one other device on the network

network. If loops aren't lining up, make sure quantization is on (Figure 8.5). And then, from the session view, learners can launch clips (loops) where this live looping all happens (Figure 8.6).

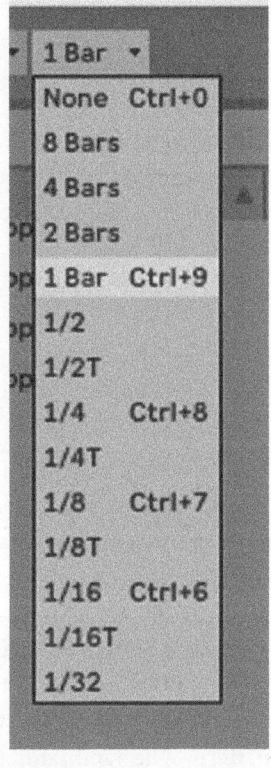

FIGURE 8.5 Quantization set to 1 Bar

FIGURE 8.6 Ableton Live session view

Chrome Shared Piano Jam

Here are three ways to set up a virtual instrument jam (which can turn into a virtual instrument band performance if you like) on Shared Piano by using whatever learners have access to.

1. Navigate to Chrome Music Lab's Shared Piano and form a group: Jam.

This exercise can be done with any combination of devices. It can also be done with or without external speakers as long as the groups are far away enough from the other groups not to cause a distraction. Have learners form groups of three to five people and tell them that their jam has to have at least three elements:

a. A rhythm track (beat)
b. A chord progression, or riff (often referred to as ostinato in traditional circles)
c. A melody of some kind

Give learners up to 10 minutes or so to come up with a jam with those elements in them to present. You may have to demonstrate each element unless this exercise is something they have done a lot of work on previously. Be sure to demonstrate with a couple of volunteers on how the result could look especially if this jam is new.

For the demonstration, using the Shared Piano hooked up to a projector, have two other learners log into the same virtual piano you are on by sharing the link at the bottom left corner. Once they are in, assign one to be the drummer (on some type of percussion) and the other to a riff. All they would need to do for a riff is pick two notes and play them in a repeating pattern. The facilitator (that's you!) takes the melody. The projector part is important so that the other learners can see and hear all the parts together. I will often ask them to stay on the "white keys" for now if they are new to the piano.

2. Join the same room via link; select instruments: Jam.

Shared Piano can have up to 10 people jamming remotely on the same virtual keyboard. It also works if they are in the same room, too, but there will be a slight amount of latency from each player regardless of how this jam is done. This being said, they will often line up well even with the latency. The user can hover over the avatar (animal faces) to see how much latency that person is currently experiencing (there is nothing you can do about it, just an interesting fact). The main benefit of using this approach for jamming together is that Shared Piano automatically records anything that is played into it. So if learners were hesitant to play in front of the class, the facilitator can scroll back in their screen and press the triangular play icon where they began their virtual performance, and Shared Piano will play it back.

3. Record; play it back; jam over the recording.

If the musician is jamming alone, they can play a riff or drum pattern and click the "Save" link on the bottom right corner (not left) to open a new window, play it back, and layer a new part over top of the recording.

GarageBand Virtual Instruments and Amp Modellers

GarageBand for iOS has a nice collection of virtual instruments that are easy to use (Figure 8.7). The touch interface of the virtual guitar is unique to the iPad and the "smart" instruments explored in Chapter 4 make the use of this app for getting a virtual band going quite easy. The user would simply touch the chord to play and the "smart" instruments generate a loop with that chord automatically. A distinguishing feature of the GarageBand iOS app is the ability to play scales,

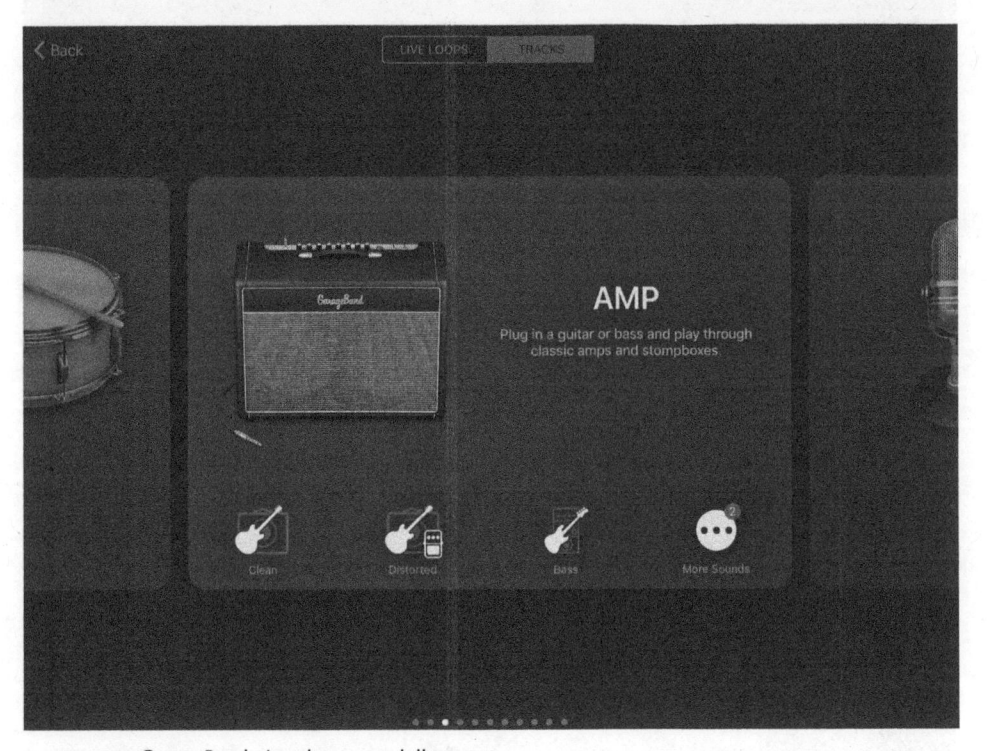

FIGURE 8.7 GarageBand virtual amp modellers

chords, and patterns on two virtual traditional Chinese instruments called the erhu and pipa, respectively (Figures 8.8 and 8.9).

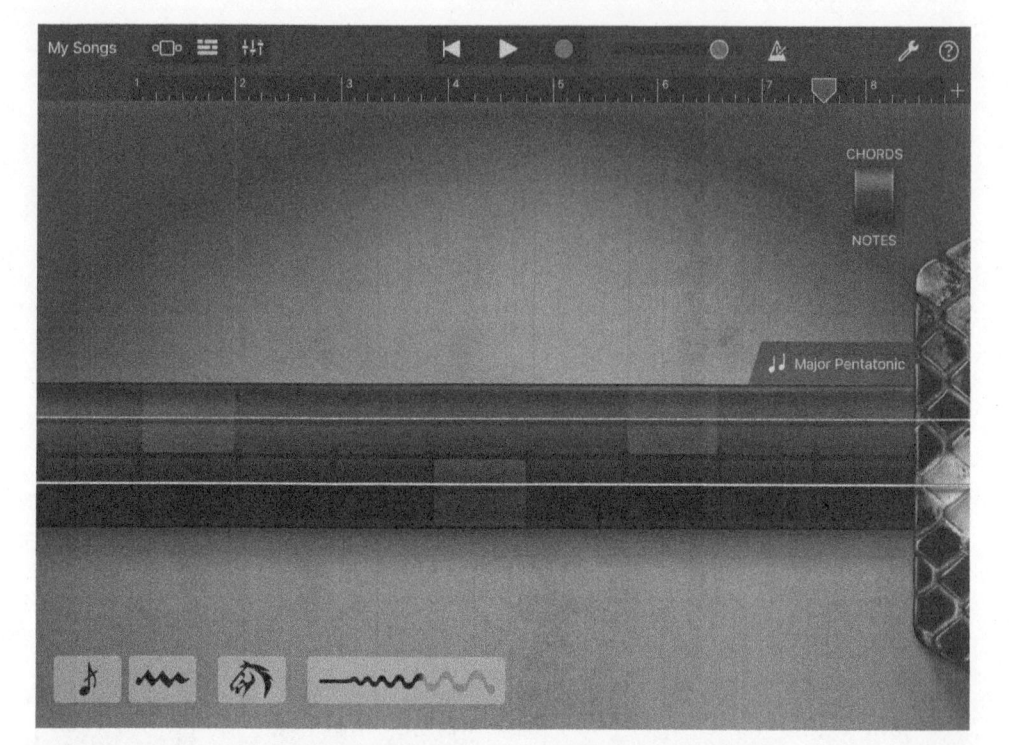

FIGURE 8.8 Virtual erhu in GarageBand for iOS

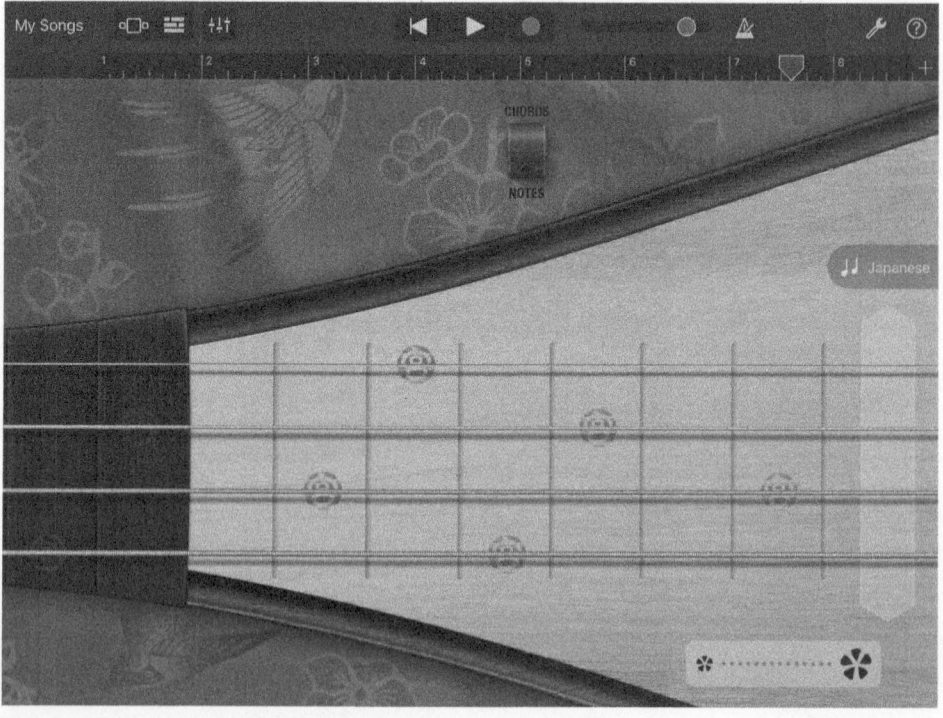

FIGURE 8.9 Virtual pipa in GarageBand for iOS

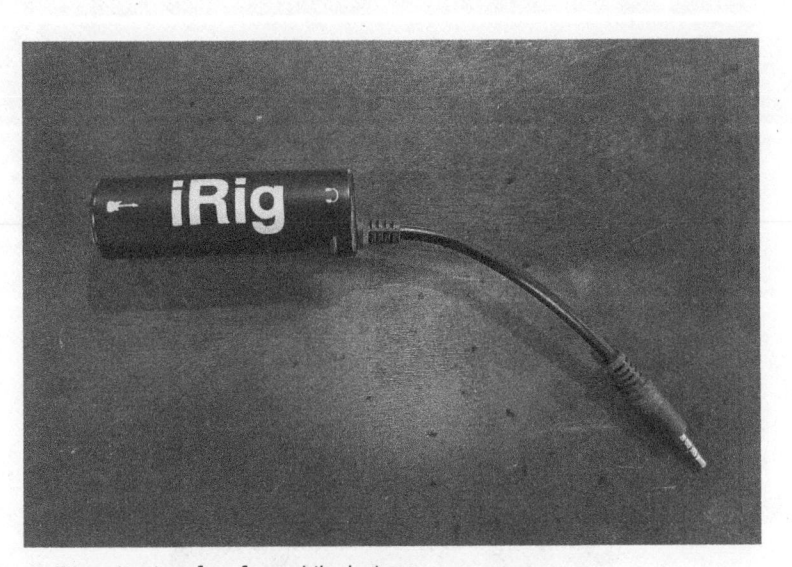

FIGURE 8.10 iRig guitar interface for mobile devices

Using the Onboard Guitar Processors

GarageBand for iOS has some very good guitar amplifier models built in. To have them work, and to get the most out of this tech, the user needs to be able to plug their electric guitar into the device. iRig and similar mobile audio interfaces come in a wide range of types for plugging pretty much anything into a mobile device. The basic guitar interface that iRig produces is not expensive and, despite the name, actually works on any mobile device, not just Apple products. The iRig and the upgrade, iRig 2, are so small that they can be concealed in the palm of your hand (Figure 8.10). They allow for a 3.5mm headphone input and a ¼″ patch cord instrument input and plugs into the headphone jack of your mobile device (or a lightning-to-3.5mm adapter). iRig even makes microphones and a plethora of other devices for mobile music making. In theory, these small audio interfaces could work on a Chromebook, too, by using a cloud-based DAW like BandLab.

BandLab for Mobile

Of course, GarageBand is only for Apple products, but BandLab does make a mobile app for Android devices. It includes everything the browser version has but includes some distinguishing features that make it easier to jam and create music anywhere. Using the BandLab Link interface (similar to the iRig), learners can plug a guitar right into it to access the guitar effects like on the cloud-based browser version. iRig products also work with this app. One of the major differences between BandLab Mobile and GarageBand for iOS is that BandLab does not currently include a similar "smart" instrument function, but it does have a looper pad that integrates with BandLab's loop packs (Figure 8.11). The Looper is designed for live music performance and manipulation, perfect for jamming or creating eBand music. This being said, GarageBand for iOS does seem more suitable for beginners, as it is easier to navigate and has presets that make it easy to create great-sounding music quickly. The "smart" instruments and the scale settings in GarageBand are useful for this function. Figure 8.12 shows what the BandLab mobile virtual piano looks like.

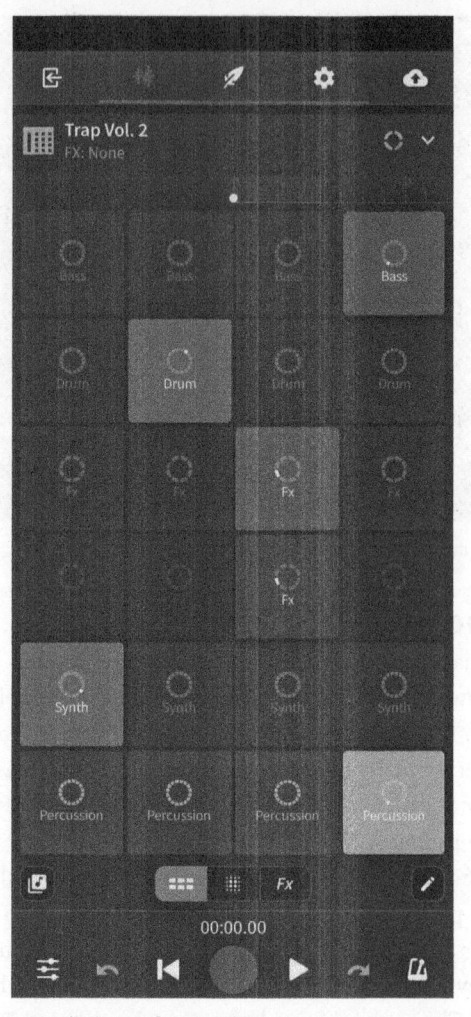

FIGURE 8.11 Live Looper in BandLab app for mobile

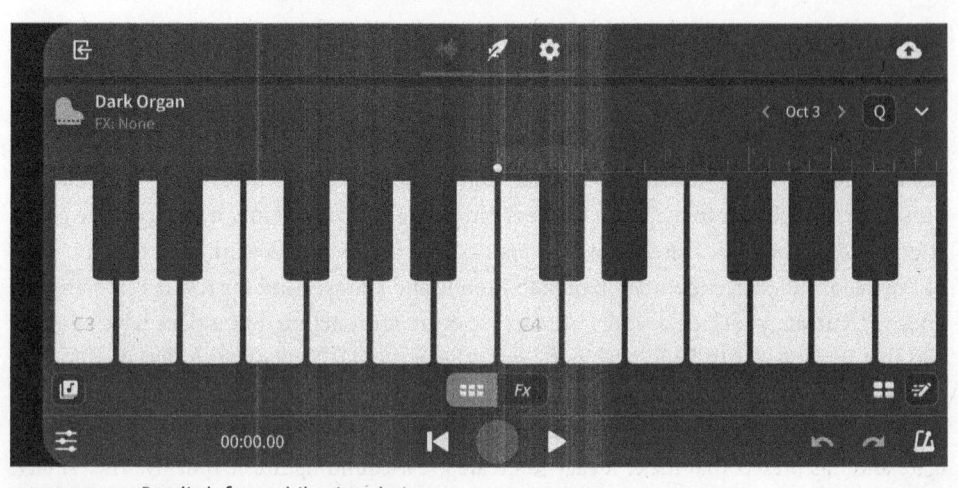

FIGURE 8.12 BandLab for mobile virtual piano

Soundtrap also has a mobile app for Android and iOS with accessible virtual instruments and is similar in functionality to BandLab.

Other Useful Virtual Instruments

Of course, a virtual instrument band will work with any virtual instrument learners can find. Here are some useful ones online and elsewhere.

Novation Launchpad Intro

There are eight loop packs and five sample packs to choose from and they can work with a device's QWERTY keyboard (Figure 8.13). It is, however, optimized for and designed for use with a Novation LaunchPad controller (Figure 8.14). If you are exploring pad controllers like the LaunchPad, they work really well in Ableton Live in the session view, where users can program all the pads on the LaunchPad to launch clips (loops) and they colour code on the device automatically. This site gives learners an idea of the functionality of this particular type of controller. There are also links to a looper DAW called Amplify Studios that can be downloaded to a hard drive. These types of controllers are designed to be used for live-loop jamming or live-loop arranging.

Sampulator

Sampulator is designed for a QWERTY keyboard and contains a collection of samples and sounds for composing. There are preset pieces to work with, but new material can be recorded into the MIDI grid and then quantized manually if need be (Figure 8.15). The only way to save currently is to log in to Twitter.

FIGURE 8.13 Novation LaunchPad Intro main screen

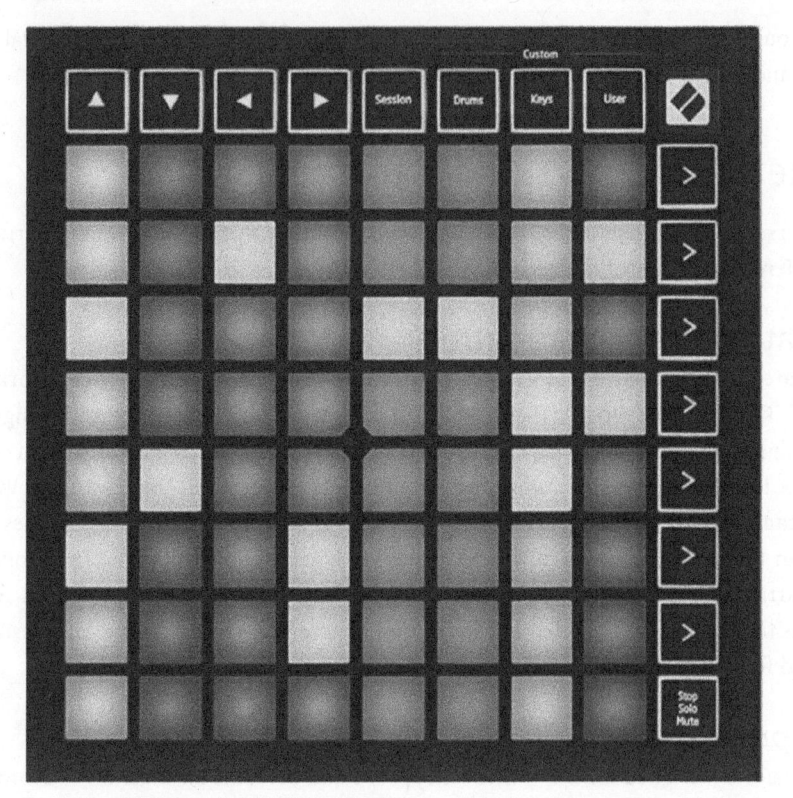

FIGURE 8.14 A Novation LaunchPad MIDI controller

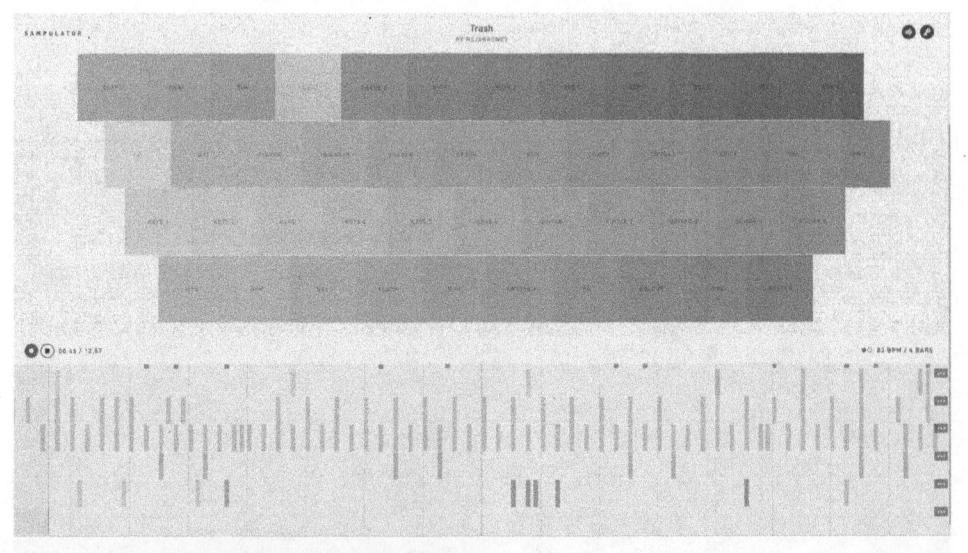

FIGURE 8.15 Sampulator main screen with piano roll

WebSID

This web app emulates an iconic Commodore 64 sound chip synthesizer by Atari. It is pretty basic but can generate some interesting sounds. It also includes a drum machine, too, though it is pretty crude. There is a Chrome App for this, which means this app can run on Chromebooks or any device quite easily (Figure 8.16). It can connect to a MIDI controller of learners' choice, too, as long as Chrome opens after your MIDI controller is plugged in.

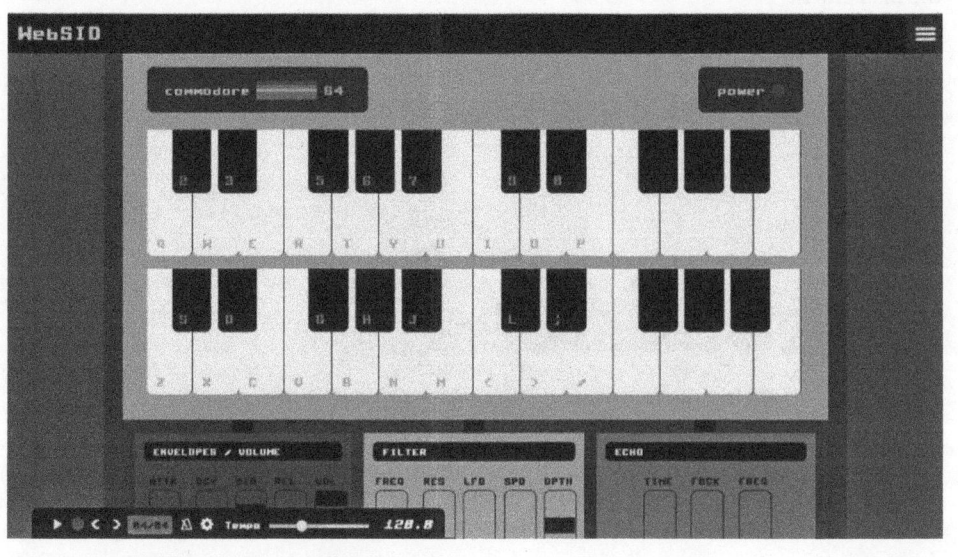

FIGURE 8.16 WebSID browser interface

Virtual Guitar Online from Apronus.com

Designed to work with a QWERTY keyboard, this virtual guitar shows chords on the guitar neck and on a piano keyboard with a good sound (Figure 8.17). It's useful if learners are utilizing held chords in their jams or compositions. Learners have the ability to record, save, and load previous compositions or compositional material. The 1, 4, and 5 chords are situated next to one another on the QWERTY keyboard to help with ease of playability.

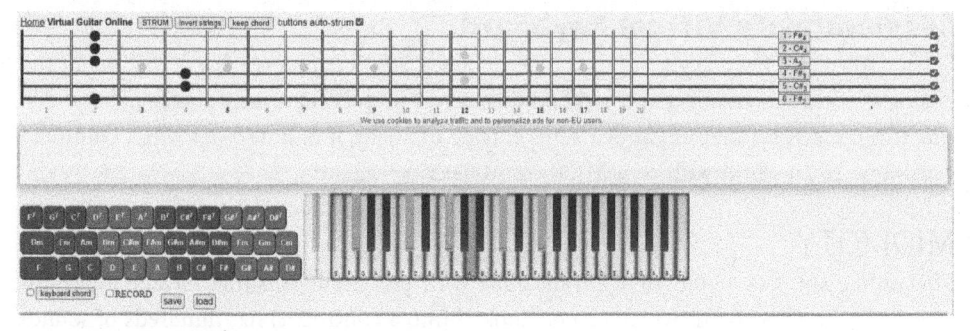

FIGURE 8.17 "Virtual Guitar Online" web screen

Online Guitar from Recursive Arts

This virtual instrument is currently designed to work only with a QWERTY keyboard and not a touch screen. It is perfect for Chromebooks or other laptop-based devices. This online guitar has a default key map that assigns particular chords or actions to the QWERTY keyboard. What is great about this feature is that the user can remap all of the keys and reassign chords to them, making it completely customizable. Users can even customize their own chords by using presets. Figure 8.18 shows the main screen with a capo added to the neck of the instrument.

FIGURE 8.18 Online Guitar from Recursive Arts

SessionTown Drums

This virtual instrument works great on PC, Chromebook, Mac, and iOS devices, but there is a bit of latency on some Android devices (Figure 8.19). The only downside is that users are unable to reassign or remap the triggers. Users have to log in with Facebook to save but if the app is being used for jamming, it will work great without the user logging in to social media.

Sessiontown's Virtual Keyboard

SessionTown also has a keyboard on its site (Figure 8.20). It contains a few decent organ and analog synthesizer sounds that could find themselves useful. There are a couple of other distinguishing features that might be useful outside of a jam, too. It also has MIDI controller capability. Yes, it works with your MIDI controller's arpeggiator.

MIDI.CITY

This online app has a built-in drum machine with preset patterns that include a few different kits. The keyboard (which can be hooked into a controller) has hundreds of sounds

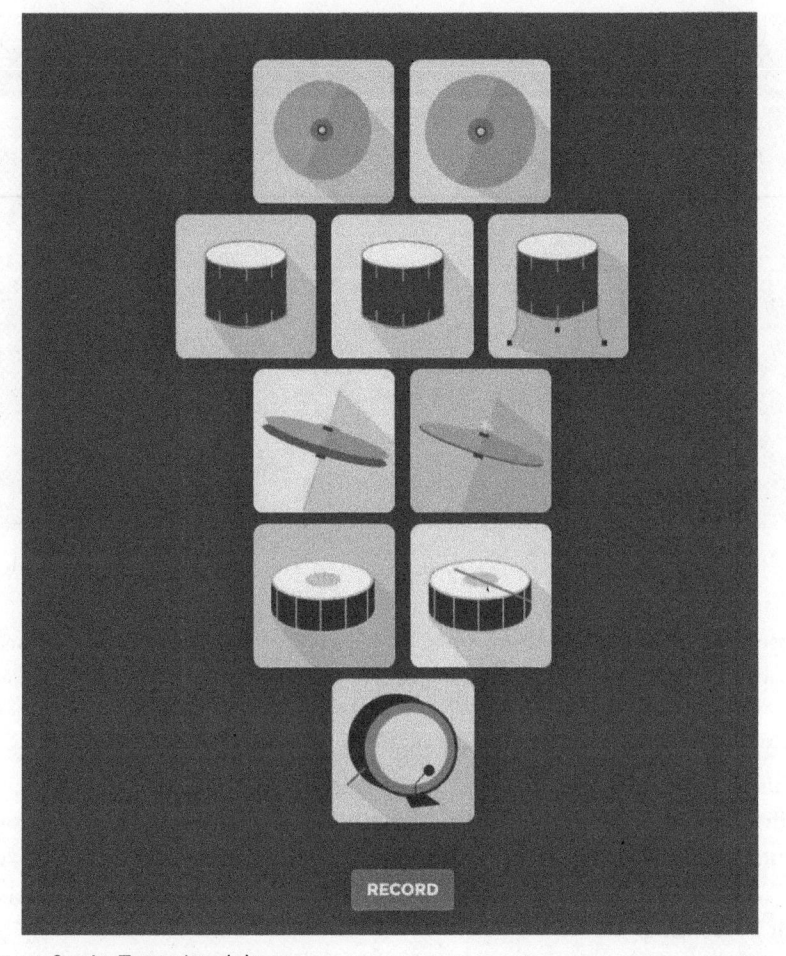

FIGURE 8.19 SessionTown virtual drums

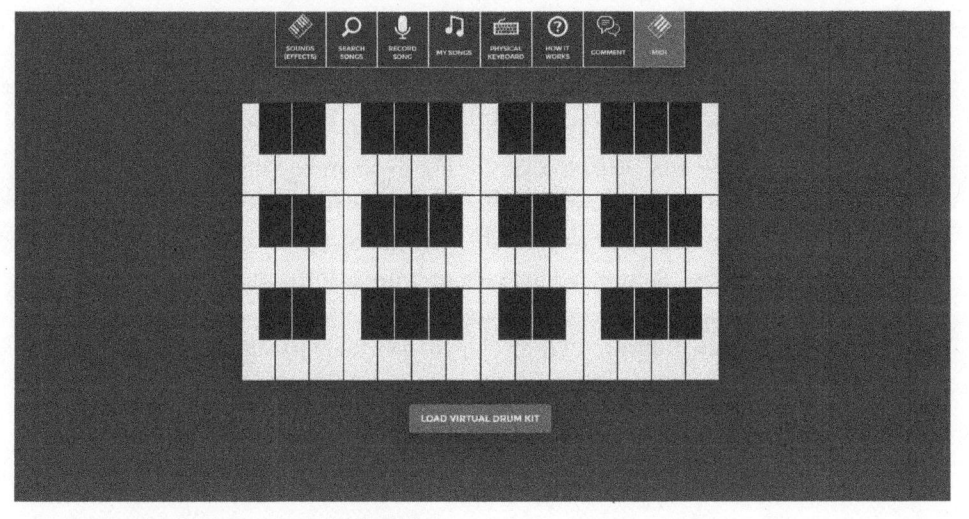

FIGURE 8.20 SessionTown virtual keyboard

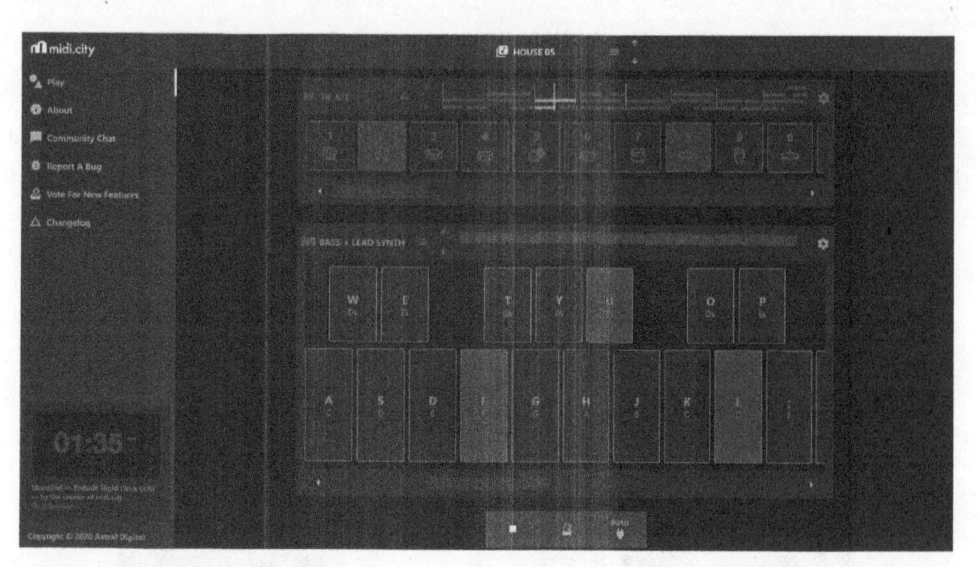

FIGURE 8.21 MIDI.CITY's main page

to choose from (Figure 8.21). Unfortunately, there is noticeable latency, but if learners use synth pads on this app primarily with a preset drum-machine pattern, learners could produce a really good chord base to build from. Pads are the opposite of leads, where they are designed to be used as soft and smooth chord changes, not melodic material like a synth lead. This way, the latency can be more easily managed and can be a good challenge for a more advanced learner of any age range. It could even be used to combine with acoustic instruments. There is currently no "Save" feature but by using a virtual audio router, Chrome Audio Capture, or Audacity's loopback feature, learners could capture sound of this instrument for a recording.

TypeDrummer

This app turns whatever learners type into the box to an electronic beat. It could be a great way to get a beat going for inspiration that is truly their own (Figure 8.22)!

Keyboard from Creatability.WithGoogle.com

This app from Google is somewhat limited for use in jamming settings but what sets this apart is its accessibility. Learners can play the virtual instrument simply by moving their heads. This capability means that the app could be an option for some learners with mobility or fine-motor differences. Figure 8.23 shows the in-browser interface set to mouse tracking.

See Chapter 10 for more virtual instruments that could be used. The aQWERTYon in particular can be incredibly useful as an eJam or a virtual instrument band component.

Makey Makey and Playtron

Invention kits like Makey Makey or Playtron are useful creative tools for classrooms. You may remember exploring these apps in Chapter 7. Whereas Makey Makey is a STEAM invention

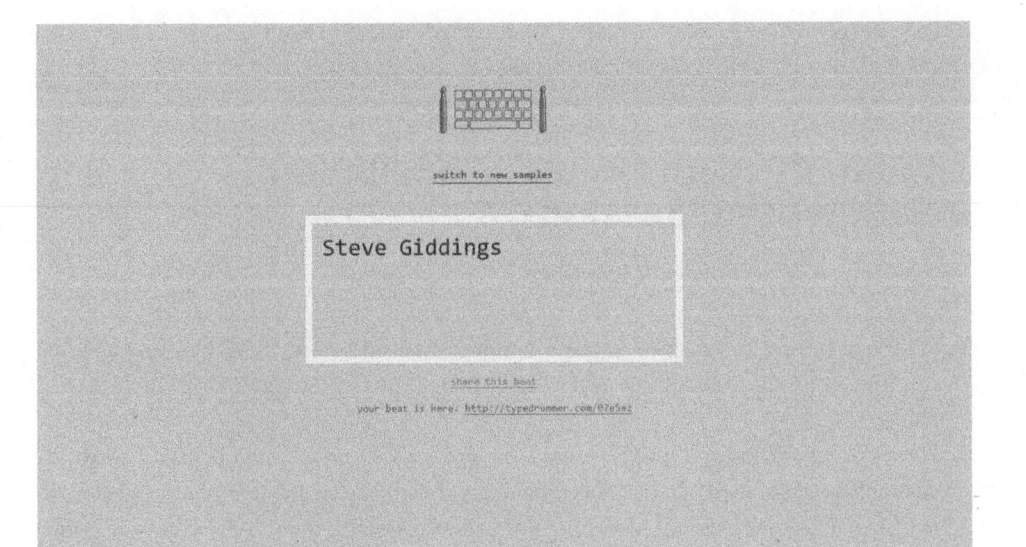

FIGURE 8.22 TypeDrummer with my name turned into a beat

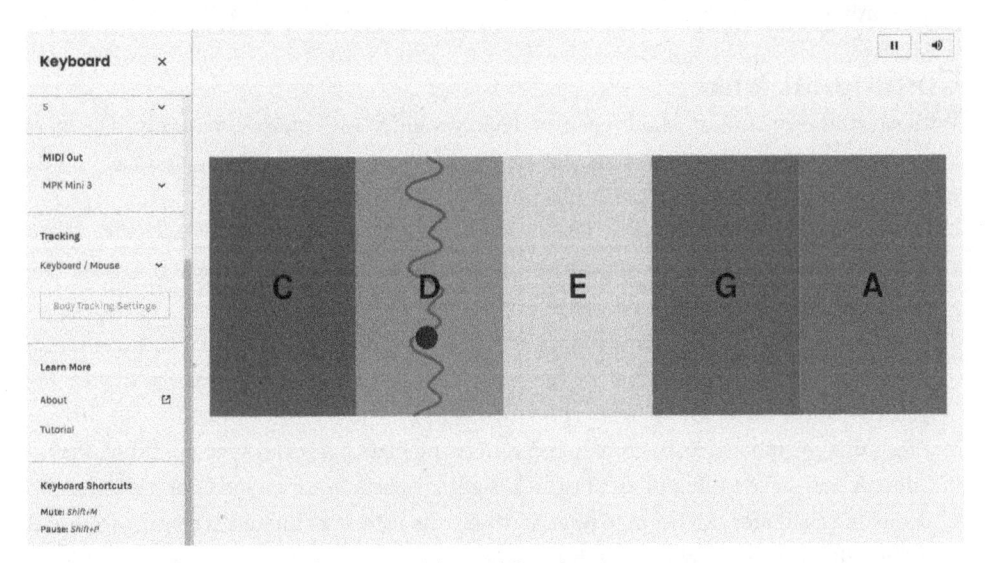

FIGURE 8.23 Virtual keyboard from Creatability.WithGoogle.com

kit that can be used for so many applications, as well as a (limited) MIDI controller, the Playtron is designed as a completely customizable MIDI controller. If learners have access only to Makey Makeys, it will certainly work. However, they will be able to program only up to six notes or sounds (using W-A-S-D-F-G keys), but that is likely all they will need in most situations anyway.

On the Playtron, which is designed as a MIDI controller, the user can input up to 16 triggers and can integrate with any of the DAWs or apps mentioned that have MIDI capability.

Then learners can design their own MIDI controllers and form a band with their own unique controllers to work with. Imagine the learning that can take place.

Getting an eJam Going or Beginning a Songwriting Session

Possible ways to start include the following:

1. Have one learner or group of learners compose a rhythm track (beat) by using a virtual drum set, creator kit, or looper. What material is presented will largely inform where the jam will go.
2. Have one learner or group of learners compose a chord progression by using smart instruments on GarageBand, or a loop that has the same bpm. The learners could also riff by using any pitched virtual instrument. Learners can select the sound as they go or they can do so after they find a riff they like.
3. Set the key of the virtual instrument like in GarageBand or on Chromebooks by using BandLab and the scale and have the learners find a solo part. Give everyone a turn to solo or mosh it.

Communal Jam

With Ableton Live Link, any Link-enabled device would fit the bpm automatically. If learners are using other devices without Link, learners will have to be more choosy, and have a little more knowledge of the functionality of some of these apps.

1. If learners have access to all of the same devices, have them open GarageBand, BandLab, or Soundtrap (or whatever app you might be using).
2. Everyone begins with the same loop, pattern, or progression and adds or changes something one at a time so that by the end, everyone is playing a different pattern that fits together to the same bpm.
3. From this cacophony, learners may begin to extrapolate parts and sync up. If not, the facilitator may have to step in and begin "assigning" parts from the material presented. To do so, the facilitator can begin to observe where the pattern of interest is coming from and ask another learner to sync up with that one.

It is in this chaos that some type of order will be achieved. There are many ways this experience could go and largely depends on learners' knowledge of the particular app's capabilities. This can also all be developed separately by learners and brought together at the end. For primary learners with touch screens, have them join in a circle and share their chosen patterns one at a time without a break to create the illusion of a larger piece. Or the facilitator in the middle with some loops can play one bar and then point to a different learner after each one to play theirs. Chapter 9 discusses the sound possibilities in lots of different ensembles, including virtual instrument bands.

Conclusion

Considering all the possibilities that open up with digital and virtual instruments, we owe it to learners to at least try to embrace these new instruments. As we know, technology changes constantly and there are new apps that can be used as virtual instruments all the time. Many of the apps mentioned in this chapter may already have updates available to increase their playability and usability. Some may not be functional anymore. In fact, at least one app went down during the writing of this book not a week after I initially researched it for inclusion. In the end, these are all places to begin with virtual instruments or virtual instrument bands and perhaps you will find something that works better for your learners, or one that didn't exist during the writing of this book. If it works for your learners, it is the right app.

9

Tech for Facilitating Creativity with Small Ensembles

Without the appropriate technology, some ensembles would simply not be able to create original music at all. Rock and popular ensembles are examples of groups that rely on technology to even make a sound. Some instruments exist in virtual form and some, like the electric guitar, need amplification to be heard or to conjure a particular creative musical or stylistic effect. For rap and hip-hop groups, a microphone, turntables, or some type of drum sequencer are often needed for a backing beat. In a group of musicians playing rock music, technology is essential for creating, as these groups tend to compose music together in small groups using electric guitars, microphones, and keyboards. Although many of these are not digital technologies, they are still pieces of technology that facilitate creativity on different levels, whether it be a blues jam, a hip-hop cypher, or a rock band rehearsal. Here are some of the essential pieces of gear needed to facilitate creativity in a popular music ensemble.

What Your School Likely Already Has

A PA System with Five to Eight Channels

As long as there are enough channels for a couple of microphones and a couple of other instruments, learners can get by in a lot of situations. For example, a bass and piano *can* be plugged directly into a sound system without any extra equipment, but the more ¼″ TS cables (explored later) used, the more line humming is compounded. To curb the line hum, and make things easier to mix in rehearsal or concert, you will need to use direct-injection or direct-input (DI) boxes (to be discussed later).

Guitars also *can* be plugged into the system, but that characteristic rock guitar sound is difficult to reproduce with this setup. Guitars need specialized amplifiers or pedals and footswitches to reproduce that characteristic sound.

Technology for Unleashing Creativity. Steve Giddings, Oxford University Press. © Oxford University Press 2022.
DOI: 10.1093/oso/9780197570739.003.0010

Two to Three Vocal Microphones with XLR Cables

Vocal microphones have a fairly standardized look to them for the most part. They can be used for vocalists or horns. They usually have a pretty specific pickup pattern (often called polar pattern), meaning they can pick up sound only from the front, not the sides. This pickup pattern is called cardioid. Hyper-cardioid is another common pickup pattern for vocal microphones. These types of microphones pick up from the front and also a little from the back (discussed more in depth later).

A Keyboard or Electronic Piano

It is very common for schools, especially elementary schools, to have a keyboard or an electronic piano. If there is an acoustic piano, it can be mic'd with the top open.

A Keyboard Amplifier

These are pretty versatile amplifiers that can be plugged into pretty much anything. If your school has one, it can be used for a monitor or to amplify a keyboard or a bass, and even can be used for a backing track.

What You Would Need, and Your School May not Already Have

Guitar Amplifier(s)

But Wait: What Is an Amplifier?

An amplifier is the part that amplifies the sound of the plugged-in instrument through the speaker. It is not the speaker itself. The knobs and switches are part of the amplifier. They can be analog or digital. Often, professional electric guitarists and bass players will have a speaker cabinet that is separate from the amplifier. This way, players can customize their sound by mixing speakers and amplifiers. These setups are usually with tube amplifiers that use vacuum tubes to control the electrical signal that creates the warmer tone many guitar players strive for, as in Figure 9.1. Figure 9.2 shows vacuum tubes inside a guitar amplifier. Combo amplifiers contain the amplifier and the speaker together in one cabinet. They are often much more portable than a separate speaker and amplifier, as in Figure 9.3.

Solid State and Digital

Tube amps and most solid-state amplifiers are analog technologies. Solid state basically means that the amplifiers use closed circuitry to produce tones and generate amplification, not vacuum tubes. Schools with jazz ensembles will very likely own a solid-state combo amp or two for guitars. To get a desired sound, or to customize the sound in any way past some distortion on these amps, you need pedals, and various foot-controlled devices, making it challenging and expensive to find exactly what might be needed for a particular sound.

FIGURE 9.1 Half stack amplifier and speaker cabinet

Digital amplifiers are also considered solid state, but have a computer chip that runs the amplifier. These are often called amp modelling systems because they can emulate many of the industry-standard sounds, including some iconic tube amp sounds without the extra equipment (or tubes). They are ideal for schools because they are very portable and versatile. Examples of these are Line 6 Spider and Fender Mustang series of amps, as in Figure 9.4. The Fender Mustang series has a four-button footswitch (Figure 9.5) sold separately that lets the learner program different settings to each button and also contains a looping station for spontaneous multi-part composition and improvisation (more on looping stations later).

Sound Systems

A basic PA system with a mixer and two speakers will do for rehearsal and in some performance situations. Performing, however, usually is done in a much bigger room,

FIGURE 9.2 Tubes inside the amplifier

FIGURE 9.3 Combo amp

FIGURE 9.4 Older model GT40 Mustang II amp modelling system

FIGURE 9.5 Four-button footswitch for the Mustang series of amps

which requires additional equipment. These items will make your groups sound better, will help your young musicians play better, and can really help your performances sound and look professional to help facilitate creative activities. Following is the basic sound equipment technology your school will need to facilitate various creative activities.

You will need a mixer with at least 12 channels, with at least one monitor mix (AUX) that can be controlled on each channel. Learners will need a separate channel for every instrument in the band. You can usually get away without micing the drums, but in bigger halls you may need to mic them. If they are electric, learners will need to put them through the mixer by using DI. An acoustic kit will at minimum need a bass-drum mic and an over-head. Thus, if the drums are being mic'd in this way, they need two separate channels per kit. In more advanced setups, often every drum is mic'd individually with those two additional overhead mics to pick up cymbal sounds.

Powered Mixer Setup

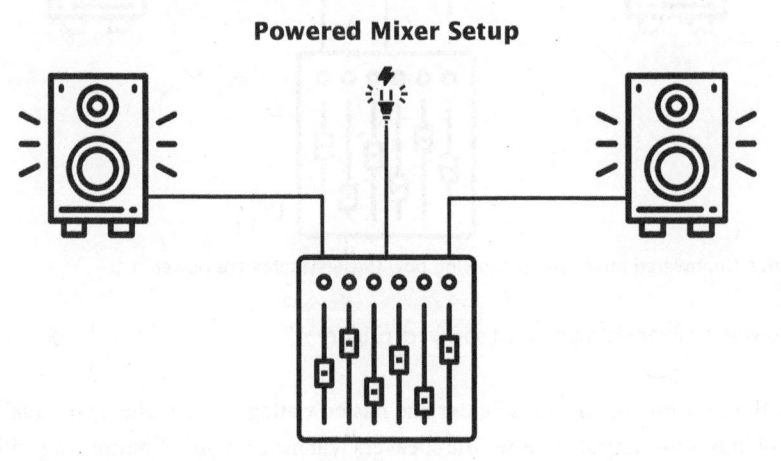

FIGURE 9.6 Powered mixer setup showing how these systems plug in

Types of Sound Systems

There are a few different setups for a sound system, but I am only going to discuss the three most common that you would likely come across.

1. Powered mixer with unpowered speakers (Figure 9.6)

With this setup, the mixer will usually be bulky and heavy with a wattage rating on the back, and it is the only piece that needs to plug into an outlet. The amplifier is built into the mixer. This means that the speakers that go with these mixers draw their power from the mixer, which houses the amplifier that gives it power. There is only one plug in for the mixer and none for the speakers.

An advantage of this setup is that learners need only one outlet for the entire system. Even if more speakers are added for monitoring purposes, they all draw their power from the mixer because the amplifier is built in. This design makes it easy to set up anywhere.

A disadvantage is that it can become very difficult to add speakers unless you know a lot about wattage and voltage. Unpowered speakers have an ohm rating and unless you know the rating of each piece of equipment, it can be difficult to mix and match. Many powered mixers, though, have an unpowered section for powered speakers at the front of the unit.

Unpowered Mixer Setup

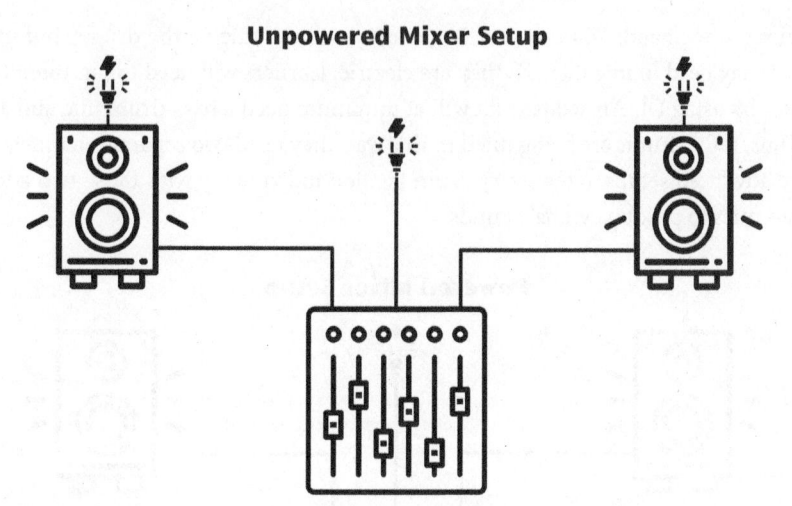

FIGURE 9.7 Unpowered mixer setup showing how these systems are powered

2. Unpowered mixer with powered speakers (Figure 9.7)

With this setup, the mixer is lighter and has no wattage rating. There are usually faders instead of knobs for output volume. The speakers will have an on/off button and will have to be plugged in, meaning that each speaker has its own amplifier that needs power.

An advantage of this system is that mixing and matching is easy. Each speaker has its own wattage and has built-in amplifiers.

A disadvantage of this system is that power outlets are needed for every piece of equipment you plan to use. Every mixer and speaker will require its own power source.

3. Digital setups

Digital systems have become the industry standard but there aren't a whole lot of schools that have embraced them at this point. Advantages of these systems are that they have a memory and can store mix data within them so that learners can access the mix of a particular group at any time. Also, the mix can be controlled wirelessly via an iPad or other tablet. This setup means the mixer can be backstage and the sound engineer can control it from front of house. Also, because the setup is digital, the live performances can easily be recorded to an SD (security digital) card or similar storage device. They also give the sound person more control over effects and can be customized much more easily than on the analog boards. There is no need for a long cable snake (discussed later), either, which means a little less setup time. Disadvantages are that a lot of things still need to be plugged in. Digital boards also tend to be more expensive than analog systems. I would also be concerned about software updates that may not be serviceable by the school's governing body.

At Least Two Main Speakers

This requirement is usually shortened to just mains. These are the speakers that the audience will hear that plug into the mixer. If you have an unpowered mixer, you need powered speakers and vice versa.

Up to Three Monitors

Monitors are the speakers on the floor in front of the stage facing the performers. They help the musicians hear one another better because of the directionality of many speaker cabinets. For example, if a performer is behind the main speakers it can be very difficult to hear what is coming out of the speakers, so the performers need additional speakers facing them, called monitors, that have a separate mix from the mains. A separate mix means that the volume can be adjusted for those monitors separately from the main speakers. Some mixers have two or more monitor mixes. This means that each monitor can be adjusted separately from the others, customizing the monitor mix to each musician. This is a much more advanced setup. Monitors work the same as speakers. If you have an unpowered mixer, you will need powered speakers to act as monitors. Any speaker can be a monitor.

At Least Two DI Boxes

You may need only one DI box if your keyboard and bass amplifiers are equipped with a built-in DI. You will be able to tell if it has DI built in if the amplifier includes XLR outputs (Figure 9.8).

DI boxes have two main purposes, as follows:

1. To change the signal going to the mixer so that all of the signals going to the board are the same.

FIGURE 9.8 XLR output jack

The DI takes the signal generated from a ¼″ cable and converts it to XLR, which are balanced lines, meaning they give off virtually no hum. Quarter-inch cables are not grounded and therefore generate a humming interference.

2. So the amplifier can act as a monitor for performance.

Without a DI hooked into an amp, the sound from the instrument only goes out the main speakers with nothing coming back to the musician other than the stage monitors, a situation that can be challenging. The DI box lets musicians control their stage volume separately from the main volume so that the person using the DI box can hear themselves during a performance. To have this control, simply plug the instrument into the input hole on the DI with a ¼″ cable and then connect the input labelled "in/thru" on the DI to the input on the amplifier. The XLR goes to the mixer and then the musician can control the keyboard amp like a monitor. Figure 9.9 shows a picture of a double DI box with a wiring diagram on the top to help.

FIGURE 9.9 DI box showing a wiring diagram on top

A 75–100-ft Cable Snake

If you are using an analog board, a cable snake is a good idea. It's a piece of equipment that helps the person operating the soundboard to be far away from the stage so that they can better gauge the sound in the room and not be in the way of the performers.

It has a box with XLR and ¼″ channel inputs and speaker outputs on one end and male and female cable ends for the soundboard/mixer at the other. It really cleans up the performance area and instead of running 12–15 (or more) different cables across the room, there is only one. Think of the snake as a large extension cable for your mixer. Each cable is labelled and sometimes colour coded (Figure 9.10).

FIGURE 9.10 Cable snake with 12 input channels and four output channels

Figure 9.11 shows where everything plugs in and some of the important parts of the mixing board you should know. AUX SENDS are your monitor mixes (what the musicians hear). They can control how much of each instrument is coming out of the monitor. The monitor mix will be different from the main mix (what the audience hears). Adjusting the AUX SENDS on each channel will not affect your main mix. An XLR-to-¼″ adapter is often needed for this setup.

Some mixers will have stereo sends for something like a backing track. Two empty channels can be used to control a backing track if need be. For this you would need a 3.5mm (⅛″) male stereo cable (TRS) to two mono ¼″ male speaker inputs (TS). Figure 9.12 shows two common backing track hookups. Volume for the 3.5mm to RCA hookups can be controlled only from the main volume, meaning everything will be controlled all at once. The 3.5mm-to-dual ¼″ can be put into the stereo sends and be controlled separately from the main volume. Both are useful in different situations.

INPUTS are where all the instruments plug into. GAIN refers to how much of the instrument's signal is let into the mixer.

AUX SENDS for your monitor.

AUX SENDS are controlled on each channel here.

VOLUME CONTROL for each channel. Each channel has a MUTE function.

VOLUME CONTROL for mains.

FIGURE 9.11 A diagram showing where to plug everything in on the mixer

Extra Cables

3.5mm Stereo TRS (1/8") to RCA

3.5mm Stereo TRS (1/8") to RCA 1/4" mono TS

FIGURE 9.12 Extra cables for backing tracks or playing music

Microphones

For Live Sound

Shure SM58s are the industry standard for vocal microphones. When performers are vocalizing into a cardioid dynamic microphone it is important to hold it two finger-widths from the mouth at the farthest. I will often tell learners one finger just so they will be as close as possible (Figure 9.13). This position guarantees the best sound and best mix.

Shure SM57s are the industry standard for use as instrument microphones. They are used to mic a guitar amp for a live performance and can be used for horns and vocals, too. Figure 9.14 shows an ideal placement on the amp.

FIGURE 9.13 Two-finger widths apart

FIGURE 9.14 Mic placement on the amp

FIGURE 9.15 Beta 52A bass-drum mic

For a bass drum, the Beta 52A is your best bet (Figure 9.15). Bass-drum mic stands are also useful.

For overheads (cymbals and toms) a cardioid condenser microphone like the KSM137 will work (Figure 9.16).

You will often see each drum mic'd separately at large shows. This step isn't needed for many school shows.

Other Micing Considerations for Recording

Many of the microphones mentioned previously will work for a recording. If learners are producing a podcast, video blog, or recording vocals or small acoustic groups like a

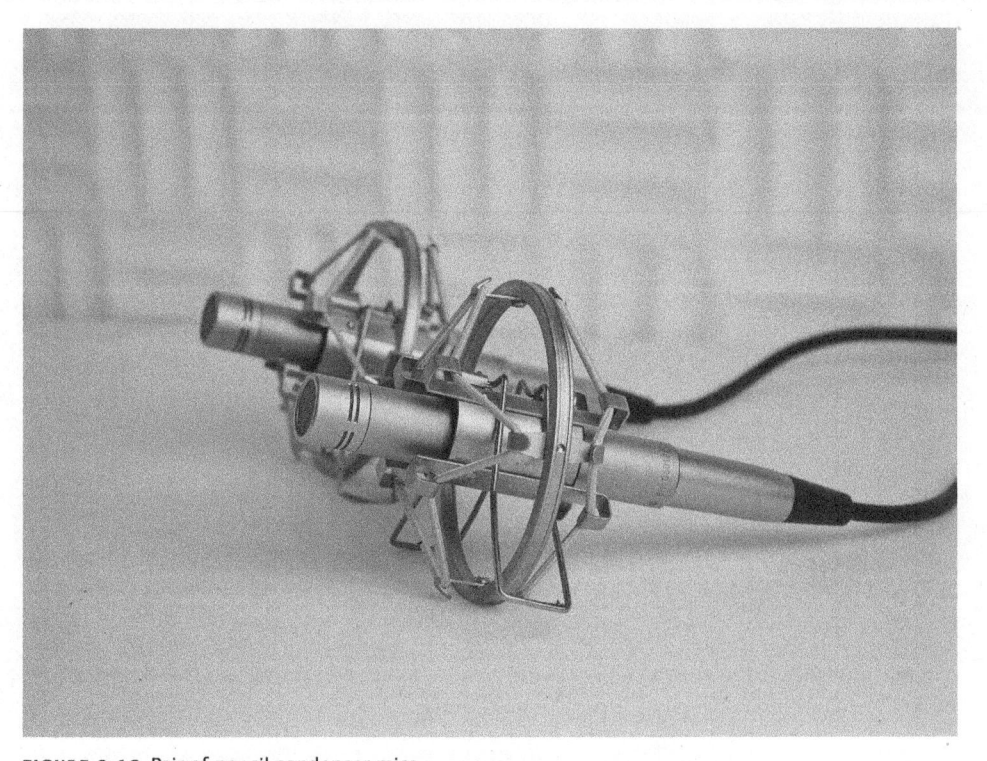

FIGURE 9.16 Pair of pencil condenser mics

quartet or string section, there are more specific microphone arrangements they might want to consider:

For vocals, wide-diaphragm condenser mics are often used. One very common and very well-priced microphone is the AudioTechnica AT2020. There is a USB version of this mic, too. It is commonly associated with being a backup mic at Abbey Road Studios, the home studio of the Beatles.

Another reasonably priced, versatile, but not as widely acclaimed mic as the AT2020 is the Apex 415B. What makes this one useful is the polar pattern selection. It is capable of cardioid, bidirectional, and omnidirectional, a versatility that is useful for recording room sound or for a small instrumental ensemble.

The more expensive but industry-standard condenser microphone is the broadcast-quality Shure SM7B and its USB counterpart Shure MV7. Other than the USB mics, they will need an interface (or a mixer) with phantom power on. Phantom power is the 48V button on your mixer or interface which sends power to microphones that need an extra boost of power which is needed for condenser microphones.

Figure 9.17 gives examples of polar patterns that learners might come across as well as some other considerations for choosing a microphone for particular applications. For more education about microphone polar patterns and other useful microphone information, the shure.eu website is fantastic.

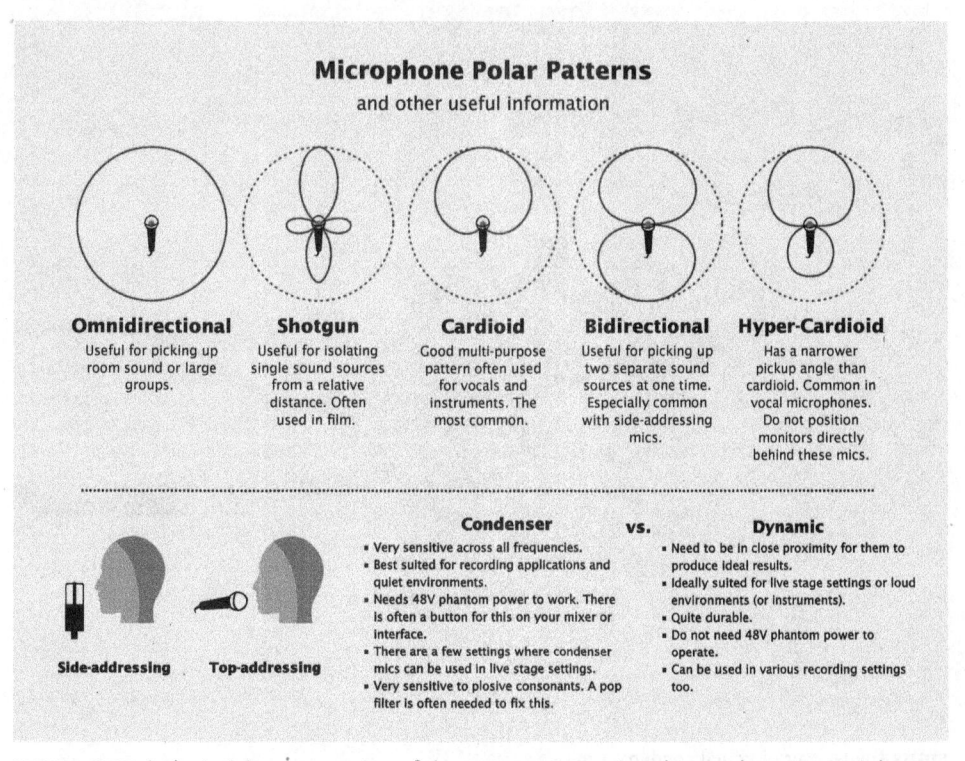

FIGURE 9.17 A chart giving an overview of the most common microphone polar patterns and a pros and cons of dynamic and condenser microphones

Instruments You May Need to Help Facilitate Creativity by Using Technology

Electric guitars: Look at the Fender line of Stratocasters. There are junior versions for smaller children.

Bass guitars: Look at the Fender Bronco for a short-scale bass to fit smaller children (or even a bass ukulele) and the Fender P Bass for all others.

Keyboards: Yamaha has some great keyboards for a variety of purposes. There is a difference between a piano and a keyboard. Pianos have weighted keys and are usually up to 88 keys. Keyboards have thinner, often unweighted keys and usually have lots of MIDI and DJ capabilities, making them versatile for most applications.

MIDI keyboards and other controllers: These can be helpful for programmed samples and finding unique sounds.

Acoustic or electronic drums: They each have their advantages and disadvantages. Mapex is a good name for acoustic drums. Roland and Yamaha have some good electronic drums. Electronic drums are great for emulating those authentic 808 (i.e., modern hip-hop) or 1980s stadium drum sounds (i.e., INXS).

Cables and Hookups

Figure 9.18 shows some common cables that learners will come across. Use this figure as a reference for terms throughout this chapter and in other sections throughout the book.

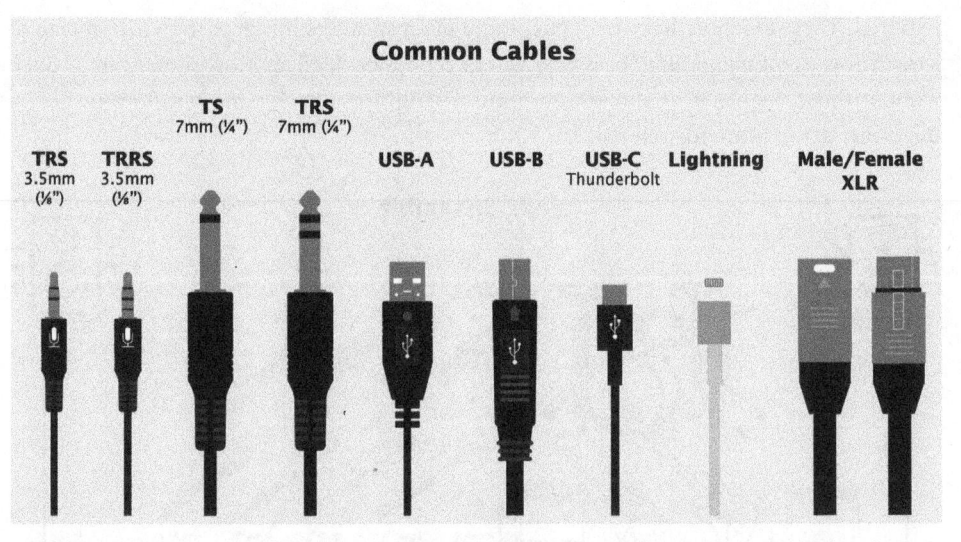

FIGURE 9.18 Common cables that facilitators and learners will come across while working with music technology

A Quick Guide to Running Sound in Any Creative Musical Situation

The gear you will need will depend on each "sound scenario" and can range from very basic to more advanced. Here are some of the basics for each kind of setup.

1. Jazz ensemble

Big band: At least one solo mic for each horn section (saxes will likely need two), a mixer with two main speakers, amplification for each electronic instrument (guitar, bass, keyboard). You will likely not need monitors.

Small combo: Depending on the melody instrument, it may not need anything. It may also depend on the venue. One vocal mic for a saxophone, horn, or vocalist is common. Figure 9.19 (next page) shows the minimum setup for a big band or similar jazz group.

2. Rock ensemble

Since rock ensembles and popular music ensemble groups are made up of mostly electronic instruments and vocalists, this is the most extensive setup learners will likely come across. Learners will need a mixing board; two main speakers; at least two floor monitors; enough vocal mics for your singers or horn players; amplification for your guitars, bass, and keyboard; a DI box for your bass, acoustic guitar, and keyboards; and an instrument microphone for your guitar amplifiers. Other micing options are at least two overhead condenser microphones for each drummer and a bass-drum mic for each bass drum. Basically, everything is mic'd or amplified for a group like this, including the guitar amp, as mentioned earlier. If you are micing bass drums, bass bin speakers are often required. These are large bass-frequency-only main speakers for large shows. If micing of bass drums is not happening, bass bins will likely not be needed. Most shows can be done without them. Figure 9.20 shows a minimum setup for a rock band but does include a three-mic drum setup for reference.

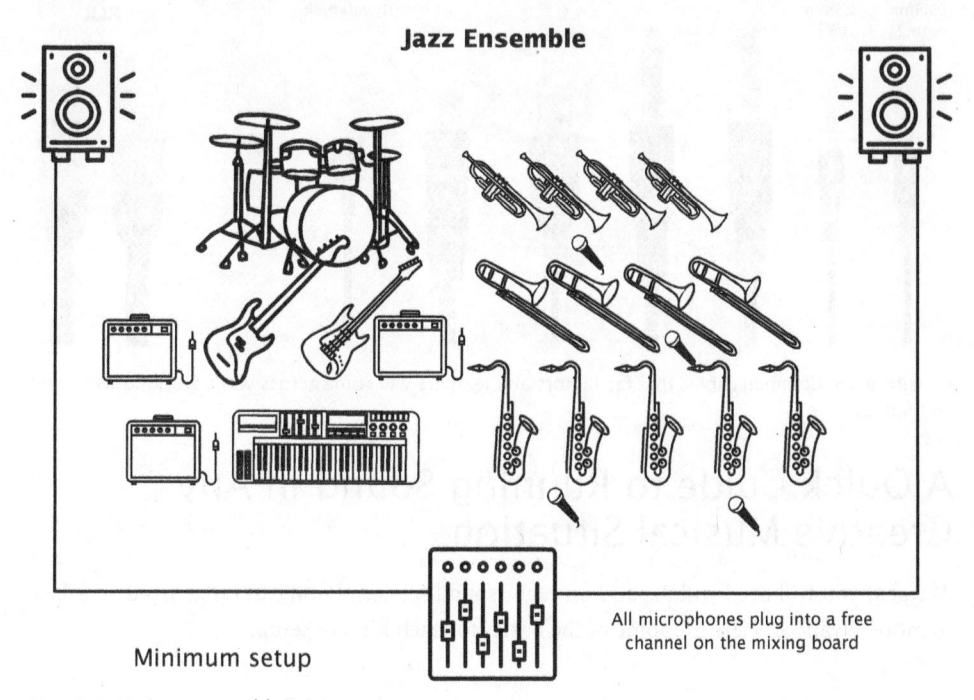

FIGURE 9.19 Jazz ensemble minimum setup

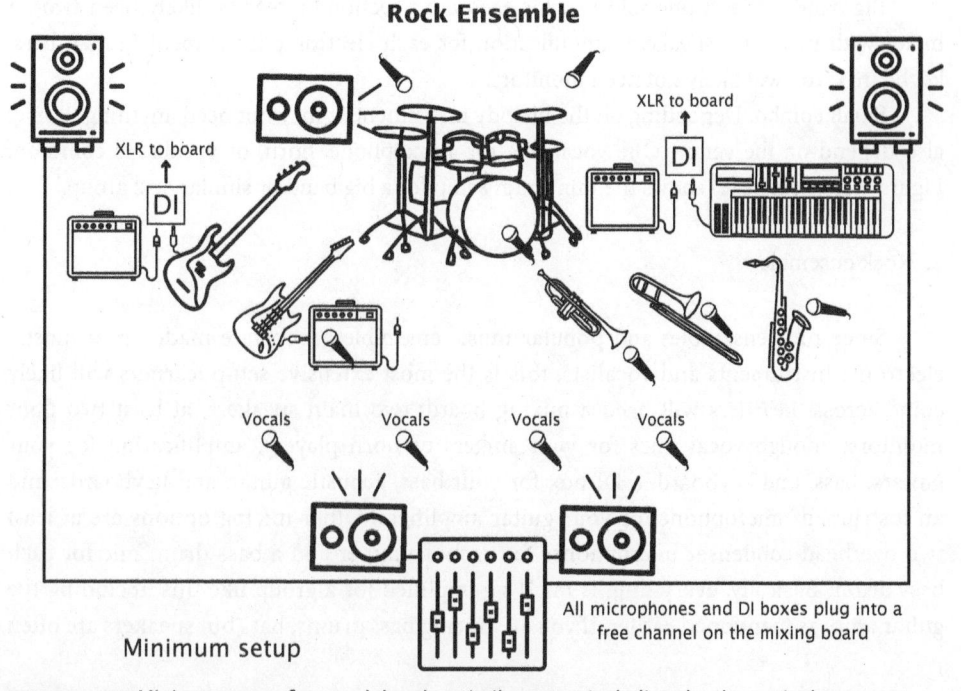

FIGURE 9.20 Minimum setup for a rock band or similar group including the three-mic drum setup

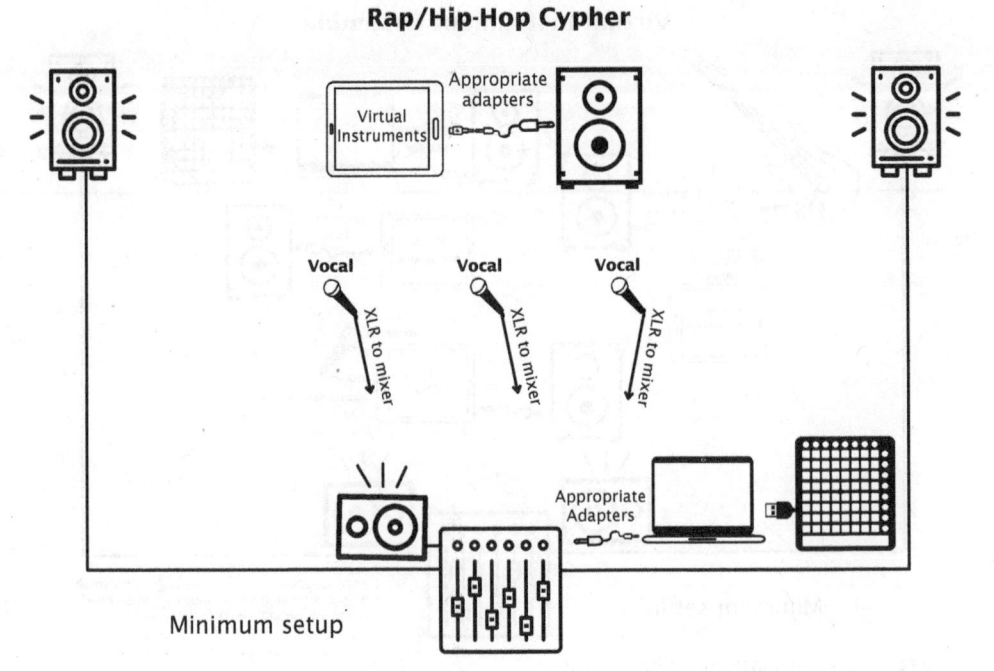

FIGURE 9.21 Minimum setup for a live rap cypher

3. Rap/hip-hop cypher

A rap cypher is often an improvised rap session where there is a precomposed beat upon which multiple rappers take turns "spitting bars." There isn't a whole lot needed other than a vocal microphone or two and a speaker that can hook up to a smart phone, laptop, or other device. Since iPhones no longer have 3.5mm inputs, and many other mobile devices are moving toward that reality, Bluetooth capability is a handy tool. For everything else, a 3.5mm stereo input (TRS) on your device will suffice. Figure 9.21 shows a possible setup for a live rap cypher. For a jam or cypher that is not being done in front of a live audience, main speakers will likely not be needed.

4. Virtual band

Each device involved will need its own amplification and 3.5mm (⅛″) cables. A number of ¼″ to 3.5mm cables or converters will be useful to change the size of the cable to fit into the 3.5mm port on most devices. If MIDI controllers are needed, USB and MIDI cables will also be needed. Figure 9.22 shows the possibilities for setting up a virtual instrument band in a live or classroom setting. For a more easily manageable setup, DI everything as you would a bass or a keyboard.

Troubleshooting Tips

There are several things I wish I had known when I started working with sound for the first time. Don't make the same mistakes I did! Here are some common issues that arise with sound.

Virtual Instrument Ensemble

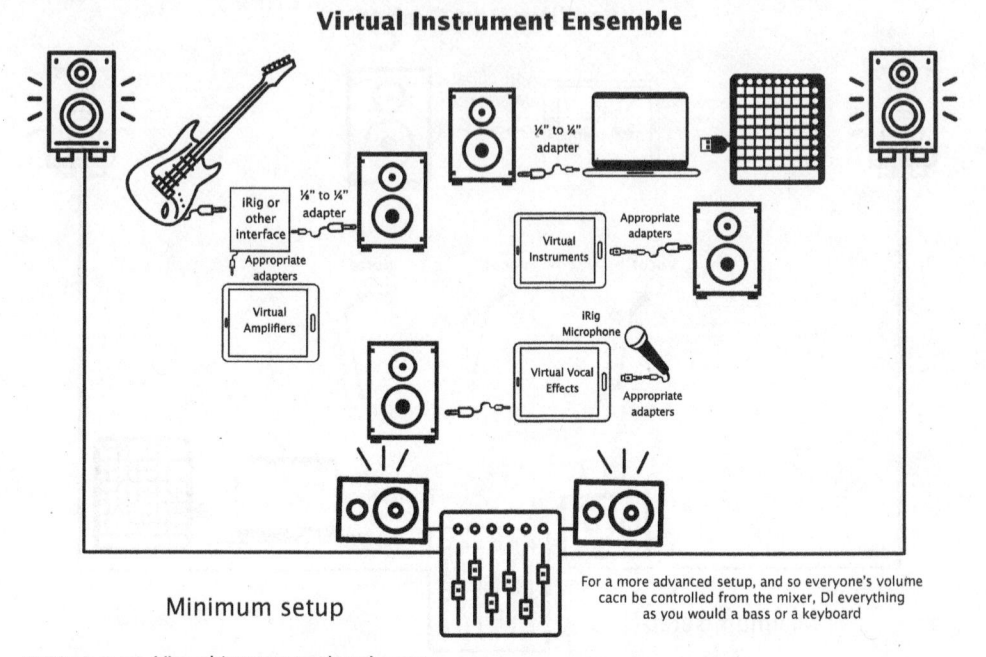

FIGURE 9.22 Virtual instrument band setup

Just because your speaker goes to 10 does not mean that it should ever go to 10: using the top setting can blow your speaker. You never start to run a marathon at full tilt, because you will tire out much more quickly—and you might die! Same with the speaker.

Speech is different from singing: understanding speech relies on the high-frequency sounds in words that the letters *t* and *s* generate. "Testing 1-2-3" isn't just a thing we say into a microphone—it is designed to help test the sound across all frequencies.

Gain versus volume: gain is how much comes into the mixer and volume is how much gets out. There is a balance between the two. Some inputs will need more gain, while others will need very little.

The "prison guard" and "gate keeper": if you think of the mixer as a "prison guard" and the speakers as the "gate keepers," it will help to understand the basics of how sound works.

Phantom power: Regular vocal and instrument microphones work without phantom power. Condenser microphones need phantom power. Look for the 48V phantom-power button at the top or the back of your mixer if everything is set up properly but the microphone is not working.

"Headphone out" is equivalent to "speaker out": if there is a headphone jack on an instrument like a keyboard, it can be used to plug an instrument into the mixer or into the DI.

Monitors: Monitors plug into AUX outs and can be controlled separately from each channel. All performers need to hear themselves, including kids.

How much amplification? As a general rule, the larger the room, the more amplification will be needed.

Approaching Creativity Authentically by Using This Technology

Rock or Popular Music Ensemble

Rock and popular music ensembles are conducive to creativity and can be done with learners as young as eight. Without the bind of notation (in most cases) creativity isn't as hindered as it might be in some other ensemble types. As mentioned earlier, many popular music ensembles can't create their characteristic sounds without some form of analog or digital technology. Here is how you can approach creating with a group of learners with electronic instruments while keeping it authentic. This approach can work with any group of instruments but it is a common way for rock musicians to approach writing songs in a group:

Have a guitarist, bassist, or keys player show a progression or riff that they composed. Or, you could just have them go ahead with something. Sometimes the best things happen in spontaneity! If nothing is coming to them, just pick two notes, or combination of notes, and have them find a repeating rhythmic pattern for those two notes—something simple. A really good way to get them playing with the technology is to experiment with the effects. On a keyboard, there are lots of banked MIDI and synthesizer sounds. Use synth leads for melodic parts, and use synth pads for backing chords.

Have your drummers play a pattern that fits into the progression. If they can't think of anything, usually a steady rock pattern will work. At minimum a kick-snare-kick-snare pattern will suffice. Electronic drums can have an interesting overall affect on the sound of the group, as there are lots of banked drum samples that sound great and some drum-machine sounds.

Have your singers experiment with melodies or harmonies. They don't have to be lyrics at this point, just hooks. If lyrics *do* come, that's fine, but there are no wrong answers if it sounds good. Sometimes singing is best added after the instruments have figured out the music and how the underlying parts will go. Try using some vocal effects with a vocoder or running them through an effects pedal like a harmonizer.

Have your other chording instrument learners copy the progression or riff being played so they have a foundation to work from. This can be accomplished during the session without stopping the groove, or by taking the time to have them show one another what is being played so everything is really clear. This depends on the learners. Once they know the progression or the riff, they can begin to experiment with variations, embellishments, melodies, harmonies, or countermelodies. In a real jamming situation, though, the performers won't stop to teach you the riff, so learning to follow or "read the fretboard" is much more authentic and *hugely* beneficial to their overall musicianship.

Once they have established a groove and are playing away, encourage them to change something if they haven't already. The drummer has a lot of control over what happens in a jam session with regard to phrasing and style. Even changing a cymbal or a drum can make a big difference in a song. If the person who came up with the original progression wants to change to a B section or a C section, that change should be encouraged. It challenges the others to follow along and generates ideas for later songwriting.

Changing the chords completely for the B section (or in this case, the chorus) is not necessary. If you must change a chord, just change one. As mentioned earlier, changing the rhythm might be enough to trigger a change, or just adding more cymbals, more distortion, or more intensity. Change the effects or the MIDI sound on the keyboard to generate interest.

Soundpainting: Improvisation for the Orchestra

There *is* a way to jam that is much more authentic to the genre and style that band, orchestra, and choir musicians would be familiar with—it's called soundpainting! Soundpainting is a language of physical gestures for facilitators and learners to enable group improvisation and composition and can be integrated with any group of instruments or combination of instruments, even technology or some hybrid version of it. It was invented by Walter Thompson, and here are the basics on how it works:

The conductor gestures *who* is playing. The gestures can specify instrument groups, small groups, or whole ensemble.

The conductor gestures *what* they are going to play. There is a plethora of different gestures indicating long tones, pointillism, stab, hit, extended techniques, improvisation, and many others. There are technology-specific gestures and the language is evolving all the time, but also the beauty of this language is that facilitators and learners could make one up. A precomposed loop or a sample would best be presented as a palette. This particular gesture can be used in soundpainting for a musician to remember a particular part and be able to use it later in another composition.

The conductor gestures *when to start* and *when to stop*.

The musicians decide *how* that instruction is to be executed. For example, if they were instructed to play long tones, they get to choose what pitch to play the long tone on.

Once the "jamming" has begun, the conductor can play with the material that the musicians have presented and take it from there. There are a number of other gestures that can be used to indicate remembering particular patterns, changing pitch, intensity, volume, and even style.

Soundpainting can be used with any combination of instruments, actors, dancers, or levels. A group of flat-out beginners can learn 20 gestures in 60–90 minutes and could give a public performance in only a couple of rehearsals. The possibilities are endless with soundpainting.

Soundpainting is an unintimidating, natural, and more-authentic-to-the-style way to introduce creative technology to a large ensemble used to traditional approaches. To learn more about this, go to www.SoundPainting.com, where you can learn about Walter and buy the workbooks. There are also a lot of videos on YouTube of this in action. You really have to see it to understand it fully.

Conclusion

Of course, for learning about technology in the music classroom, sound tech cannot be overlooked. Analog sound often works in partnership with digital and virtual instruments to create an authentic experience for the learner and the performer. Knowing what goes in where is incredibly beneficial and will help learners to create music with little stress. I'm hoping that this chapter has given you some practical advice for setting up sound and being able to know how these technologies work together within your music class and onto the stage.

Figure Attribution

All attributions listed are for Figure 9.17.

Omegatron, *Bidirectionalpattern.svg*, August 30, 2020, Wikimedia Commons, accessed May 25, 2021 https://commons.wikimedia.org/wiki/File:Bidirectionalpattern.svg (altered by author to include a microphone graphic in the center)

Omegatron, *Shotgunpattern.svg*, May 14, 2021, Wikimedia Commons, accessed May 25, 2021 https://commons.wikimedia.org/wiki/File:Shotgunpattern.svg (altered by author to include a microphone graphic in the center)

Omegatron, *Cardioidpattern.svg*, September 8, 2020, Wikimedia Commons, accessed May 25, 2021 https://commons.wikimedia.org/wiki/File:Cardioidpattern.svg (altered by author to include a microphone graphic in the center)

Omegatron, *Hypercardioidpattern.svg*, September 5, 2020, Wikimedia Commons, accessed May 25, 2021 https://commons.wikimedia.org/wiki/File:Hypercardioid pattern.svg (altered by author to include a microphone graphic in the center)

10

Other Considerations

In this chapter, other considerations that were not previously covered in earlier parts of the book will be explored. We will be examining and discussing virtual hubs for keeping learner work in one place, ways to use video and video recording apps that can be easy to use for many different purposes, and other creative music apps and software that were not previously mentioned.

Virtual Hubs for Learner Creations

So, you have gone through all the ideas in this book and everything is all on different sites and you would like one place to keep all of the wonderful creations. If your school is using Google Suite for Education, learners would likely be at least somewhat familiar with some of the Google Apps included in the Google Education Suite. Google Classroom, Google Docs, and Google Sites are just a few of the ways to showcase and keep portfolios of creations by learners.

Google Classroom

In Google Classroom, facilitators can create virtual rooms for learners to join as part of a class (Figure 10.1). Assignments can be managed from there and anything turned in can be organized through the Classroom.

Google Docs

Google Docs is the Google Suite's word processor and you may have experience with it even if your school doesn't have the Google for Education accounts, as every person with a gmail account gets free access to Google Docs. It works like most word processors but is better integrated to the Internet in terms of auto linking and embedding. It could simply be used as a list of links (for Chrome Music Lab, BeepBox, or any other link-based composition tool) to compositions that learners have done. Then it could be sent and shared with the facilitator via the "Share" button (Figure 10.2).

Technology for Unleashing Creativity. Steve Giddings, Oxford University Press. © Oxford University Press 2022.
DOI: 10.1093/oso/9780197570739.003.0011

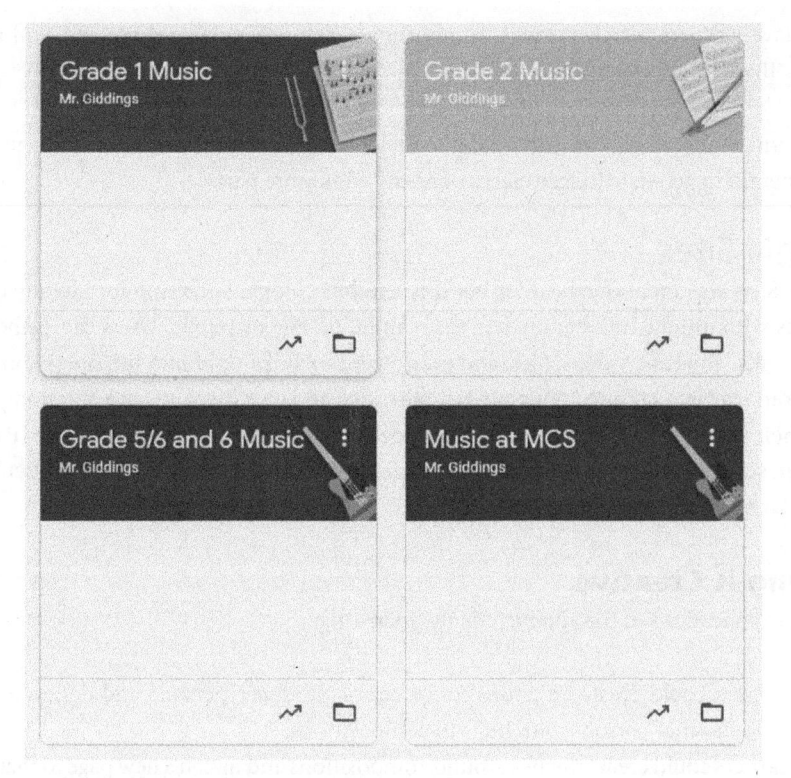

FIGURE 10.1 Google Classroom classes view

FIGURE 10.2 Google Docs share button

Flat Add-On

With the Flat for Docs add-on, users can write snippets of music right into Google Docs (Figure 10.3). This site could act as a hub for keeping original snippets of ideas or some larger works, perhaps also a draft form of a final work.

Making It Creative

Possible applications of this app include the following:

Using Google Docs' commenting feature, learners could comment on compositions with suggestions for how to improve or something they liked about it.

> Share a musical snippet in Google Docs with the Flat add-on and ask for feedback on a particular snippet.

Have learners search through compositions that others have made and find a list of themes that were found.

Perhaps there are a lot of pentatonic melodies; perhaps there is a lot of tab used. Use these themes to generate longer pieces of music with more parts.

Google Sites

Google Sites was mentioned earlier but it is another Google Suite App for literally creating websites with unique link parameters that can be private or public. Users can embed Song Maker links, YouTube videos, files, and even BeepBox links right into the site (Figure 10.4). See if your learners' compositions can be embedded and give them creative autonomy in creating their website. Currently, Google Sites does not allow for the embedding of MP3, WAV, or other sound files. However, a unique share link can be created to those particular files within Drive and hyperlinked within the site.

Making It Creative

Possible applications of the app include the following:

Learners could create an entire composer or producer persona and design a website around that persona with links to compositions.

Learners could create themes around compositions and match a new page to that theme.

Learners could create podcast episodes discussing their inspiration for particular pieces of music and embed them into the site.

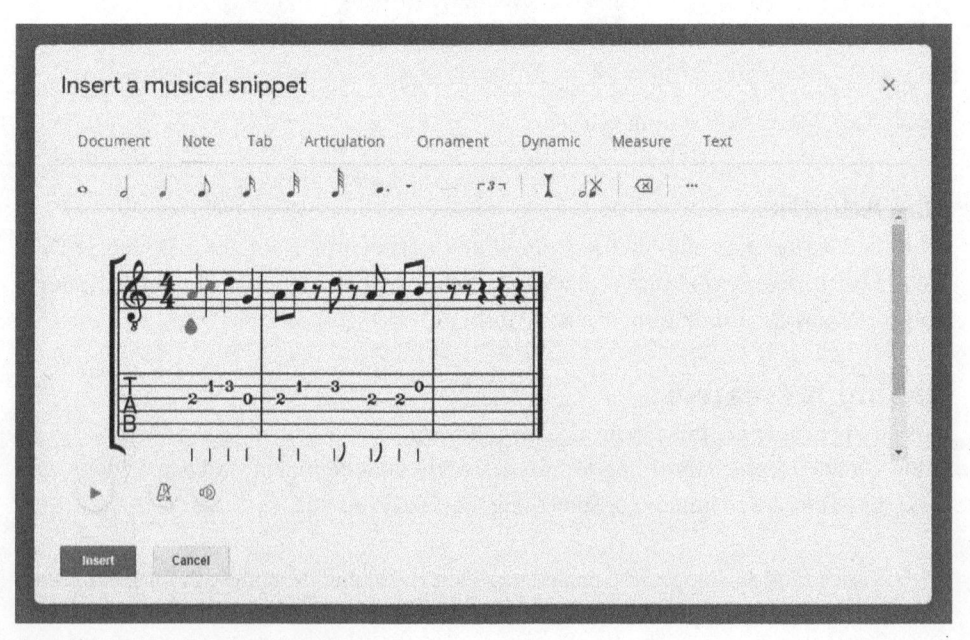

FIGURE 10.3 Flat for Docs add-on

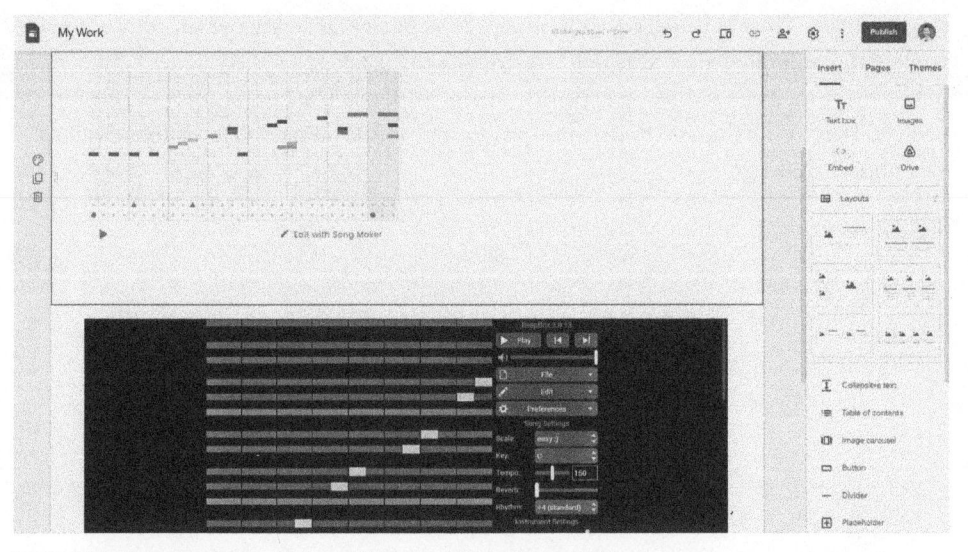

FIGURE 10.4 Google Sites with Song Maker and BeepBox embedded

Other Virtual Portfolio Hubs

If your school doesn't have access to Google Suite for Education, there are other ways to keep creations all in one place.

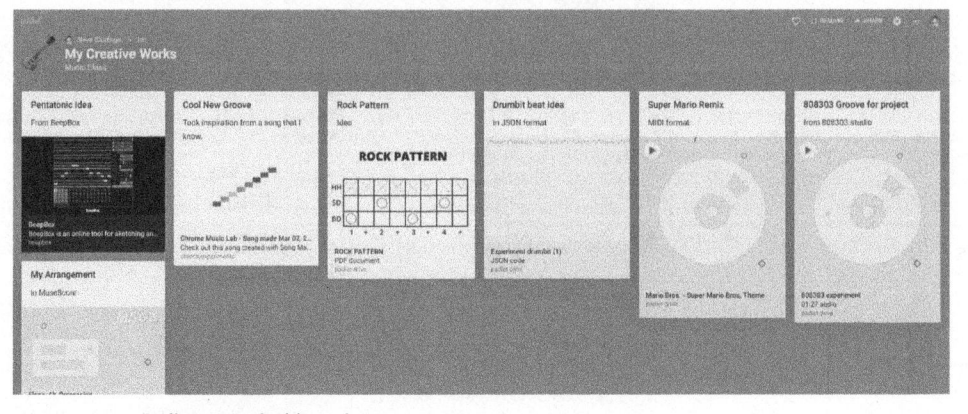

FIGURE 10.5 Padlet main dashboard view

Padlet

Padlet is a virtual hub for saving everything from links to sound files to videos. Much of these become embedded within the portfolio itself (Figure 10.5). Other file formats like MIDI or any proprietary project files need those particular softwares to work. In the free version, there is a 10 MB file limit, which means that many video files will be unable to upload, as most video files are larger than 10 MB. Every padlet can be shared like a Google Site or can remain private. It can also be shared and integrated with social media and other platforms

(Figure 10.6). There is Padlet for Education, called Padlet Backpack, which adds unlimited padlets and unlimited file size as well as extra security (such as a walled garden) if requested but seems to me to be somewhat expensive at around $2000 USD per school per year for 500 padlets. The free version is—by default—private and secure, as padlets are automatically private until shared.

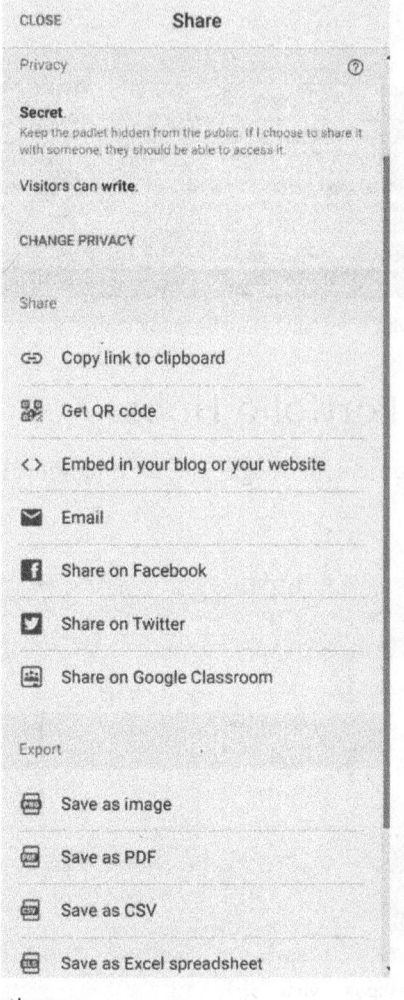

FIGURE 10.6 Padlet's share options

Wakelet

Wakelet is very similar to Padlet in a lot of ways and seems to cater to educators and the needs of learners. It is completely free and does not have a file upload limit. It reminds me a little bit of Pinterest. Wakelet has a Chrome extension for easy saving of ideas but also is COPPA- and FERPA-compliant. Figure 10.7 shows the Wakelet file stream and what the main dashboard looks like.

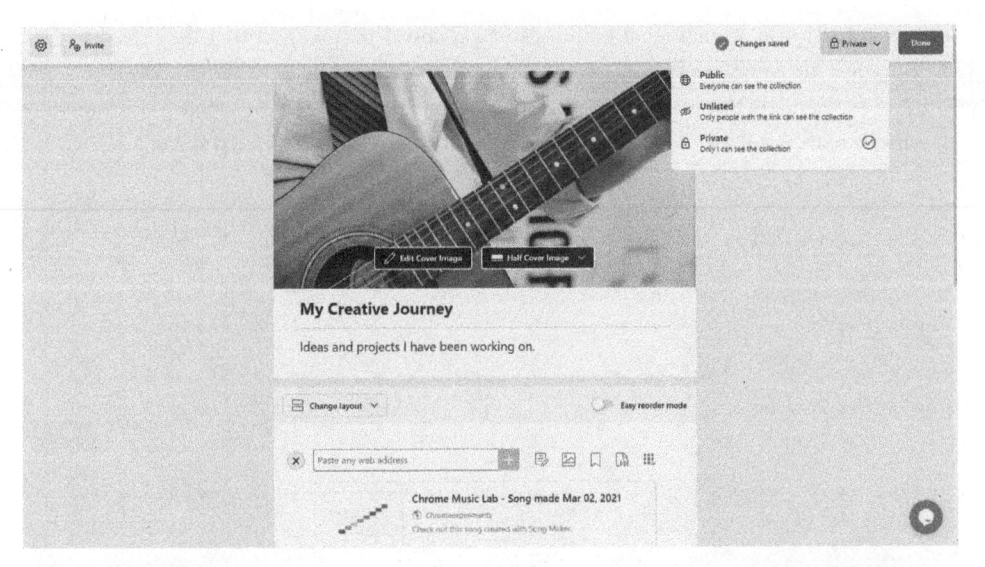

FIGURE 10.7 Wakelet stream

If learners are saving compositions in BandLab, Soundtrap, Noteflight, Flat, or any other cloud-based account site, they can even save ideas on one of these hubs by saving as an MP3, WAV, PDF, or other file just so they are all in one place.

Creative Video Software

Music and audio production technology often go hand in hand with video production. In this section, we will explore a variety of different video-making software.

Loom

Loom is a free-for-teachers screen recording software that has a desktop-based version and a Chrome extension. Users can do minor edits after recording and store them in their closed database. The videos can also be downloaded and further edited elsewhere or uploaded to YouTube. This capability is great for short tech instructional videos, but I could also see learners using this app as a hub for chatting about their compositions as sort of a virtual defense of a project, so to speak. Using the "Current Tab" feature in Loom, users can record a BeepBox composition, and sing or rap a topline over it, for instance, as a sort of multitrack recording. Loom hosts the videos that are made there, so if YouTube is blocked on your student accounts, Loom likely is not. Figure 10.8 shows the ready screen before recording happens. Another common screen recorder used by educators is Screencastify.

Flipgrid

Flipgrid is a virtual video hub for sending short video messages to learners within a class. It can be used to pose questions to learners where they reply with a video. One way to create music by using Flipgrid would be to send out a partially finished melody that every individual learner must finish somehow. It could also be a chord progression that they need to fit a melody over or some lyrics they need to change to fit a particular theme. Consider using Flipgrid for band, orchestra, and choir skills testing, but have learners create a short melody or pattern with the skills they are learning in addition to their traditional skills.

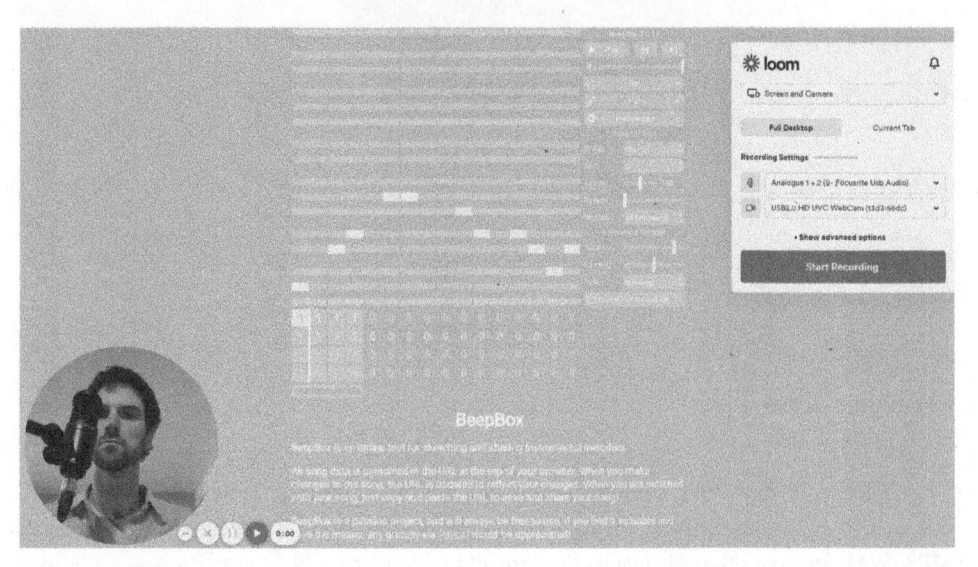

FIGURE 10.8 Loom's record screen

Acapella App

Acapella App for iOS devices automatically syncs up multitracked videos for virtual ensembles with zero latency and without the need for fancy software. Unfortunately, any I've tried for Android devices always have some latency. These types of apps can be incredibly useful for having learners create multi-part arrangements of music they love.

Cyborg Llama

Those wanting to do multilayered videos for virtual ensembles but don't have any iOS devices, there is Cyborg Llama (Figure 10.9). This is a web-based app that is exclusive to laptop and desktop devices only. When the facilitator signs up and sets up a session, the app automatically calculates the latency and corrects it so there is no need for fancy software and hardware. This has huge implications for small-group composition projects on- and offline. There is a very limited free version, a subscription version with more options, and a shared-drive version that integrates with Google Suite. Check here for more information: https://www.cyborgllama.info/try-it-now.

UpBeat Music App

Figure 10.10 shows the main website of UpBeat Music App. After trying this app with a group of friends, I noticed that it doesn't let users play together in real time. It sets up a recording session that can be calibrated quickly to line up after the recordings are done. There is a bit of a learning curve here with lots of different calibration points, but it can be a very good experience for your learners to introduce them to multilayer video editing. There are paid sections with discounts for educators and a limited free version to use.

FIGURE 10.9 Cyborg Llama website

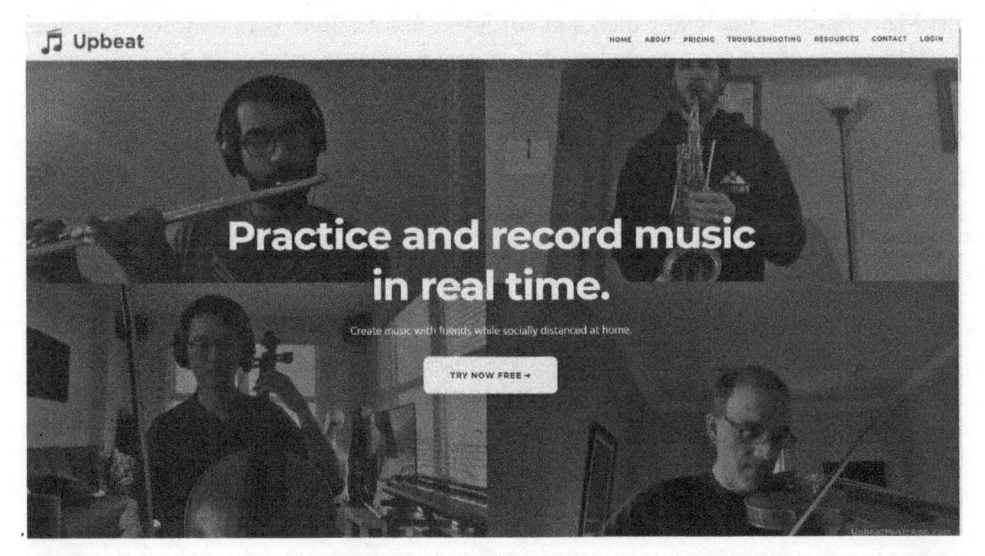

FIGURE 10.10 UpBeat Music App website

Major Video Conferencing Apps
Zoom
Many of us have become well acquainted with Zoom. And many of us quickly found out that there is no latency correction like in Cyborg Llama or Upbeat Music App.

Google Meets

Google Meets, part of the Google Suite for Education, is similar to Zoom. Google, not being a dedicated video conferencing company like Zoom, had many shortcomings that were improved upon greatly throughout 2020 and 2021 because of the high volume of users from the global pandemic.

Making These Apps Creative

Possible applications include the following:

> Have learners create call and response activities in which one asks a musical question and the other delivers an answer to finish the phrase.
> Play a piece of music with no metre so that the latency doesn't really matter.
> Have learners create a piece of music designed to be played only over video conferencing apps.

Video Editing

Da Vinci Resolve

Da Vinci Resolve, like many pieces of software, has multiple tiers of access. The free version of Da Vinci is quite powerful and could be all that learners need to put together videos. Of course, for learners to use this app, classrooms would need to be equipped with a desktop or some type of PC with its own disk space. It will not work on Chromebooks or similar cloud-based devices. Figure 10.11 shows the main editing screen of Da Vinci Resolve.

FIGURE 10.11 Da Vinci Resolve editing screen

Final Cut Pro

This app is the much more advanced version of iMovie for iOS. It runs only on MacOS and uses a one-time payment model.

iMovie

This is the app that comes with iOS devices for video editing. It is pretty powerful for what it is.

Adobe Premiere Pro

This is the video editing software from the Adobe Suite of creative apps. This company makes the well-known Adobe Photoshop, the industry standard for photo and image editing. This software uses a subscription payment model.

These video editing softwares can be used for a wide variety of creative musical expressions. Learners can create video blogs, music videos, musical video responses, and many other creative projects that you or your learners may come up with.

BandLab for Mobile

BandLab for Mobile actually has some basic video capturing and editing features to add music to.

OBS

OBS (Open Broadcast Software) is a versatile open-source video recording software perfect for recording multiple video feeds at once and for streaming live video. It is completely free and fairly easy to set up. When in doubt, though, there is YouTube. OBS is desktop based, so Chromebooks will not run it. It will run on Windows, MacOS, and Linux devices. This app can be used for broadcasting performances live with multiple camera feeds, creating instructional videos, or putting together a music video with multiple camera angles (Figure 10.12).

FIGURE 10.12 Open Broadcast Software (OBS) scene with three separate video feeds

Record them all in once screen or open multiple instances of OBS to record separate feeds to edit together later.

Cloud-Based Video Options

WeVideo

WeVideo is a versatile cloud-based video editing software designed for use in schools (Figure 10.13). It is free to try but does cost per seat. There are templates for anything learners might want to create, a GIF creator, the ability to record the screen or from a webcam right into the software, and a dedicated podcasting feature. A teacher can buy one seat for the school to have learner access, or any number of seats designed for use in a school. The app can work on Chromebooks or any device and is COPPA- and FERPA-compliant. It is fantastic for creating high-quality edited videos for musical projects. Like some of the cloud-based DAWs, the education plans have a walled-garden and collaborative features and can integrate with school software packages like Google Classroom, Schoology, or Canvas.

FIGURE 10.13 WeVideo main editing screen view

Canva

Canva is a free-to-use cloud-based graphic design program with a wide range of video editing options to choose from, too. Users can create entire graphics and videos from templates or from scratch or can be downloaded to use in other video projects. Using Canva, a learner could create an entire brand package for a podcast that they are making, or design a promotional video or poster for an upcoming concert. The most advanced version, Canva Pro, is available free to educators who can prove they teach somewhere. Once the request is approved, Canva for Education is COPPA- and FERPA-compliant, integrates with Google

Classroom Google sign-in, and is optimized for Chromebooks. Figure 10.14 is a depiction of the main dashboard screen in Canva.

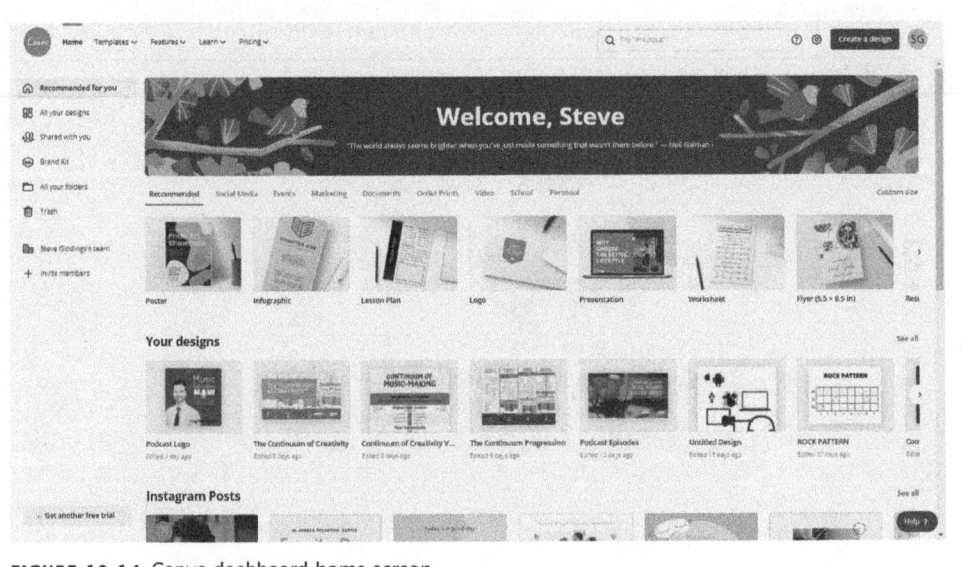

FIGURE 10.14 Canva dashboard home screen

Other Creative Apps

This section of the chapter will go over some other creative music apps that didn't come up in the earlier parts of the book and that you might want to use for your creative musical endeavours with learners.

aQWERTYon

From the same people who invented GroovePizza comes the aQWERTYon. There are currently two versions of it. You might be able to tell by the name that it is some kind of virtual instrument that uses your QWERTY keyboard. Scales can be customized to include only the notes of that scale. Figure 10.15 shows only the notes of the C blues scale, but here are a plethora of other scales and structures to choose from. This online app is great for jamming, or writing music within a DAW, or even just planning out ideas without a MIDI controller. The aQWERTYon website suggests playing along with your favourite YouTube videos.[1] It's designed to help make improvisation, composition, and theory approachable. A distinguishing feature of this virtual instrument is that it is WebMIDI enabled, meaning that it can act as the main MIDI controller for your MIDI projects in any DAW or notation software by setting up a virtual MIDI port by using LoopMIDI or similar virtual MIDI hubs. Virtual ports can be set up only on desktop computers with dedicated disk space. Learners

---

1. aQWERTYon 2017, https://musedlab.org/aqwertyon, accessed on December 4, 2021.

can record system audio or record as a MIDI track right into their favourite DAW or notation software, too.

The original aQWERTYon at https://apps.musedlab.org/aqwertyon/?sound=rock_organ& gives learners pre-chosen YouTube videos to jam to with using QWERTY keyboard transposed to the right sound and key.

FIGURE 10.15 aQWERTYon set to C blues

ChordChord

ChordChord is a unique web app for generating chord progression and beat ideas (Figure 10.16). It has a random generator with a collection of sounds and patterns that it applies

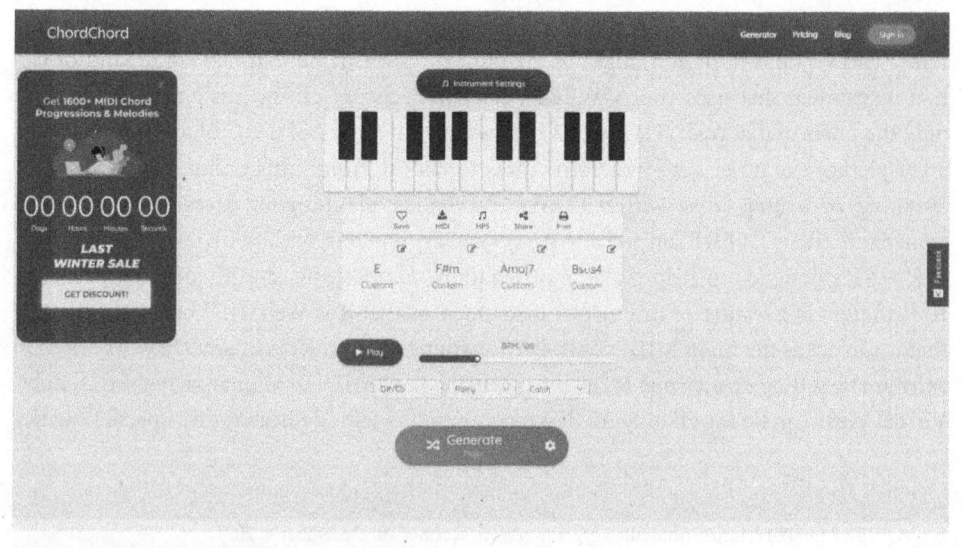

FIGURE 10.16 ChordChord's main screen

to the progression. After the user generates an idea, the chords can be customized to the musician's liking. Using the free version, users can generate a share link much like Song Maker or BeepBox and share their ideas that way. With the paid premium version, the ability to save progressions to a profile, download as MIDI and MP3, and download a file as a PDF chord chart is enabled (see Figure 10.17). Of course, learners can always use Chrome Audio Capture or other audio capture device to save the progression and open it as a WAV file in learner projects.

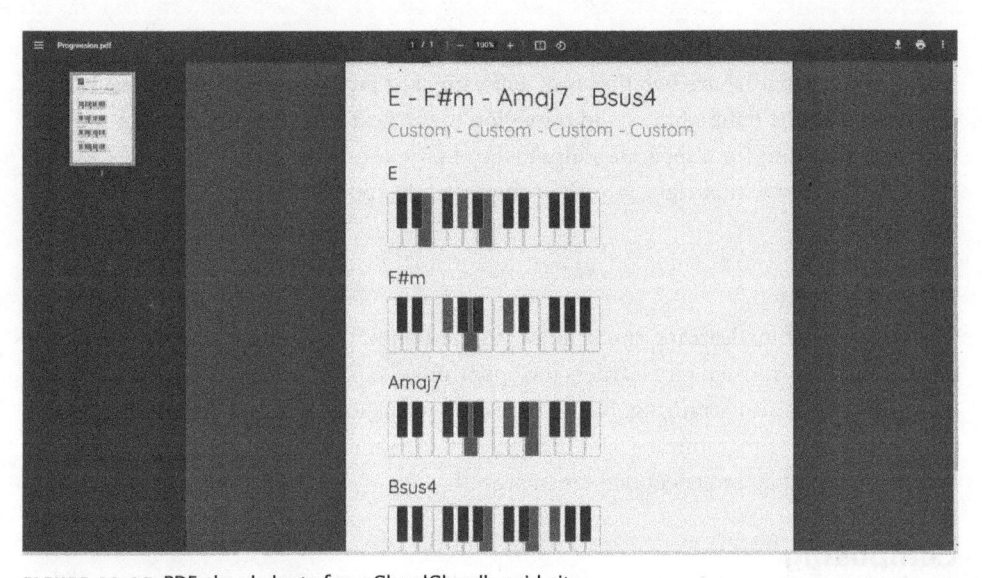

FIGURE 10.17 PDF chord charts from ChordChord's paid site

Cornelius Composer

This is part of a collection of apps by Classplash designed for teaching younger kids how to sight-read European staff notation, and some composing by using that notation. It was written by using a game engine, so many of the apps in the suite are games and Cornelius Composer is both a notation software and a game for learning staff notation. There is a subscription-based option for schools and it is designed to work on almost any platform, including Chromebooks.

Jam Tracks from YouTube

YouTube, as you are likely aware, is a treasure trove of information and useful tools. If learners are looking for a backing track to help with improvisation on any instrument, there are jam tracks in every style, genre, and key to help with learner creative projects. If learners are exploring Baroque music, put on a Baroque backing track and improvise a Baroque melody over it like a true early European music practitioner. The Western classical backing tracks on YouTube are largely actual Baroque and Classical accompaniments of written pieces. Many of the others in other genres are designed specifically for the purpose of jamming. Instead of playing the actual melody, try improvising a new melody over it in the same key, or using it in a DAW project. But what if learners are looking for a blues jam track in Bm? There's that, too. What about a jazz standard to practice jazz chops? Done. There are many options.

RhymeZone

Rhymezone is a useful online rhyming dictionary and thesaurus for writing lyrics for any genre. Add lyrics to existing melodies, or write a new melody go with the lyrics. Try it out!

Mixxx and Virtual DJ

Mixxx and Virtual DJ are two pieces of software used for DJs to line up two tracks for a live set or find the tempo for a good transition to the next tune. Use it to line up and sync two different stems from separate songs to do a new mash-up of these two songs. Learners can record the new mix right into the software and export it for use in other projects if they wish.

Blob Opera

This online machine-learning app is more than just a fun time filler. It has the potential to enable creativity, and can give learners the opportunity to play with the concepts of not only composition but also arranging, blend and vowel formation, ear training, voice types and ranges, computer programming, and theory! Here are some ideas for including Blob Opera into your lesson plans to encourage creativity.

Composing

This use seems like the most obvious one. It gives learners the ability to record a composition. Remember that a recording can be a composition, too. This app defaults to an A-major tonality and lets the user play with a melody within the parameters of that particular key. Learners could plan out a melody and find those pitches in Blob Opera and compose a short piece of music with them for any grade level.

Plug in a MIDI controller and things get interesting. Once the MIDI controller is in, all the chromatic notes become available. The user will have to be comfortable with ranges because each blob will take over if the user is in their range, and if there is overlap, there will be a bit of a fight for which blob sings the particular pitch—an incredible learning opportunity for a young choir. Turn on the arpeggiator on your MIDI device and watch what happens! The blobs are touch sensitive, too, so the softest touch on your MIDI device will be "oooo," and the heaviest will be "AH."

Blend and Vowel Formation

The blob opera makes it pretty obvious when one of the blobs is not on the same vowel as the others. Learners can achieve all different vowel sounds with a MIDI device by using different velocities. This exercise can be a great way to introduce blending in a choir by illustrating the idea clearly. Have learners explore what emotions different vowel sounds evoke with a particular melody.

Ear Training

Use Blob Opera to help find inner harmonies. The user has the ability to isolate parts within a chord and within the preset songs, too, by turning off particular parts or "soloing'" out others. Use a MIDI controller to help regulate how loud a particular harmony is. Ear training and learning by ear are much more effective on one's own instrument (as discussed earlier).

Arranging

Using their ears or a written melody part, learners can input the melody by dragging the mouse (to get the harmonies) and record it when they feel ready. To create the effect of a re-peated note, they can change the vowel sound. Or using a click track and a MIDI controller they can play each part separately (more advanced) and record each part into Audacity with the loopback feature or an Internet tab recorder like Chrome Audio Capture and arrange their work into a DAW. There is a bit of a latency from when the controller is pressed to when the blob makes the sound, but it is pretty consistent and something learners could get used to using.

Programming

Users can learn about machine learning and how to program their own musical experiments by using Scratch, or the facilitator can start a crash course in Google Machine Learning and guide learners through the machine-learning process. Another popular machine-learning music app by Google is the Bach Google Doodle, which we will discuss later.

Common-Practice-Period Voice Leading

I'm not an expert in common-practice-period theory but this app definitely seems that it at-tempts to follow those rules. You can figure out what chords the blobs are singing and analyze what they are doing. Try not to use "right" and "wrong"; instead, talk about why something sounded the way it did, because if it sounds good, it's probably fine. Use the arrangements provided with the app or use your own.

Part Singing

Use the app to introduce or advance part singing. Input the part into Blob Opera with a MIDI device and record it. After the parts are recorded together on Blob Opera, take out parts and add them back in when needed.

Transcribing

Either by using a preset piece or by composing one, have learners transcribe the parts into a standard notation of their choice.

Jamulus and JamKazaam

Jamulus and JamKazaam are both ways to jam or rehearse online in real time with low-la-tency audio. They give users the ability to connect to a server or host a private network. They facilitate jamming or rehearsing from a distance or within a LAN within a school.

Google Doodles

The Google home page has a new doodle almost daily to celebrate a person or a holiday from another part of the world. Occasionally, there are musical ones. One of the most popular in recent history was the Bach Google Doodle: a machine-learning app that has analyzed many, many J. S. Bach pieces to find patterns and generate a Bach-style four-part harmony based on the melody the user composes. These doodles are often very accessible for learners of any age or experience level. Learners as young as five years old can have success with these.

FIGURE 10.18 Bach Google Doodle

Bach Google Doodle

This particular Doodle turns the user's melody into the style of Bach. Figure 10.18 shows how it gives users the ability to download the piece as a MIDI file, meaning it can be imported to a notation software or DAW. Thus, learners can write entire pieces—in short snippets at a time—in the style of Bach and add a drum machine to it! It seems to integrate well with Finale and MuseScore (Figure 10.19). It's not great with other notation software I've tried. It

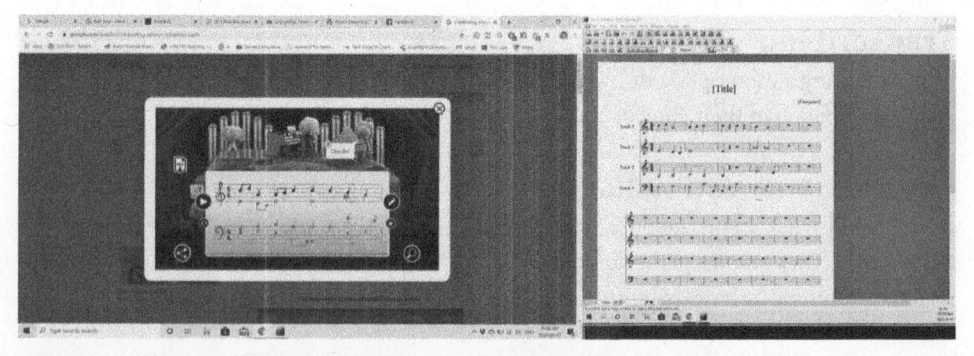

FIGURE 10.19 Bach Google Doodle transferred as MIDI information to Finale NotePad

works very well on most DAWs. This particular Doodle also has the ability to switch to rock organ sound and to save as a link to share on the web.

Clara Rockmore Doodle (Theremin)

This app celebrates the life of Clara Rockmore; theremin virtuoso. After a quick lesson and a short concert, learners can actually play the theremin right in the browser and it emulates a really nice theremin sound. Easy mode gives pitch names, and scales to work with (Figure 10.20). With easy mode off, it is very free flowing, with no pitch hints other than the user's ear—much more like playing a real theremin. This app could definitely be used as a virtual theremin for other compositional projects.

FIGURE 10.20 Clara Rockmore Doodle in easy mode to the key of D

Les Paul Doodle

This Google Doodle celebrates the contributions of Les Paul with an interactive guitar doodle. Learners can record their compositions and save them as a link.

Robert Moog Doodle (Moog Synthesizer)

This Doodle lets the user play with a Moog synthesizer in the browser. Learn how a synthesizer works with this app and record compositions.

Hip Hop Doodle

Learn about the history of hip-hop and mix beats with the virtual turntable. Beats can be saved as a link and sent through email.

Oskar Fischinger

This doodle lets the user compose music in the style of abstract film artist Oskar Fischinger. Compositions can be saved via a link.

Looping Stations and Apps

Looping stations are useful for individual music making. A single musician can create loops of themselves beatboxing, playing an orchestral instrument, singing, or making any musical sound to emulate the groove that an entire band would make and then perform over their own loops. These are useful for live performances and put a new meaning to the one-person band. There are pedal- and foot-controlled loopers for instrumentalists, and tabletop loopers controlled with the fingers for producers, or vocalists. With these, learners could plan out a composition or improvise one and perform it live by layering all the parts together and building the piece in front of one another in real time. Something to know about these stations is that often timing is everything. The composed loops don't line up automatically to the beat, so there is a bit of a learning curve to begin. Figure 10.21 shows an example of a small pedal looping station.

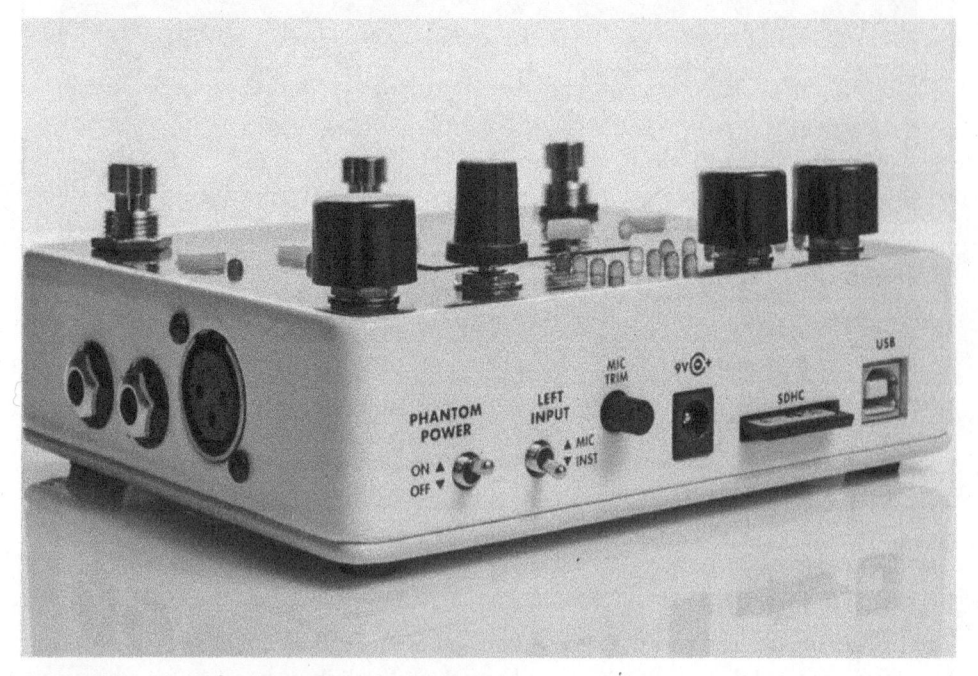

FIGURE 10.21 Basic foot-controlled looping station

There are apps that emulate the basic premise of these looping stations and can be used for live performance or a recording.

Loopy HD (iOS) and Loopify (Android)

For iOS, there's Loopy HD (which is Ableton Link enabled), a useful, visual looping station. Users can record loops of anything they would like with up to 12 tracks with the ability to bump tracks together to make room for more loops. The equivalent looping station for Android devices is Loopify. It has very similar layout and functionality to Loopy HD. Both have latency correction built into the app so the tracks will line up during recording. They are both intuitive with regard to getting the loops to automatically line up. Headphones are a must for an app like this. Figures 10.22 and 10.23 show some of what the interface in Loopify looks like. Loopy HD is similar in layout to this app.

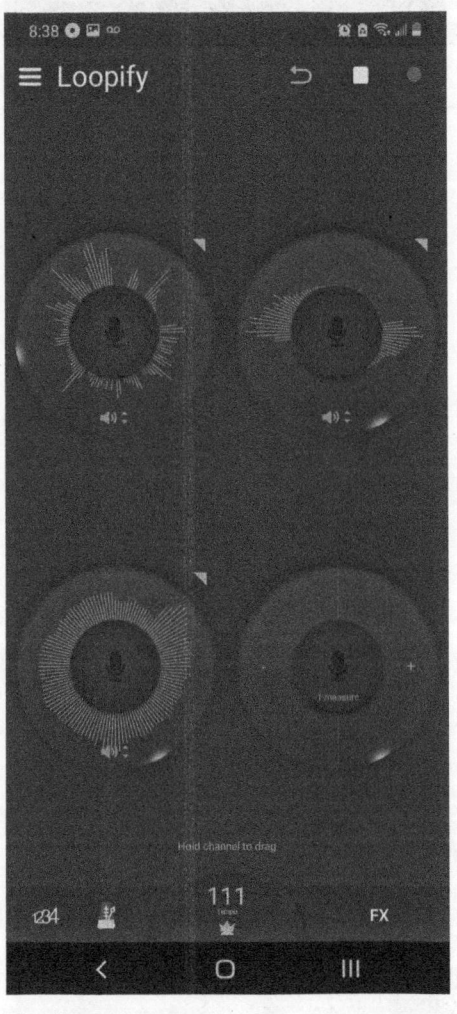

FIGURE 10.22 Loopify looping view

Super-Looper

Super-Looper is an online looper compatible with Chromebooks (Figure 10.24). It works differently from the way Loopy HD and Loopify do, though. Instead of being able to record sounds, Super-Looper lets the user record samples only by using the QWERTY keyboard as a pad controller of sorts. There is also an iOS app for Super-Looper.

GroovePad (iOS and Android)

GroovePad is a versatile live-looping station similar to the one in the BandLab Mobile App. It contains pre-made loops that will fit together with a variety of loop packs available. There is an FX controller built in as well for controlling filters and sounds for live mixing and beat dropping. On Android, the pro version is available on a subscription basis.

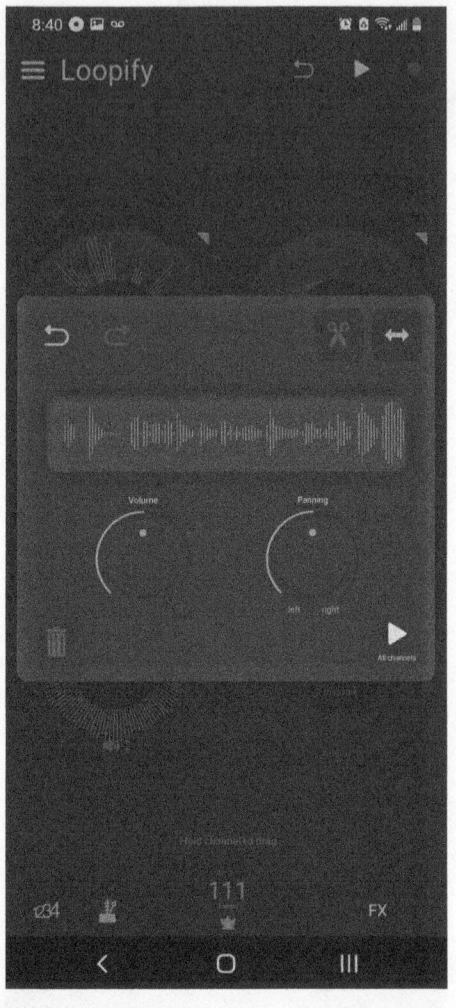

FIGURE 10.23 Loopify settings

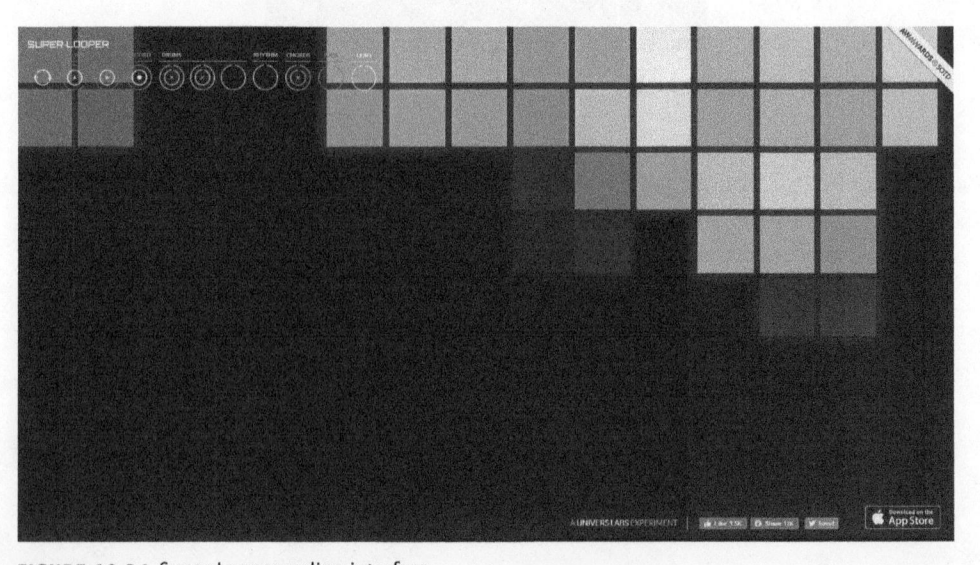

FIGURE 10.24 Super-Looper online interface

Quantiloop Pro (iOS)

Quantiloop is a live looper designed to integrate with other Apple music-making apps but also has its own unique functionality for looping. The layout resembles a foot-controlled or tabletop looping station.

GarageBand Live Loops (iOS)

Built into GarageBand for iOS is Live Loops, with many loop packs to choose from, and with an easy-to-use interface, Live Loops is designed for (as the title suggests) live looping similar to a pad controller like the Novation LaunchPad. It can also function as it does in the web version of BandLab where loops are selected to be used in a composition in tracks mode. Users have the ability to record their own loops to preexisting loops as well by using GarageBand's amplifier presets and recording capabilities. These types of apps are designed for live DJ performances or as a live backing track for an improvisation, or cypher. Each loop pack contains a prearranged piece. Each column can be activated all at once by using the arrow button at the bottom and will automatically default to one-bar quantization. This means that once any loop is pressed, it will finish and begin the next loop at the nearest bar (this process can be adjusted), so poor timing isn't an issue at all. In the preset arrangements, if each column is pressed in order from left to right in four- or eight-bar phrases, it sounds like a fully developed, coherent beat, which can be useful for improvising toplines, for cyphers, or for live dance parties by using the EDM (electronic dance music) loop pack. Each loop within those presets can be operated manually, too, so learners can create their own arrangements by using the preset loop packs, improvise shows, and record or perform them live. Figure 10.25 shows

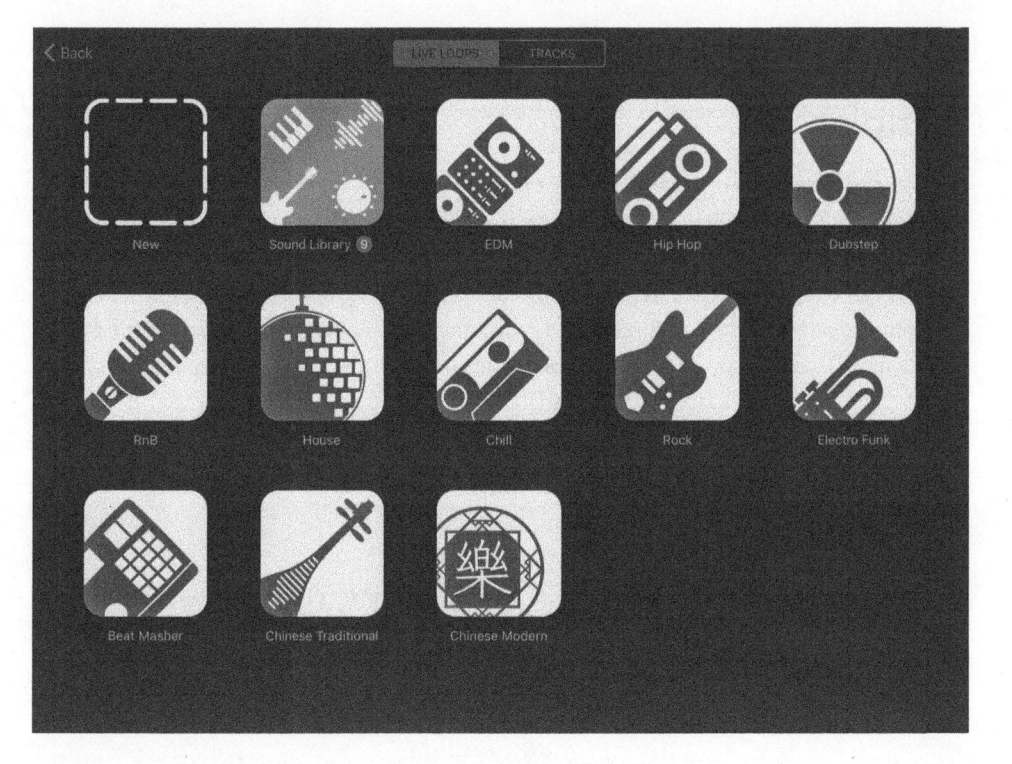

FIGURE 10.25 GarageBand Live Loops loop-packs main dashboard

the main screen for Live Loops. Figure 10.26 shows the Live Loops interface with the loop launcher screen.

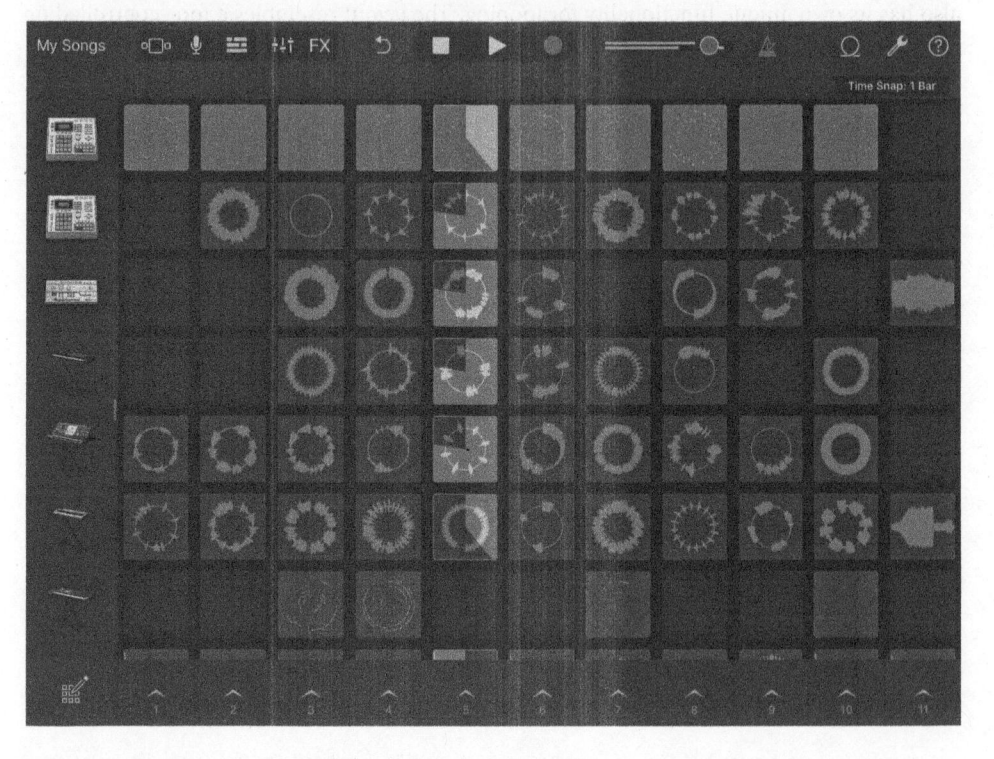

FIGURE 10.26 GarageBand Live Loops loop launcher screen

Samplers

GarageBand has a built-in sampler app that is easy to use, but as mentioned, it is available only for Apple products. Sampling is useful for recording found sounds or other pre-recorded sounds and triggering them to a MIDI pad controller like the Novation Launchpad or the Ableton Push. Samples can often be assigned to pitches on a keyboard MIDI controller, too, to make for some interesting creative works. Until recently, finding free, non-Apple sampling software has been a challenge. BandLab—on the non-education side—added a sampler to their arsenal of apps within their free cloud-based DAW. This is also available on the mobile version. It is only a matter of time before this feature is available on the BandLab for Education platform, too.

Auto-Tune Apps

Auto-Tune was mentioned earlier as a tool for helping learners to improvise unhindered to find usable material for a topline or another compositional element. It can also be used to explore different scales and flavours from a melody line. It often gets a bad rap, but the distinctive sound that Cher uses in her later material shows that it is often used to produce a particular timbre. The term "Auto-Tune" often refers to any pitch-correction software effect, but Auto-Tune is the pitch-correction plug-in designed by Antares Audio Technologies that has become the industry standard to the point where any pitch-correction plug-in is now referred to as Auto-Tune.

GSnap Audacity Plug-In

GSnap is a free pitch-correction-effect plug-in for Audacity (Figure 10.27). It gives users the ability to set the key, and a scale from the common modes and pentatonic scales. There are YouTube tutorials on how to use it and troubleshoot it.

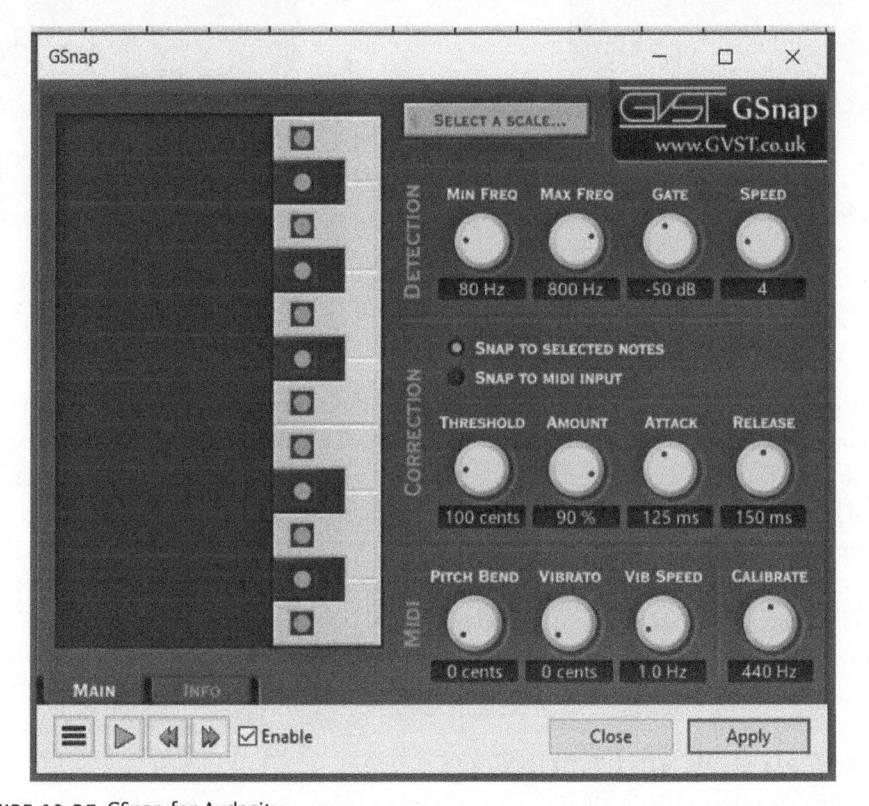

FIGURE 10.27 GSnap for Audacity

Soundtrap

Soundtrap for Education accounts have free access to Antares Auto-Tune (Figure 10.28). The Soundtrap mobile app functions similarly to the way the web version does, but support for Soundtrap for Education on mobile is limited. BandLab currently does not have built-in Auto-Tune; however, many apps can export an auto-tuned voice to WAV, M4A, or MP3 format to use in other software.

Plug-Ins for Any DAW

Whatever DAW you use, there are pitch-correction Auto-Tune or Auto-Tune-like plug-ins for you.

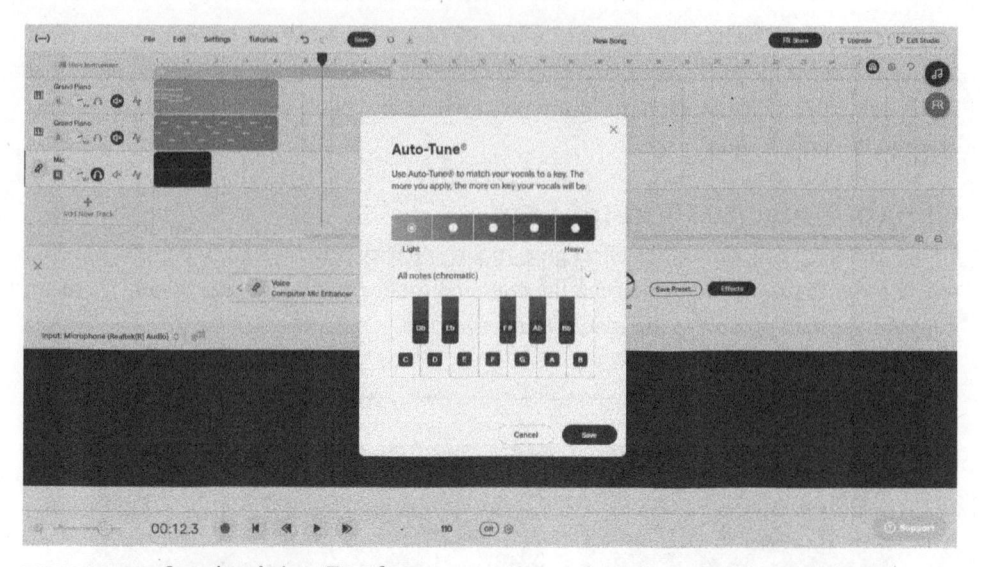

FIGURE 10.28 Soundtrap's Auto-Tune feature

There are a few apps to explore that use Auto-Tune-like features:

Voloco (iOS and Android)

Voloco is a versatile auto-tune app. Users have the ability to download effected vocals in M4A file format in the free version, but also in lossless WAV format in the paid version. The free version can be used to collect material and effected vocal tracks that could be used for material later in a composition. A good copy could be recorded after importing these ones with the new vocal line for better-quality recording.

Tune Me (iOS and Android)

With this app, vocal lines can be easily recorded over a beat. Ideas can be easily exported to any location, too.

AutoRap (iOS and Android)

This app turns any speaking, singing, or words into a coherent rap song. Select a style and just speak naturally into the app and generate. It will automatically auto-tune and auto-rap where appropriate. This capability could be used as a great way to generate ideas for a rap in which there is a theme with a few words and rhymes.

Conclusion

I'm hoping that the apps and tech tools in this chapter will open up more creative options for learners to explore. Many of these apps are being updated and new ones are being added all the time. This means that even though these may be a place to begin, there could be brand-new apps that work better or do more of what you and your learners are looking for that didn't even exist until recently. Regardless, there is always a tool that does most of what you need and for everything else, there are work-arounds in partnerships with other apps and software.

Conclusion

Throughout this book we explored how important creativity and technology are to music education but also how important it is to reimagine how a music program could look through the lens of informal learning, technology, and creativity. We explored DAWs, notation software, how they can work together, and innovative ways to use these tools in your classrooms. We also explored the tech you need to get started, how everything hooks up, and how to adapt your programs to include more aspects of creativity, technology, and informal learning.

It is important for you to know that although, going in to writing this book I knew much of this information, there is so much more about creative music tech that I had to learn during the writing process. It is impossible to learn it all, and the best you can do is to keep on learning. YouTube is a treasure trove of information, tutorials, and lessons for you to explore music technology. I've learned a lot on Twitter by following the likes of Ethan Hein, Will Kuhn, Adam Patrick Bell, Samuel Wright, Robbie Burns, and Katie Wardrobe. As well, I was able to learn so much through exploration of my own, akin to the informal learning approach. Also in keeping in line to one of the major themes of this book, trust the learners; chances are pretty good that many of them will be able to figure it out themselves.

I'm also hoping that the pages of this book struck some inspiration for you. Of course, you *can* use my lesson ideas to a T, but I'm hoping that it also gave you enough information to come up with creative technology ideas for you and your learners to thrive in this creatively inspiring technological environment.

Technology for Unleashing Creativity. Steve Giddings, Oxford University Press. © Oxford University Press 2022.
DOI: 10.1093/oso/9780197570739.003.0012

MASTER LIST OF APPS

DAWs

Ableton Learn
Ableton Live
Ableton Live Lite
Audacity
BandLab
BandLab for Education
Cakewalk
Cubase
FL Studio
GarageBand
Logic Pro
Pro Tools
Reason
Soundation
Soundation4Education
Soundtrap
Soundtrap for Education

Notation Software

1Chart
Chord Sheet Maker

Cornelius Composer
Dorico
Dorico for iPad
Dorico SE
Finale
Finale NotePad
Flat for Docs Add-Oon
Flat for Education
Flat.io
HookPad
HookTheory Classroom
MuseScore
Noteflight
Noteflight Learn
ScoreCloud
Sibelius
Sibelius First
Sibelius Mobile

MIDI Sequencers

808303.studio
Bach Google Doodle
Beepbox
Drumbit
Drumbit Pro
GroovePizza
JummBox
Mario Paint Composer Emulator
ModBox
Oskar Fischinger Google Doodle
Paint Composer
TypeDrummer

Chrome Music Lab

Arpeggios
Kandinsky
Melody Maker
Rhythm
Shared Piano
Song Maker

Loopers and Looping

Ableton Link
Amplify Studios
BandLab for Mobile
GarageBand Live Loops
GroovePad
Incredibox
Loopify
Loopy HD
Quantiloop
Super-Looper

Samplers

BandLab (non-EDU)
BandLab Mobile
GarageBand iOS

Virtual Instruments

aQWERTYon
BandLab
Blob Opera
ChordChord
Chrome Shared Piano
Clara Rockmore Google Doodle
GarageBand
Hip-Hop Google Doodle
Keyboard from Creatability.WithGoogle.com
Les Paul Google Doodle
MIDI.CITY
Novation LaunchPad Intro
Online Guitar from Recursive Arts
Robert Moog Google Doodle
Sampulator
Scratch
SessionTown Drums
SessionTown Keys
Soundtrap
TypeDrummer
Virtual Guitar Online
WebSID

Coding

BitBucket
Blockly
EarSketch
GitHub
GitHub Education
MakeCode
Scratch
Sonic Pi

Virtual Audio Routing and Virtual Loopback

Audacity Loopback
LoopBack
LoopMIDI
OBS
VoiceMeeter
WebMIDI

Web and System Audio and Video Recording

Chrome Audio Capture (GitHub Version)
Loom
OBS
Screencastify

Virtual Hubs

Google Classroom
Google Docs
Google Sites
Padlet
Padlet Backpack
Wakelet

Video

Acapella App
Adobe Premiere Pro
BandLab for Mobile
Canva for Education
Cyborg Llama
Da Vinci Resolve

Final Cut Pro
Flipgrid
Google Meets
iMovie
Loom
OBS
Screencastify
UpBeat Music App
WeVideo
Zoom

Pitch-Correction Software and Apps

AutoRap
GSnap for Audacity
Soundtrap
Tune Me
Voloco

Virtual Amplifiers

BandLab
GarageBand
Soundtrap

MIDI File Databases

BitMidi
MidiWorld

Stem Databases

Amazon Music
Facebook Groups
Skio
Splice Contests
Traxsource
Wavo

App Sites

Apple App Store
Chrome Web Store
Google Play Store

Software Packages

MusicFirst Classroom

Remote Audio Rehearsing

JamKazaam
Jamulus

Other

Chrome Transpose Extension
Melodyne

Index